Generations in Twentieth-Century Europe

Also by Stephen Lovell

DESTINATION IN DOUBT: Russia since 1989

THE RUSSIAN READING REVOLUTION: Print Culture in the Soviet and Post-Soviet Eras

SUMMERFOLK: A History of the Dacha, 1710–2000

Generations in Twentieth-Century Europe

Edited by

Stephen Lovell

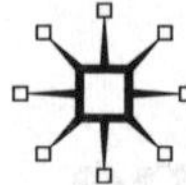

First published 2007 by
PALGRAVE MACMILLAN
Houndmills, Basingstoke, Hampshire RG21 6XS and
175 Fifth Avenue, New York, N.Y. 10010
Companies and representatives throughout the world

PALGRAVE MACMILLAN is the global academic imprint of the Palgrave
Macmillan division of St. Martin's Press, LLC and of Palgrave Macmillan Ltd.
Macmillan® is a registered trademark in the United States, United Kingdom
and other countries. Palgrave is a registered trademark in the European
Union and other countries.

ISBN-13: 978–0–230–00891–5   hardback
ISBN-10: 0–230–00891–7   hardback

This book is printed on paper suitable for recycling and made from fully
managed and sustained forest sources. Logging, pulping and manufacturing
processes are expected to conform to the environmental regulations of the
country of origin.

A catalogue record for this book is available from the British Library.

Library of Congress Cataloging-in-Publication Data

Generations in twentieth-century Europe / edited by Stephen Lovell.
      p. cm.
   Includes index.
   ISBN 0–230–00891–7 (alk. paper)
   1. Europe—History—20th century. 2. Generations—Europe.
   3. Conflict of generations—Europe. 4. Intergenerational relations—
   Europe. I. Lovell, Stephen, 1972–

   D425.G46 2007

   305.2094'0904—dc22   2007023304

10   9   8   7   6   5   4   3   2   1
16   15   14   13   12   11   10   09   08   07

Printed and bound in Great Britain by
Antony Rowe Ltd, Chippenham and Eastbourne

Contents

List of Tables

Acknowledgements

This book has resulted from the conference 'Generations in Europe', held at New College, Oxford, in April 2005. I gratefully acknowledge the contributions made by a number of institutions: the Leverhulme Trust; the British Academy; New College, Oxford; the Faculty of Medieval and Modern Languages, the Modern European History Research Centre, the European Humanities Research Centre and the Management Committee for Russian and East European Studies, all at the University of Oxford; and the Centre for Twentieth-Century Studies, King's College London. In addition, I am even more than usually grateful to my co-organizer, Catriona Kelly, who provided much of the intellectual impetus and took upon herself the lion's share of the planning and practical arrangements, as well as to Andy Byford, who did more than anyone else to keep the conference running smoothly when it finally took place.

My other great debt is to the Leverhulme Trust, whose award of a Philip Leverhulme Prize ensured that the manuscript would be put together without too much delay.

Notes on Contributors

Catriona Kelly is Professor of Russian and Co-Director of the European Humanities Research Centre, University of Oxford; and a Fellow of New College. She is the author of many books, the most recent being *Comrade Pavlik: The Rise and Fall of a Soviet Boy Hero* (Granta, 2005). She has just completed a major Leverhulme-funded study of childhood in twentieth-century Russia: *Children's World: Growing Up in Russia, 1890–1991* is scheduled to be published by Yale University Press in 2007. She now plans to write a study of cultural memory in Leningrad and St Petersburg from 1961.

Anna Krylova is Assistant Professor of History at Duke University. She is the author of articles on Soviet history and ideology in *Slavic Review*, *Kritika*, *The Journal of Modern History*, and other journals. Her current project is a history of Soviet women fighters in World War II.

Sandra Souto Kustrín is a Research Fellow at the Department of Contemporary History, Institute of History, Spanish National Research Council (CSIC). She has published widely on the labour movement, youth, and collective action in interwar Spain; her articles have appeared in Spanish, French, and British journals (*Hispania*, *Mélanges de la Casa de Velázquez*, and *The European History Quarterly*). She is the author of: *'Y ¿Madrid? ¿Qué hace Madrid?' Movimiento revolucionario y acción colectiva (1933–1936)* (Madrid, Siglo XXI, 2004) and (with Paul Preston) of *La guerra civil. Las fotos que hicieron historia* (Madrid, La Esfera de los Libros, 2005 [2nd edn 2006]). Her current project links governmental policies, youth and youth organizations, and conflicts in Spain between 1876 and 1939 from a comparative perspective.

Stephen Lovell is a Reader in Modern European History at King's College London. He is the author of *The Russian Reading Revolution: Print Culture in the Soviet and Post-Soviet Eras* (2000), *Summerfolk: A History of the Dacha, 1710–2000* (2003), and *Destination in Doubt: Russia since 1989* (2006); and co-editor of the following: *Russian Literature, Modernism and the Visual Arts* (2000), *Bribery and Blat in Russia: Negotiating Reciprocity from the Middle Ages to the 1990s* (2000), and *Reading for Entertainment in Contemporary Russia: Post-Soviet Popular Literature in Historical Perspective* (2005).

Holger Nehring is a Lecturer in History at the University of Sheffield. He is interested in the history of protest movements and is currently working on a book on the protests against nuclear weapons in Britain and West Germany in the late 1950s and 1960s. His recent publications include: 'The Growth of Social Movements', in Paul Addison and Harriet Jones (eds), *A Companion to Contemporary Britain, 1939–2000* (forthcoming, Oxford, 2005), and 'Westernisation – a New Paradigm for Interpreting West European History in a Cold War Context', *Cold War History* 4/2 (2003/4), pp. 175–190.

S. A. Smith is Professor of History at the University of Essex. He is author of many articles and the following books: *Like Cattle and Horses: Nationalism and Labor in Shanghai, 1895–1927* (Duke University Press, 2002); *The Russian Revolution: A Very Short Introduction* (Oxford University Press, 2002); *A Road is Made: Communism in Shanghai, 1920–27* (University of Hawaii Press, 2000); (with Diane P. Koenker), *Notes of a Red Guard: The Autobiography of Eduard Dune* (University of Illinois Press, 1993); and *Red Petrograd: Revolution in the Factories, 1917–18* (Cambridge University Press, 1983). The present chapter arises from his current research project, funded by the Arts and Humanities Research Council, which examines the efforts of Communist regimes in the Soviet Union and the People's Republic of China to transform popular culture along lines of science and rationality by eliminating the beliefs and practices they categorized as 'superstition'.

Nicholas Stargardt is a Lecturer in Modern History and Fellow of Magdalen College, Oxford. His publications include *The German Idea of Militarism: Radical and Socialist Critics, 1866–1914* (Cambridge, 1994) and *Witnesses of War: Children's Lives under the Nazis* (London, 2005).

Pat Thane is Professor of Contemporary British History, Institute of Historical Research, University of London. Her main publications are: *The Foundations of the Welfare State* (Longman, 1982, 2nd edn 1996); *Women and Gender Policies. Women and the Rise of the European Welfare States, 1880s–1950s*, co-ed. with Gisela Bock (Routledge 1990); *Old Age from Antiquity to Post-Modernity*, co-ed. with Paul Johnson (Routledge 1998); *Old Age in England. Past Experiences, Present Issues* (Oxford University Press, 2000); *Women and Ageing in Britain since 1500*, co-ed. with Lynne Botelho (Longman, 2001); *Labour's First Century. The Labour Party 1900–2000*, co-ed. with Duncan Tanner and Nick Tiratsoo (Cambridge University Press, 2000); *The Long History of Old Age*, ed., with illustrations

(London: Thames and Hudson, 2005), also published as *A History of Old Age* (Getty Museum, LA, 2005); and *Das Alter. Eine Kulturgeschichte* (Primus Verlag, Darmstadt, 2005).

Richard Vinen is a Reader in Modern European History at King's College London. His publications include *The Politics of French Business 1936–1945* (1991), *Bourgeois Politics in France 1945–1951* (1995), *France 1934–1970* (1996), *A History in Fragments: Europe in the Twentieth Century* (2000), and *The Unfree French: Life under the Occupation* (2006).

Bernd Weisbrod is Professor of Modern European History at Göttingen University where he is also acting chair of a group of contemporary historians in Lower Saxony and director of a graduate school on 'Generations in History'. In his Ph.D. he investigated the economics and politics of heavy industry in the Weimar Republic (1976), and his *Habilitation* dealt with Victorian social policies, especially with regard to pauper children and juvenile delinquency (1986). His most recent work deals with post-1945 German academia (*Akademische Vergangenheitspolitik. Beiträge zur Wissenschaftskultur der Nachkriegszeit* [Göttingen: Wallstein, 2002]) and the politics of violence (*The No Man's Land of Violence. Extreme Wars in the 20th Century* [Göttingen: Wallstein, 2005]).

1
Introduction

Stephen Lovell

Generation has never been so ubiquitous in public discourse as in our own present day. For journalists, politicians and advertisers it is often the first recourse when making sense of voter behaviour, consumer preferences, or simply the *Zeitgeist*. The baby-boomers have duly been succeeded by Generations X and Y, not to mention a number of more refined categories. In 2000, for example, the young German novelist Florian Illies shot to prominence by publishing *Generation Golf*, an exploration of the values and world view of those who, like the author, had grown up in the blandly affluent eighties. Three years later, Illies felt the need to provide a sequel, which showed the 'fun generation' of his first book confronting economic uncertainty, undergoing a 'quarter-life crisis', and turning into the 'fear generation'.[1] In 2006, the sociologist Jean Twenge published *Generation Me*, a more analytically ambitious attempt to diagnose those Americans, born from 1970 onwards, who had 'never known a world that put duty before self'.[2]

Here, as in so many other places, there is a discrepancy between common parlance and scholarly usage. While members of the general public have become increasingly conversant with generation, historians have remained rather uncomfortable with the concept. They have not ignored generation, but they have construed it in subtly yet significantly different ways: some scholars emphasize socializing institutions, while others stress family life; some try to identify long chains of historical succession, while others focus on the unique experiences of a single cohort; some favour quantitative survey data or oral history, while others see generation as primarily a discursive phenomenon to be traced through the close reading of texts and the investigation of a given society's 'memory wars'. Yet age-related allegiances and forms of behaviour have never received the sustained attention that has been lavished on other key markers of modern identity such as class, ethnicity and gender. Although generation has since the 1980s increasingly become a preoccupation of academic research, it has been a focus of discussion primarily in the social and political sciences. Historians have sensed that generations are important, being closely bound up with the *longue durée* of social change, with the distribution of economic resources, and with the never-ending competition for political legitimacy and authority. But they are quite understandably set on their guard by the fuzziness and multifacetedness of the generation concept (which often combines, or confuses, the senses of cohort and life stage), as well as by the apparent incommensurability of the research methods that are required to pin it down: how, they implicitly ask, can a demographer, an anthropologist, a political scientist, a literary scholar and an intellectual historian (all of whom make use of the term 'generation') convince themselves that they are engaged in a coherent collective endeavour?

That is one rather complicated question that lies at the heart of this book. In more straightforward terms, the chapters that follow can be regarded as an attempt to find out how, if at all, age mattered in twentieth-century Europe. Their working hypothesis, unsurprisingly, is that age *does* matter, and starts to matter in a rather different way in the modern era. While it is certainly the case that distinctions between young and old, juniority and seniority, are ancient and fundamental to human cultures,[3] they appear to gain new prominence and to be put to new purposes in the last third of the eighteenth century and the beginning of the nineteenth. At around this time, in several European cultures, the word 'generation' was made to do more work than hitherto. The concept it evoked became more complex, socially significant and culturally resonant. As Raymond Williams observes, 'the full modern sense of **generation** in the specific and influential sense of a distinctive kind of people or attitudes' did not begin to take shape until the mid-eighteenth century and only entered its heyday in the mid-nineteenth.[4]

Williams included 'generation' as one of his 'keywords' of modern culture: a term that, although in English it dated back as far as the thirteenth century, underwent a radical semantic shift in the late eighteenth and early nineteenth centuries. We can infer a number of social and historical reasons for this development. Certain groups in society (in the first instance, young, well-off, well-educated males) were stimulated by new institutions (universities, bureaucracies), places (notably cities) and events (notably the French Revolution) to find a solidarity with their coevals that might override previous loyalties (such as those within a family, clan or social estate). This sense of generational distinctiveness could find expression in several striking ways. It might bring political mobilization as young men competed with their fathers for access to the levers of power in the modern state. It might foster a youth culture or lifestyle, as in the Romantic movement. And generational consciousness might instil in men and women of any age a sense of their own historical location and direction. The modern concept of generation was complemented from the very beginning by a notion of history as a sequence of unique phases of development. Educated nineteenth-century Europeans were often preoccupied – or depressed – by the extent to which they were constrained by the past, and the concept of generation was a satisfying way for them to find an advantageous accommodation with it. Instead of being borne along by History, they could become its chosen ones.

This kind of account does, however, bring its own dangers. We need to be wary of taking nineteenth-century intellectuals at their own estimation. The idea of a decisive shift to modern generationality also has a distinctly teleological colouring: as 'traditional' societies undergo modernization (or enter modernity), so the argument runs, their patriarchal order is overturned and the older generation loses its privileged social and discursive position. In many histories, accordingly, 'generation' is practically a synonym for 'youth'.

Youth, however, does not have things all its own way, even in an era of modernization. Even a historical cleavage as bloody as the French Revolution did not put an end to the conflation of politics and the family. Beheading a paterfamilias was traumatic for the collective imagination, however great the provocation had been.[5] Although John Locke dealt a hefty blow to family-based justifications of political authority, and even though eighteenth-century Americans seriously considered the idea of replacing the legal code every nineteen years so as not to saddle the younger generation with the decisions of their elders, family metaphors abounded in the early years of the Republic. The Founding Fathers were just too powerful, and too convenient, to be passed over in favour of their offspring.[6]

The nineteenth century, then, saw no entirely clear transition from a familial, even genealogical sense of belonging to a lateral sense of allegiance within a particular cohort. On the contrary, the advantage of the generation concept is that it can play on the ambiguity between 'horizontal' and 'vertical' ties. People never need to decide whether, ultimately, they belong with kin or with coevals. The modern European cultures discussed in this volume all make it possible to speak of 'generations' existing both across the family dinner table and in the electoral system or the welfare state. The generation concept potentially offers both a mechanism of change and a source of solidarity and cohesion (though, of course, it may also bring rupture and conflict). It is to do both with succession and with simultaneity.

Either way, generation always implies relativity. To belong to a generation, you need to have a location in time that is in some ways specific. It may just be that you have been born 30 years after your parents. Perhaps you have witnessed an epoch-defining event or undergone a socializing experience that represents a caesura in your own biography and a source of solidarity with those who have the experience in common. The generational clock may be ticking at different speeds in several different areas of existence: the individual life cycle, the cycle of family reproduction, social institutions (schools, armies, welfare states and so on), and history.

Given that generations can exist in several different dimensions, it is worth clarifying what they can contribute to historical knowledge. Above all, they are part of the way societies organize their time. Far from being natural or inexorable, generations require decisions to be made about how to measure the temporal positions of different groups and about where to draw the lines between these groups. Generations sometimes do not take shape until some time after the event that ostensibly gives them their meaning. We should not assume that our retrospective sense of the social coherence of a historical generation matches that of its members. Equally, we should not expect generations to be inclusive or fair. Almost invariably they will leave out people who, by dint of their date of birth or experiences, ought to belong. The right to speak in a generation's name is frequently hard-won. In the nineteenth and twentieth centuries, European societies periodically fought memory wars to determine which generations had the strongest claims to exist. Such wars tended to be waged – and won – by educated, articulate and well-connected males. In nineteenth-century Russia, for example, the struggle over collective memory was carried on largely by the Russian intelligentsia, a group that numbered no more than a few hundred thousand. On the eve of World War I, there were only around 35,000 university students in Russia, and the number of active opinion-formers was, as everywhere, considerably lower than the annual intake into higher education – somewhere between 5000 and 10,000.[7]

It often takes a lot of discursive effort for the idea of a generation to coalesce, given the essential fluidity of the concept. Although we all know now that nations are 'invented' or 'imagined' communities, there is a decent chance that nationality, once ascribed to an individual, will stick to him or her. With generation the situation is rarely so clear-cut for two main reasons. First, because the individual can postpone only temporarily, not indefinitely, his or her move from one generation to the next; today's youthful rebel may well be tomorrow's conservative patriarch.[8] Second, because it is not clear where the lines between neighbouring cohorts should be drawn.

For all that generations are hard to pin down, to write about them is more than an exercise in hair-splitting intellectual and cultural history. They are closely bound up with politics and economics – that is to say, with the distribution of power and resources in a given society. Generations can have considerable coercive power once they have taken shape as distinct social constituencies or interest groups. If your age marks you out as a member of the youth cohort, it is hard to avoid being treated as a 'young person'. When you enter the category of 'old person', your outlook and life-chances are likely to depend heavily on the ways in which your society treats its senior members. Generational issues seem to be articulated with particular vehemence at moments when societies are facing fundamental choices about the allocation of collective resources and the redistribution of political authority. Prominent examples include countries suffering the teething troubles of modernization: France in 1789, Germany and Italy in the middle of the nineteenth century, Russia in the late imperial era. 'Modernization' is a vexed and currently unfashionable term, but it does seem to imply the growth of a bureaucratic state that takes upon itself ever more elaborate functions: not just the collection of resources (through taxation, conscription, bureaucratic service) but also their targeted distribution. In the process, the state does much to define generations. Youth is the section of society that undergoes socialization in institutions such as schools, universities and armies. By setting up pension systems, the modern state also does much to create old age as a social generation rather than a biological fact.

So far I have tried to explain why generations might be interesting to historians. They are part of the way a society understands itself: they may serve as an effective means of reconciling succession and solidarity or else as a painful reminder of tensions and cleavages. They are also bound up with the ways that different groups lay claim to power and authority. They have to be taken into account when a society is debating how to distribute collective resources. They clearly have some relation – though not always a direct one – to the structure of families, to socializing institutions and to major historical events.

What is less clear, however, is how we might find a coherent way of combining these different aspects of generational history. Is generation perhaps a weasel word that tempts us to make arguments based on lateral association rather than analytical argument? How, quite simply, can we try to pin down generation and write its history? In the next section I survey the various heavyweight attempts that have been made to grapple with these questions.

Theories and histories of generation

In a lecture on the history of generations, Sir Herbert Butterfield recalled the wish expressed in the Fourth Book of Ezra that 'God, instead of creating the human race in a series of successive generations had put all men to live on the earth contemporaneously'. Not only would this, in Butterfield's words, have 'shortened the long tale of human misery', it would also have put historians out of business. Human beings do, however, come along in an unceasing flow, which means that academics can continue to make a living from disentangling continuity and change. As Butterfield himself admitted, it is hard – especially with respect to societies historically remote from our own – to establish whether generational turnover represents smooth transmission of political experience or conflict and rupture.[9]

David Hume, torch-bearer for the Scottish Enlightenment, had similar questions in mind as he inquired into the origins of political legitimacy. He indulged himself in a thought experiment that forms a neat counterpoint to Butterfield's. What would happen, Hume wondered, if one set of human beings were to die out suddenly and be succeeded, like a silkworm or a butterfly, by a whole new generation? How would people then run their affairs? He imagined that they would do things very differently. They might, for example, 'voluntarily, and by general consent, establish their own form of civil polity, without any regard to the laws or precedents, which prevailed among their ancestors'.[10] Thus would be eliminated all tension between old and new, traditional and modern; the newborn cohort would be free to find the form of government and social organization that best suited it, without being constrained by past arrangements. In such a case, government by 'original contract' would be not a myth of unsullied democratic descent but a political reality.

But the thrust of Hume's argument was that life does not work in this way. Flux, not a revolutionary cycle of extermination and rebirth, is the condition of human society. It is only individuals who enter and depart the scene all at once; groups and cohorts may become eroded, depleted or blurred around the edges, but they are never altogether effaced. For this reason, when we assert that our political system is based at some level on universal consent, on a truly democratic social contract, we are deluding ourselves. Authority as currently exercised has never arrived in the present via a morally unblemished ancestral line; nor has property. In the beginning, there have always been sordid acts of violence and usurpation.

In Hume's view, however, it is no bad thing that we are not free to remake civil society from scratch when we appear on earth. Wholesale change – revolution, in other words – is liable to bring with it confusion, conflict and error. Flux may not always carry us along in the right direction, but for the most part it is a helpful guiding force. The coexistence of generations may not always be frictionless, but it does ultimately ensure the smooth regularity of progress.

I cite Hume's essay partly for its intrinsic interest, but also because it attracted the attention of two of the most prominent modern theorists of historical generations, François Mentré and Karl Mannheim. Both these writers took up Hume's metaphor of the butterfly, but to rather different effect.[11] They agreed that history could never be stopped and restarted, but they thought of the self-reproduction of human society in terms not of flux but of succession and alternation. They argued that generations were not simply carried along by the flow of time but had a life of their own – a conclusion they were led to draw above all by observing the rise of 'mass society' before and after World War I. Generations in the modern world that Mentré and Mannheim saw around them tended to think of themselves as distinct social or cultural entities, as historical agents in their own right. By the early twentieth century it was highly plausible to see generations as providing the pulse of modern history, and not just in the sense that the tempo of human civilization depends on the rate of alternation between old and young, and on the nature of the relationship between them. Historically adjacent cohorts were profoundly divided by their experience of World War I, and in the alienated mass societies of post-war Europe generation was looming just as large as the other main social identities – class and ethnicity. Generation provided a point of intersection for biology, society and politics, and hence a powerful agent of mobilization – as fascism would soon demonstrate.

But for all that generations would appear to be an important element in modern history, it is far from clear how useful they are for historians. On closer inspection they turn out to be extremely elusive. It is hard to be sure where one generation ends and the next begins. The Annalistes, pioneers of scientific 'total' history who came to prominence in the same post-war era, had no truck with the concept of generation in historical analysis. As Lucien Febvre wrote dismissively in 1929: 'it would be better to drop it [generation]'.[12] For the adherents of 'total' history, generational history represented much too partial and arbitrary a reading of the past. Karl Mannheim to some extent concurred with this kind of critique. As he noted in his seminal essay on the subject, generations are an exceptionally complex problem in historical sociology, because they invite both 'positivist' and 'romantic-historical' approaches, while being satisfactorily defined by neither of these. On the one hand, it is tempting to seek exact correlation between the average life span and the rate of historical progress. This was the thrust of the writings of Auguste Comte and his nineteenth-century successors, whose main concern was to find a scientific key to what they saw as the inexorable development of modern society.[13] On the other hand, it might seem plausible to ascribe to each generation an 'inner aim', and to each era a *Zeitgeist*. There are, in other words, two opposing ways of viewing generational time: 'a mechanistic, externalised concept of time' that can be used as 'an objective measure of unilinear progress by virtue of its expressibility in quantitative terms'; and 'subjectively experienceable time' that pulls people together into cohorts by virtue of the fact that they have been 'submitted to the same determining influences'. Mannheim himself was more sympathetic to the 'romantic-historical' than to the 'positivist' approach, but he argued that neither method was satisfactory in isolation. The task of the historical sociologist was to give the generation concept its due without consigning it entirely to the objective or the subjective realm; to acknowledge both the fluidity of time (which eroded objectivist certainties) and the multidirectional character of social processes (which placed limits on the effects of subjectivity, and made the *Zeitgeist* concept nebulous). For Mannheim, as for Wilhelm Dilthey, the generations represented a complex dialectic between layers of social experience, not a chain of succession or a straightforward series of conflicts.[14] The essays by Hume and Mannheim suggest that there is a tension, at the very least, between two basic senses of generation: as a source of historical continuity and as a manifestation of historical rupture.

This brief summary of Mannheim's essay will perhaps make clear another difficulty facing the historian of generations. As soon as we try to gain historical purchase on this slippery concept, we become aware that generations do not always succeed one another smoothly, that not all generations last the same amount of time, that not all generations speak with the same voice. Are generations defined by the shared experience of a particular cohort, or are they more diffuse than that? Does a generation always define itself by opposition to its seniors (or juniors)?

If we turn to more recent writings on the subject, we can find lucidity but no great reduction of complexity. In an incisive survey of the literature that existed in the early 1970s, Alan B. Spitzer concluded that the term 'generation' is used by historians and historical actors in six conceptually distinct senses, and that it is usually unclear how much we can ascribe a cohort's values and behaviour to its historical location, how much to the collective experiences it has undergone, how much to rites of passage or recurrent patterns of generational self-affirmation and so on.[15]

It is hard to argue with Spitzer that the generation concept is often fudged in practice, but this does not preclude further investigation. This book starts from the conviction that history is not an exact science, and that 'What is a generation?' is a *question mal posée*. It is more interesting to inquire when and why social, cultural and political differences are seen in terms of generation rather than of anything else, and how it is that certain generations come to see themselves as separate. For not only do generations make history; it is also the case that history makes generations. The very concept of generation, as used by Mannheim, Mentré and other twentieth-century commentators on the subject, implies chronological consciousness, a sense of one's own unique position in history. It suggests that a society has turned away from a genealogical sense of generation – an awareness of one's own place in a long chain of familial succession – to a less vertical, more horizontal sense of chronological belonging. And this in turn suggests that writing a national history through the prism of generations might be a good way of doing the things that historians often want to do: of finding a way to combine society, politics and culture, and using a society's understanding of itself (its culture) to inform – not to distort – the study of political movements and social structures.

The point will perhaps become clearer if we consider the three main peaks of interest in the historiography of generations in modern Europe. The first of these is the French Revolution and the following decades. Of course, the awareness of generational difference was not an invention of 1789; it is very old indeed. But the idea usually advanced by scholars is that the revolutionary period brought awareness of horizontal allegiances with one's coevals, not just of succession from the older generation, and that it made generational consciousness a historical phenomenon. To be young in 1789 or 1815 or 1830 was very different from being young in 1740 (as was Hume). Hume could not see any way of isolating a historical generation, of observing it take shape in the shifting sands of time. A few decades later, at least for some intellectuals of the revolutionary era, these sands had hardened into a historical rock face. The members of the revolutionary cohort had a number of good reasons to believe in their own distinctiveness from their predecessors. For a start, the relationship between the generations was transformed by legislation. Revolutionary discourse gave sons the same rights as their fathers. Partible inheritance was imposed at a stroke of the revolutionary's quill. But declarations of revolutionary principle were not the only catalyst for generational consciousness. Perhaps more critical was shared historical experience and institutional background. On these grounds the youth cohorts of 1789 and 1815 differed profoundly. The Napoleonic period raised young men's social and occupational expectations; many of them gained a good education in the prestigious new imperial institutions. Even more importantly, the collapse of the Napoleonic Empire was a collective trauma that gave the 'generation of 1820' (defined by its main historian as the cohort born between 1792 and 1803) strong collective self-definition.[16] At approximately the same time, 'youth' became a broadly applied signifier across Europe. It was a vehicle for aspirations to national renewal; it was bound up with the aesthetics and politics of Romanticism; it connoted opposition to the purportedly inert and corrupt Restoration era. Young people were accordingly well represented on the barricades of the nineteenth century. The effect of revolution, then, was not just to establish a historical divide between pre- and post-revolutionary generations, but also to instil in educated young men a historical consciousness that would provide a generational dynamic for later European history.

The second main focus of work on generations in European history has been the era of mass politics (say, 1890–1930), when new, much larger, groups of people moved to the cities and discovered horizontal age allegiances. These people were not the relatively tight-knit elite younger generation of the first half of the nineteenth century; they did not have a clearly projected romantic nationalist, or liberal, or republican ideology. They were politically volatile and, especially after their own collective trauma of the World War I, profoundly disaffected.[17] As I suggested above, it is not by any means a coincidence that the founding works of the sociology of generations (those by Mannheim, Ortega and Mentré) date from this era.[18]

The third peak of historiographical interest in the question of generations is the post-war era with its youth countercultures and protest movements. In an era of peace, prosperity and stability, and given the breakdown of existing social identities (notably class), it was generational, not economic, alienation that turned people into political actors in 1968. If this insight is pushed further, generational identity can be taken to epitomize (post-) modern Western civilization. We are so depoliticized and individualized, or so the argument runs, that it is only an apparently apolitical characteristic – our age – that is capable of mobilizing us and making us feel solidarity with others. What is perhaps most striking about the Parisian and Californian student cohorts of the 1960s is how little their values and life experience differed from those of their parents – as opposed, say, to the young people of late-modernizing countries such as Bulgaria, Rumania and indeed the Soviet Union.[19] As Pierre Nora has suggested, to be a member of a generation is the only way for us to feel individual while forming part of a social group, to feel we are making a personal choice when we enter a group to which we belong by an accident of birth.[20]

If we survey the full course of the twentieth century, the broad trends are clear enough: generational identities have become more numerous, less politicized, less nation-specific and more consumer-orientated. These changes mean that Mannheim's classic essay from 1928, though it remains an essential starting point for reflecting on the concept of generation, now appears to have certain limitations. It could not of course take into account the plebeian turn that many European cultures took from the 1960s onwards, nor the sexual revolution that has meant that generation can no longer be automatically gendered male. Mannheim was himself reacting against the 'great men' approach to defining generation that he found in the work of François Mentré, but his own essay now appears distinctly 'romantic-historical' in some of its particulars. Nor could it be expected to foresee the consequences of demographic ageing and the growth of welfare states, which have greatly increased the prominence of older generations. Coming shortly after a world war and in the midst of social turmoil and political extremism in many parts of continental Europe, Mannheim's analysis naturally emphasized the role of generational agency in bringing about social and political change. A historian writing on the more secure, prosperous, stable and individualistic phases of the century might be more inclined to emphasize the role of generation in creating social solidarity.[21]

There is, in other words, ample justification for examining the whole of the twentieth century, not just the youth politics of the interwar period, for the light it can shed on generation formation. Twentieth-century history throws up so many ways in which generations might plausibly be measured. One is in terms of great events, especially the conflicts and cataclysms that marked the first half of the century. Another is in terms of political design: the century saw the rise (and later fall) of states with unprecedented coercive powers for whom the moulding of youth was crucial to their projects of social transformation. The twentieth century, like the nineteenth, had a thick overlay of 'generationalizing' commentary by various opinion-formers, but the range and the nature of such commentary was transformed by the explosive growth of mass culture and of new media (notably cinema and television, though the internet may not be far behind). Last, but certainly not least, the societies in which generational identities were taking hold themselves underwent fundamental changes: rural–urban migration, advances in medicine, improvements in health care and education, steep rises (and a few sudden falls) in the standard of living and the arrival of widely available birth control. All this meant that the life experiences and trajectories of neighbouring cohorts might differ as never before.

Yet these differences did not necessarily lead to a sense on the part of youth of generational distinctiveness, let alone of rupture. The family remained a powerful socializing institution. One recent exemplification of this point comes in an opinion survey of March 1998, when Russian under-30s, who had undergone their formative years in one of the most unsettled parts of later-twentieth-century Europe, were asked about their relationship with the older generation. Well over half of them (58 per cent) declared that they were not significantly different from their parents.[22] It is also clear that authoritarian regimes, given the immense resources and discursive energy they expended on affirming a particular vision of youth, suffered notable failures in their programmes of generational socialization. As Dorothee Wierling has shown, the GDR 'generation of 1949', although told insistently by the Communist Party that it had unique historical value and a special generational mission, is more adequately defined by the experiences it underwent in the less political and more everyday aspects of its collective biography: the high hopes and self-confidence born of the post-war era, when members of this cohort were the pride of their parents and the chosen ones of the regime, dissipated in the 1970s, when the educated specialists of the post-war generation confronted a lack of fulfilling employment in East German society. In other words, the 1949 cohort, despite the best efforts of the regime, can be regarded as a generation *an sich* but not *für sich*.[23]

This dichotomy – between generations as publicly declared identities, as social constructs, and generations as anthropologically verifiable communities of coeval experience – is hard to escape in the historiography of modern generations. It will insinuate itself into this book too. In the chapters that follow, some authors (Weisbrod, Krylova, Nehring) will be mainly concerned to track the generational narratives of a given society, their proponents and their political purposes. Others (Smith, Kelly, Souto Kustrín, Stargardt) will be more interested in the ways in which collective experiences really differed from one era to another and can properly be called 'generational'.

This does not mean, however, that historical analysis of generations must be split down the middle between those scholars who debunk the generational 'myths' put about publicly by hegemonic male intellectuals and those who seek 'real', sociologically identifiable generations through microscopic social-historical investigation. The relationship between 'real' and 'imagined' generations is a creative tension rather than an absolute divide. It is certainly wise to remain conscious of the arbitrary character of much 'generationalizing' and to be suspicious of narrowly deterministic accounts of generation formation (which hold, for example, that young people sign up for a protest movement on account of their domestic grievances against their parents, or their student milieu, or their year of birth). But generation is a socially rooted identity that has political and economic implications. In this light, it is hardly more arbitrary, or less 'real', than class or nationality.

Here, then, is one historiographical divide that this volume is designed to cross. Another is geographical. Most writing on the history of generations – with a few exceptions such as books on the 'generation of 1914' or the 68ers – is concerned with a specific national context. Scholars usually find acute cases of generational sentiment in the culture they happen to study. Pierre Nora has claimed that generational allegiance is a key to French political history.[24] Historians of Germany have several good grounds for arguing the special prominence of generational identity in their object of study: the proliferation of small city universities and consequent tension between students and artisans; the statization of the civil service and the professions; and the cult of youth as a part of nation-building.[25] Historians of Spain, besides pointing to the epoch-defining moment when Spain lost its last American colony in 1898, can cite abundantly the thinker who is perhaps the most famous (though certainly not the most convincing) generational theorist of the lot: Ortega y Gasset.[26] Hungarians can claim a globe-trotting Budapest 'generation of 1900', one of whose members, Karl Mannheim, would write the single most influential essay on generations.[27] Historians of Russia can point to the first militant generational subculture, whose epicentre was St Petersburg in the 1860s, as well as to the obsession with youth socialization in the Soviet period.[28] The truly exceptional case is perhaps Britain, which largely lacks the generational narratives so abundant elsewhere.[29]

This book aims to establish a genuinely comparative context for interpreting the role of generation in twentieth-century Europe. It brings together material on Britain, France, Spain, Italy, Germany and the USSR, and thus loosens the structuring geographical binaries in the historiography of modern Europe: North and South, and (especially) East and West. It might appear that the countries of the Soviet bloc are a special case in the history of twentieth-century generations, given the state's domination of the public sphere in those societies and the consequent obscurity in the documentary record of issues such as generation conflict and student rebellion. But, as the chapters on Soviet history in this volume suggest, the political indoctrination of youth was only one part of the story. No less crucial were the social contexts in which projects to bring into being a 'new Soviet person' were carried out. In this light, Soviet generationality appears to be the outcome of processes of modernization which, although hypertrophied at some moments and highly attenuated at others, provide a meaningful comparator for modernization in Western democracies (and not something else entirely).

The structure of this book

The chapters that follow form three main thematic clusters. The first of these concentrates on the role that generation has played in political discourse in twentieth-century Europe. In Chapter 2, Bernd Weisbrod examines the tendency in Germany to conceive of generational change as a dramatic and/or heroic departure by elite groups of young men from the traditions of national regeneration. He shows that this habit of thought continued into the post-war era, when two further generations were identified as political for their efforts to break the mould and transform a political culture of defeat. In Chapter 3, Richard Vinen investigates the role of World War II in generational self-definition in France, while in Chapter 4 Holger Nehring examines the rhetoric of generational belonging in West European protest movements in the 1960s. Weisbrod, Vinen and Nehring all investigate the politics of memory in post-war Europe and the often highly tangential relationship between generational declarations and cohort experience.

The next group of chapters takes a step away from political discourse: it offers a series of case studies of particular cohorts and inquires whether, and in what ways, cohort experience amounts to generational identity. In Chapter 5, S.A. Smith investigates the enormous efforts made by the Bolsheviks to do battle with 'vestiges of the past' and socialize young people comprehensively as 'Soviet'. His study of the early Soviet campaign against all forms of 'superstition' leads him to more general reflections on the relationship between modernization and generational formation. In Chapter 6, Anna Krylova takes a different perspective on the 'first Soviet generation' that the Bolsheviks were so desperate to bring into being. By attending both to public discourse and to first-person forms of expression, she argues that the opposition between 'false' generational ideology and 'authentic' cohort experience cannot be sustained usefully. In Chapter 7, Sandra Souto Kustrín investigates the connections between age groups and the acute political conflict of interwar Spain, putting this close-grained social and political history in dialogue with the various social theories that have been devised to explain the youth militancy of the 1920s and 1930s. In Chapter 8, Nicholas Stargardt takes as his object of study the 'war children' of Nazi Germany – a cohort that would appear at first glance to have undergone one of the most devastating and generation-defining collective experiences of the twentieth century. On closer inspection, however, Stargardt finds that there is just as much to divide this cohort as to unite it. In Chapter 9, Catriona Kelly examines post-Stalin children, who constitute a Soviet cohort apparently much *less* clearly defined than its predecessors. The children of the 1950s and 1960s did not figure in public discourse to the same extent as those of the 1920s or 1930s, and they had not undergone shattering historical experiences such as revolution, collectivization and world war. Yet, as Kelly argues, the post-Stalin era saw many small changes – expansion in the state-funded childcare network, improvement in health care infrastructure, increase in the provision of extra-curricular activities and growing availability (in theory) of consumer goods – that together led to major cultural shifts.

The third and final section of the book offers a reminder that generation is not just about childhood and youth. Every society contains several generations that define themselves in relation to each other as well as to historical events and socializing experiences. This multigenerationality only became more pronounced in the twentieth century, as Europeans lived longer and saw the state taking a more extensive role in the intergenerational distribution of resources. Chapters 10 and 11 offer case studies of these processes in Britain and Russia that, given the wildly different political and social histories of those two countries, have a surprising amount of common ground. In both places, modernization and the rise of the welfare state have brought the issues of intergenerational equity and entitlement to the fore while at the same time leaving intact, or even strengthening, the co-operation and interdependency between old and young. The book concludes, then, with an agreeable paradox of contemporary generational history. Generational asseverations have in recent times increased in intensity and frequency (as I suggested in the first paragraph of this 'Introduction', people have never previously had so many ways of generationalizing their experiences), but in other respects the scope for intergenerational intimacy is greater than ever: new communication technologies mean that old and young can keep in touch at any distance, the family occupies a sacred place in popular culture and public discourse, intergenerational wealth redistribution within the family remains crucial (given that education, housing and long-term health care are unprecedentedly expensive), and the fall in the birth rate ensures that attention and economic resources have never been lavished by so many parents and grandparents on so few children and grandchildren. Generational history, like most other history, is not straightforwardly linear, and it is not wholly implausible to suggest that, when historians come to write their accounts of the 'Generation Z' of the early twenty-first century, they will note a turn 'back' to a filial piety that may never previously have existed in European history.

Notes

1. Information from the Random House website: http://www.randomhouse.de/book/edition.jsp?edi=135500.
2. Quotation from Twenge's website: http://www.generationme.org/aboutbook.html.
3. Justification for this view can be found in David Lowenthal's wide-ranging *The Past is a Foreign Country* (Cambridge, 1985), esp. Chapters 2 and 3. For a long view – extending back to late antiquity – of generational conflicts between 'Ancients' and 'Moderns', see J. Le Goff, *History and Memory* (New York, 1992), p. 27.
4. R. Williams, *Keywords: A Vocabulary of Culture and Society*, 2nd edn (London, 1983), p. 140.
5. L. Hunt, *The Family Romance of the French Revolution* (London, 1992).
6. Lowenthal, *The Past is a Foreign Country*, pp. 117–21.
7. V.R. Leikina-Svirskaia, *Russkaia intelligentsiia v 1900–1917 godakh* (Moscow, 1981), p. 8 (university students) and pp. 124–5 (regularly published writers).
8. This is the thrust of P. Abrams, 'Rites of Passage: The Conflict of Generations in Industrial Society', *Journal of Contemporary History*, 5 (1970), 175–90.
9. H. Butterfield, *The Discontinuities between the Generations in History: Their Effect on the Transmission of Political Experience* (Cambridge, 1972), quotations on p. 1.

10. D. Hume, 'Of the Original Contract', in idem, *The Philosophical Works*, ed. T.H. Green and T.H. Grose, 4 vols (London, 1882–86), vol. 3, p. 452.

11. F. Mentré, *Les Générations sociales* (Paris, 1920), p. 180; K. Mannheim, 'The Problem of Generations', in his *Essays on the Sociology of Knowledge*, ed. P. Kecskemeti (London, 1952), p. 277.

12. Quoted in J.-F. Sirinelli (ed.), *Générations intellectuelles: Effets d'âge et phénomènes de génération dans le milieu intellectuel français* (Paris, 1987), p. 14, n. 4.

13. Note A. Comte, *Cours de philosophie positive*, vol. 4, pt. 1 (Paris, 1839), esp. Lesson 51, 'Lois fondamentales de la dynamique sociale, ou théorie générale du progrès naturel de l'humanité'. On later nineteenth-century approaches, see V. Drouin, *Enquêtes sur les générations et la politique 1958–1995* (Paris, 1995), Chap. 1, esp. p. 19.

14. Mentré found a way out of these difficulties by taking literary 'generations' as his measure. In this way, he was able to mark out the whole of French history from 1515 to his own present day. Nations without a literature, he argued, did not have a history either, and so were unsuitable for generational research.

15. A.B. Spitzer, 'The Historical Problem of Generations', *American Historical Review*, 78 (1973), 1353–85.

16. A.B. Spitzer, *The French Generation of 1820* (Princeton, 1987).

17. On the political incoherence and volatility of youth movements, note Philip Abrams's observation that 'just because it cuts across familiar lines of social differentiation the appeal to youth cannot follow up its attack on existing systems with any socially coherent, viable or widely acceptable proposals for an alternative system' (Abrams, 'Rites de Passage', 179).

18. See R. Wohl, *The Generation of 1914* (London, 1980).

19. On generations in the post-war French bourgeoisie, see R. Vinen, *France, 1934–1970* (Houndmills, 1996), p. 140.

20. P. Nora, 'Generation', in idem (ed.), *Realms of Memory: Rethinking the French Past*, vol. 1 (New York, 1996), p. 508.

21. See J. Zinnecker, '"Das Problem der Generationen": Überlegungen zu Karl Mannheims kanonischen Text', in J. Reulecke (ed.), *Generationalität und Lebensgeschichte im 20. Jahrhundert* (Munich, 2003), esp. pp. 45–7.

22. B. Dubin, 'Mezhdu vsem i nichem', in Iu. Levada and T. Shanin (eds), *Pokolencheskii analiz sovremennoi Rossii* (Moscow, 2005), p. 252. More poignantly, 45 per cent of these respondents said that they wished their own children and grandchildren to be different from them.

23. D. Wierling, *Geboren im Jahr Eins: Der Jahrgang 1949 in der DDR: Versuch einer Kollektivbiographie* (Berlin, 2002).

24. Nora, 'Generation', p. 503.

25. See M. Roseman (ed.), *Generations in Conflict: Youth Revolt and Generation Formation in Germany 1770–1968* (Cambridge, 1995).

26. D.L. Shaw, *The Generation of 1898 in Spain* (New York, 1975); J. Ortega y Gasset, *The Revolt of the Masses* (London, 1932). For a justifiably sceptical assessment of Ortega's writings on generation, see Chapter 7 by Sandra Souto Kustrín later in this volume.

27. J. Lukacs, *Budapest 1900: A Historical Portrait of a City and Its Culture* (London, 1988), pp. 137–81.

28. One of the most robust interpretations of this kind belongs to Lewis S. Feuer in his *The Conflict of Generations: The Character and Significance of Student Movements* (London, 1969).
29. The reasons for this are a matter of some speculation. One possible explanation is the relative paucity of epoch-defining historical events in modern Britain. Another is that, until quite recently, the major student centres in Britain were non-metropolitan. English exceptionalists might also claim that Britain is a place where empire has on the whole made the elite more, not less, integrated, and where the Church has also served as an integrative institution for educated young men.

2
Cultures of Change: Generations in the Politics and Memory of Modern Germany

Bernd Weisbrod

When the Düsseldorf faculty officially took leave of Wolfgang Mommsen, the prominent historian of Wilhelmine Germany, Max Weber and the British Empire who passed away in 2004, his equally famous colleague Hans-Ulrich Wehler reminded everyone that he and Mommsen belonged to the same generation.[1] We were both, he said, 45ers, still reluctant at the end of the war to leave our disappointments behind, and more and more intent on breaking new ground without, however, ever questioning the authority of our academic fathers. There were differences, of course, he explained, but on the whole, their common experience in Germany's painful post-1945 transition gave them a sense of democratic purpose that outlasted their own doubts. After all, they were the group that Helmut Schelsky back in the fifties had dubbed the 'sceptical generation' – one that encompassed Helmut Kohl and Hans-Jochen Vogel, Günther Grass and Hans Magnus Enzensberger, Ralf Dahrendorf and Jürgen Habermas, Joachim Fest and Rudolf Augstein, Hans-Ulrich Wehler himself and, of course, Hans and Wolfgang Mommsen.[2] This is a long list of politicians and academics, writers and journalists, still very young when the war was over, who on looking back can lay claim to the transformation of the Federal Republic from *Volksgemeinschaft* to liberal democracy. For some time they had seemed to stand in the shadow of the 68ers, the self-appointed political generation which was readily credited with the second coming of the democratic spirit in the Federal Republic, at least *ex post*, but now, maybe, it was their turn to claim responsibility for the post-war culture of change that had transformed West Germany for good.[3]

This is just one typical example of the automatic and retrospective approach to generations in modern Germany that divides historical actors into neat configurations of 'them' and 'us' and presents historical consciousness as being located in age cohorts whose members lie on all sides of the many deep political divides in German history. This is an important phenomenon with much deeper roots than might be suggested by the 'instant' generations that are now being invented by the day from Florian Illies's *Generation Golf* to Paul Nolte's *Generation Reform* or, more recently, the claim of our outgoing foreign minister Joschka Fischer that he is the last real 'rock 'n' roll politician' whereas all the newcomers just belong to a 'play-back generation'.[4] This frequent use of the generation paradigm in contemporary Germany may have to do with new political ambitions in the wake of unification, although the new 89ers do not seem to match any of the alleged credentials of the 68ers.[5] But, historically speaking, this German habit of seeing genera- tions as political actors calls for some caution. First, all generations are cultural constructs and usually come in particular kinds and times and for particular purposes of self-promotion. Second, it should be open to question whether there is anything particularly German about the gen- erational forces at work in history, since modern Europe has seen many apparently transnational generational movements: from the 1848ers to the 1968ers, and since 1945 a European generation of social climbers that may in the years to come give way to a welfare generation (even if, as the case of the 'Lost Generation' of the Great War shows, these 'European' generations all come in their very national guises).[6]

What kinds of generations are in question here? At first the answer looks rather simple: these are 'political generations' which, maybe, in the German case, offer an explanation for the dramatic shifts in and after the major catastrophes and crises in modern history. No wonder that the concept is so inflationary. But when the concept of 'political generations' is taken seriously it appears that only three generations are fit to carry that somewhat dubious title in the twentieth century: the two youth generations of the World Wars and the 68ers.[7] It can, indeed, be argued that they were all confronted in their politically formative period by major dramatic events and consequently managed to trans- form their experiences into a shared pattern of lasting political orienta- tion in life. In another count, however, 11 such political generations can be detected over the course of the twentieth century, with a num- ber of cohorts held together just by the fast turnover of events in their respective periods of youth.[8] In a nation at war, a few years could make all the difference – 40 per cent of males born in 1920 were killed in World War II, a much higher percentage than suffered by any other cohort born before or after. At the same time, the war experience itself was shared by a great variety of younger and older fighters and also, it has to be said, by civilians whose survival chances depended hugely on whether they lived in the East or the West, in the city or the country.[9] But what marks out the three 'real' political generations, according to Herbert, is firstly their ability to define and distinguish their own generational status against any other generation, and secondly when and whether they managed to sense and establish a new 'cultural hegemony in the making'. Self-styling and political success, therefore, seem to be prerequisites in this kind of definition.

When looking back at Karl Mannheim's classic definition of 1928, it becomes clear that common impressions in youths make for a potentiality, not the formation of a generation itself.[10] On the contrary, collective experience is here modified by a quasi-Hegelian dialectic. As in the Marxist distinction between class position and class consciousness (*Klasse an sich* and *Klasse für sich*), Mannheim argues that any given 'social location' of generations (*Generationslagerung*) needs generational 'stratification of experience' to find itself in a 'generation as actuality' (*Generationszusammenhang*) with actual 'participation in the common destiny' out of which certain 'generation units' (*Generationseiheiten*) may arise, sometimes in opposition to each other but bonded by a shared feeling of generational unity (*Generationsgemeinschaft*) against the previous generation. It is not just generation consciousness that is needed here, but also generation actors, so to speak, who usually in small groups strive to find the '*Gestalt*' of their generation to be revealed in 'collective strivings' (*kollektive Wollungen*). Mannheim has rightly been criticized for two judgements that he makes in this otherwise well-received exercise in the sociology of knowledge. Although 'generational impulse' may be a way to understand the processes by which elite groups set themselves up as generations, it may, like class ideology, overstep the bounds of its 'natural' supporters and targets and rally different cohorts to its cause. Secondly, to privilege active male youths with the awakening of the generational potentiality follows the typically twenties' adulation of – male and bourgeois – youth as constituting a political programme on its own (as in the *Jugendbewegung*, which was adamant about its style but less so about its politics). Dynamic social change will only yield its generational programme, Mannheim says, to a privileged few who find ways to unfold the potential of their 'generational entelechy' as an inner necessity but also as a development of the wider framework of 'entelechy trends' of the '*Zeitgeist*'. On the other hand, so he argued, too much speed and strife could nip that 'embryo entelechy' in the bud.[11]

This was a rather vague idea of the self-revelation of a hidden task which Mannheim took over from the art historian Wilhelm Pinder, who used it to great advantage in order to argue that all artistic styles are really due to such *Entelechien*, in historical time and in artists alike, and that artists can only considered to be artists by that index. So the argument, as Lutz Niethammer shows, is not really about generations at all, but about the group conditions of hegemonic cultural discourse over time.[12] Here Karl Mannheim's Budapest mentor Georg Lukács may have given the cue with his idea about the historical necessity of revolutions. More importantly, however, Günther Gründel was certainly lurking in the background as a member of the conservative-revolutionary 'Tat' circle who in 1932 defined the 'mission' of the young generation. He called on his own generation – the *Kriegsjugendgeneration* – which had been deprived of the war experience itself to put an end to the crisis of complacency after the breakdown of the useless dividing lines of class and tradition in Weimar Germany, and to transform their humiliation into a serious and revolutionary endeavour of youthful self-control and determined pursuit of national salvation.[13]

There is, of course, more in Mannheim than just a sociological reading of the 'youth as politics' programme of the nationalist right. But even in his studied objectivism we can detect a glimmer of that 'holy spirit' of the *Jugendbewegung*, which Eduard Spranger, in his influential *Psychologie des Jugendalters* of 1924, likened to the enthusiastic feelings of religious rebirth and conversion on a fundamentalist scale. This youthfulness, so he argued, was culturally redemptive (*kulturerlösend*) irrespective of any political programme: 'We can detect here a unique escalation of a particular phenomenon of puberty, which is never totally absent, into a great social and cultural sea-change. And where this revival is not in contact with church or free theological meaning, it will appear in the form of immanent mysticism, i.e. a wholly secular religiosity which streams from the untouched depths of life.'[14]

The marriage of this youth cult with the *völkisch* ideology did indeed foster a sense of purpose in the student generation of the twenties, which is little surprising considering their baptism of fire in counter-revolutionary and nationalist battles in the early Weimar Republic. But as is suggested by the case of Werner Best, radical student activist and later mastermind of the SS *Reichssicherheitshauptamt*, the generational sense of purpose was as much a matter of retrospective self-styling as of political strife in the making of a violent career.[15] The stylish outfit of this career may have suited the political purpose, i.e. self-victimization through violent self-empowerment, but it is doubtful whether *völkisch* socialization as such was sufficient to create a whole ideological generation of perpetrators. They were driven, it seems, more by the repercussions of violent politics in their own imagination than by any collective experience in their early socialization. This begs two questions. Firstly, does Best's 'heroic realism' really mark him out as a protagonist of the 'generation of sobriety' of the twenties?[16] It is true that he dressed up ruthlessness as emotional cool, but the heroism of the dead does not figure highly in the emotional regime of sobriety with its literary codes of disinvolvement and self-effacement (as in Berthold Brecht's famous poem 'Verwische die Spuren' ['Leave No Traces Behind!']).[17]

And secondly: if this problematic generational reading of Nazi perpetrators is taken one step further, for example, in an analysis of the new administrative SS elite as a 'generation of the relentless' (Michael Wildt's interpretation), we tend to short-circuit the cross-generational appeal of an admittedly young political movement.[18] It is true, 60 per cent of the new SS administrative elite did belong to the same *Kriegsjugendgeneration*, but on checking their own testimony we find more and more evidence for what rather looks like institutional self-generationalization. The new agencies of terror in the Third Reich did, of course, recruit the young and willing, who could feel rewarded for the *völkisch* battles of their student days by rapid advancement through the echelons of the 'dual state'. But their sense of cohesion as a generation in many ways only ratified their institutional success and socialization in the practice of violence. In any case, as is well known, '*ganz normale Männer*' of all ages could be perpetrators. There is, therefore, a danger in the recent biographical focus of perpetrator research: once the youthful socialization of a generation is put centre stage, ideology tends to be upgraded as a driving force of the 'Third Reich', whereas in many cases it appears that the camaraderie of career networks, institutional practices of violence and war-related ruthlessness were simply read backwards into a generational sense of purpose and belonging. As with many highly ambitious Nazi upstarts, institutionalized radicalism and excessive duty in the firing line of racial war could easily compensate for the lack of early party membership. In the end, it might be said that excessive male bonding through violent excesses superseded any generational sense of purpose and belonging which might have been called on for group cohesion and legitimation.[19]

This, in a way, reverses the usual assumption about cause and effect in the formation of generations. Like other biographical illusions they should be considered the problem of which they pretend to be solution: generation consciousness – *Generationalität* – very often dresses up an *ex post* interpretation of shared experience which lends extra credibility to successful leadership and tends to camouflage political disputes over authority and distribution as conflict between generations. This also applies to the generation of 1945, which with its typical wartime exposure in anti-aircraft batteries (*Flakhelfersyndrom*) was confronted with the total collapse of authority, political and parental alike, and forced to find its own way and make a new world. No doubt, this intermediary or 'sandwich' generation – a typical 'in-between generation' (*Zwischengeneration*) in Mannheim's terminology – bridged the gap between those generations tainted by the Nazi *Volksgemeinschaft* and the political generation of 1968. But in many ways the 'fatherlessness, speechlessness and historylessness' identified in this cohort by Heinz Bude was less significant than what they shared with other post-war European societies: the sense of new opportunities for normal family life and social advancement presented by the unique mid-century 'boom', in which a 'silent' generational success story was perceived as a personal reward for individual achievement, as Pat Thane has argued for the British case.[20]

If we turn our attention to politics, it has become more and more evident in recent historiography that the opening up of the public sphere, the return of the past in moral debates and legal prosecution, and the internationalization of academic standards and public discourse were well on the way before the 68ers brought the conflict about political authority to a pitch. Yet this may also be a somewhat belated acknowledgement of the valuable democratizing causes to which members of this 'generation' contributed, which were conceived not primarily as generational but as genuine political conflict, as, for example, in the *Spiegel* affair of 1962.[21] Of course, to take just this example, the gradual replacement of 'consensus journalism' under Adenauer by 'critical journalism' in the sixties owed a great deal to the example of new men like Rudolf Augstein and to the Anglo-Saxon model of reporting, which, however, underwent quite similar changes from the fifties to the sixties.[22] But the opening up of new job opportunities in the media market, the new format of TV reporting, the relaxing of cold war tensions at home and abroad and the emergence of different 'attention regimes' in a prospering society all contributed to a cultural change in the public sphere. Political contest almost came as a necessary concomitant after new standards of social and political security had been secured, but this can hardly be explained just in terms of the new generation of 45ers, whose liberal minority never managed to win majority support (unless, maybe, in their old age).[23]

The same was true of the 68ers, of course, who were still called by their political name APO (Extra-Parliamentary Opposition) well into the seventies, until, in the light of the new social movements of the eighties like feminism and environmentalism, they were dubbed the 68ers, and then moved on, miraculously, to attract almost anybody of any standing and approximately their age into their generation. And yet, in spite of their immediate political defeat (though in the wake of their heroic stance against the German tradition of the *Obrigkeitsstaat*), they are credited with the label of honour of a 'real' political generation. Why? Because they fit the Mannheim bill of a small elite of bourgeois male youths in revolt who managed to acquire hegemonic status and co-opt all sorts of fellow-travellers in their wake – albeit only after a rather contentious showdown with terrorism in the seventies which might yet prove to have been the real test of a new democratic era in West Germany.[24] In the event itself, elite group behaviour should not be mistaken for generation consciousness, whatever the impression given by the new youth culture of self-determination in lifestyle and music (which, anyway, was much stronger in the US and Britain than in the continental student revolts).[25] A good case in point here is the autobiographical reflection and psychoanalytic retrieval of the group experience and collective memory of the sixties in Italy by Luisa Passerini, which in Italian is called *Autoritratto di Gruppo* and in English *Autobiography of a Generation*.[26] In the German case, as Norbert Elias has argued, the great urge for redemptive meaning in post-war bourgeois youths ('das Sinnverlangen bürgerlicher Nachkriegsgenerationen') might have added a particular poignancy when the stage was set in 1968 for a symbolic renunciation of anyone over 30, who as such was deemed to be contaminated with the horrors of the German past. 'Fascism' as a depersonalized label of guilt did help to turn the moral tables on the *Deutsche Herrengeneration*.[27] But memory wars of this kind are hardly sufficient to explain the political romanticism of a leftist escalation of civil disobedience and provocative anti-authoritarianism which, after all, had its equivalents in almost all West European states and the United States. Political youth movements have a very German tradition, but in this case one should at least acknowledge that the revival of the German Left was also a response to the rather unusual situation whereby communism was considered an extraterritorial enemy – unlike in most other countries of Western Europe – before burying such political issues in some generational community born in troubled times.[28]

But can German terrorism nonetheless be considered a generational conflict (as Elias argues)? As we see from the confessions of one terrorist from a working-class background, Bommi Baumann, the violent break that his co-terrorists underwent with their anti-violent bourgeois socialization was hardly proof of intergenerational conflict in the particular form of 'bourgeois terrorism'. The rhetoric of liberation produced by Ulrike Meinhoff, who was from a different generation anyway, was certainly not restricted to an intellectual version of Marxism: it showed all the signs of the agitated excitement of moral outrage and self-empowerment as soon as the last vestiges of bourgeois decency, as a mother and a woman, were shed.[29] It is hard to detect in the deadly onslaught against the 'police pigs' (*Bullenschweine*) and the 'character masks' (*Charaktermasken*) a desire to rebalance the power disparities between old and young *tout court*. But this is what Elias argues for the 'young-bourgeois' generation of the 68ers in their pressing sense of oppression and inequity between workers and employers, women and men, colonized and colonizers. In any case, 'hunger for meaning' (*Sinnhunger*) should not be conflated with the murderous drive to engage in holy battle with the bourgeois state, not even as the tip of a generational iceberg. Professional and political frustrations may come in many forms, and sometimes even in the form of moral outrage. Elias acknowledges himself that the threshold of political violence may have been lower in the aftermath of violent regimes such as those in Italy and Germany, but neither the lengthening of the political moratorium for bourgeois youth in the life cycle nor the moral urge in a 'generation' allegedly devoid of political options can explain the violent doublebind between terrorists and state in West Germany. Elias seems much closer to the mark when comparing national codes of civilized conduct, which in Britain means keeping a distance from violent transgressions and finding pride in political restraint on both sides, civil society and the state, irrespective of generations.[30]

As with many other generational labels in modern German history, an inbuilt evasion of hard political facts seems to lie behind the frequent recourse to an imagined community based on common experience over the life course. As was remarked back in the twenties in the great boom of generational studies, here, maybe, is the hidden logic in the making of historical generations: a perceived need to overcome exhausted notions of cultural change – class, religion, region, even race, as Karl Mannheim suggests – with a new epistemology of social mobilization and political community that establishes a fresh claim for strong group cohesion and a new departure. For a while this cuts across the established frames of reference in which historical transitions are normally negotiated, and which we usually find well in place, even after such 'political' generations have had their say. This is also one of the great misunderstandings of the more recent debate on the pampered generation of the welfare state. This group seems to be neither heroic nor tragic enough to qualify for Mannheim's *Generationsentelechie*, especially if it is conceptualized as the transformed generation of 68ers who in their self-serving nostalgia had it both ways, in revolt first and then living on the next generation in old age.[31] But this only detracts from the very real redistributional battle which rages at present in all Western countries not so much between generations but between rich and poor, those with property and those without, those who are market-clever and those who are duty-bound, who all hand down their lifetime's chances and assets to their very own next family generation.[32]

Even the most relentless German exercise in generation formation has not succeeded in grounding generation consciousness in a very obvious community of fate: the GDR generation of 1949, which was officially feted as the symbolic promise of a splendid youth and a long and successful advance through life, lacked a sense of generational unity even though it was certainly confronted with a most incisive experience in its formative period – the building of the Wall.[33] Moreover, as a new research project in Jena has discovered, the 'children of the wall' might have common memories, and some very small elite groups did actually experience a youth revolt in the wake of its demise, but the break-up of political networks and the self-exhaustion of a society under constant pressure prevented the formation of a 'generation of 89'.[34] Much depends, obviously, on the distribution of market chances for the winning team and little on a demonstrative break with the last GDR generation. On the contrary, family allegiance is valued highly by children whose parents have to live with broken biographies, just like after World War II. As is well known from oral history interviews, individual life stories when told in hindsight tend to be told in terms of common experience. This helps to validate personal memory but also allows acquired knowledge to be read back into the established personal storyline. But even the common experience and excitement of the 'peaceful revolution' of 89 in East Germany seems to have lacked the transformation of its popular slogan '*Wir sind das Volk*' into the sense of generational necessity and purpose that looms so large in the 'accepted' notion of generational change in modern German history. It is true, historical change of tremendous consequences was crystallizing in this generation, but so far, it seems, their self-generationalization has failed simply because they could not lay claim to victory after all.

This leads to the final aspect of generational discourse in Germany that marks out cultural change as an outcome not necessarily of pro-active, but of re-active, mobilization. In the field of memory studies, as in political conflict that dresses up as generational conflict, psychological notions of family relations are read into the public discourse about 'Holocaust memory' so as to deliver a rather clear-cut understanding of the first, second and third generations after the Holocaust, which even allows for connections to be made between the two sides (German and Jewish) of victimhood.[35] This is due to the psychological understanding of secondary traumatization in children of the Holocaust and, conversely, the pressures on the children of perpetrators to 'hear' the guilt in the silence of their parents.[36] In both cases the transgenerational transmission of family histories is interrupted by the horrible truth of an unspeakable family secret. This is normally only revealed by way of proxy projection across the generational divide with the third generation of grandchildren rediscovering what was hidden from them by the emotional protection which their parents had granted their own parents. This psychological mechanism can be shown in the ways in which family narratives change over time, and in which the 'middle generation' negotiates the outcome of this process.[37] But in the Freudian approach according to which no generation can ever hope to hide its emotional state from the next, this is less a matter of narratology than of the unavoidable internalization of the missing object of identity formation. This 'telescoping' of generations in psychoanalytic terms tends to lend itself not only to a forward projection of traumatic experience but also to a backward projection of victimhood, which may itself be the outcome of an explicit framework of collective memory as well as of an unspoken assumption about the historical competition over victimhood.[38] The assumed psychological dynamics of Holocaust-related repression or traumatization across the generations, therefore, not only implies a fair amount of de-contextualization but also overlooks its own historicity as an intellectual tool for coming to terms with a very private past (whereas Holocaust consciousness, by complete contrast, is clearly a historical function of public memory politics).[39]

When looking at memory generations in this way it is evident that memory wars are hardly explicable in psychoanalytical terms alone. The collective efforts of post-war Germany in her search for a 'usable past' were clearly conditioned by the instrumental use of German victimhood for political rehabilitation.[40] But the very private pain of loss and defeat was only deferred and frequently lingered on in mental states of delusion.

In many ways, they were only covered up by the later back-projection of the concept of trauma, which was neither available at the time nor very appropriate for coming to terms with the devastating effects of war experience in the present.[41] This process of selective forgetting and traumatic remembering in competing memory cultures is more than just some sort of generation formation from above. Shared memories as such are in no way generation-generators, nor is it to be assumed that public framing of such memories can go uncontested. The photographic memories of the Holocaust, although suppressed and channelled in many ways, were also negotiated by the images of the war – as cover and container – that abounded in post-war Germany memory culture.[42] This was contested ground not just between generations, but also between political players of the same generation, as is indicated by the revealing debates about the rehabilitation of *Wehrmacht* soldiers – with or without the military plotters of 20 July – and the recent public viewing of *Wehrmacht* crimes.[43] Generational memory may thus be considered the outcome of an ongoing and contingent reframing of private experience in hindsight. Psychological theories of emotional parenting and deferred family mission do not seem to account for these complicated processes in establishing post-war memory generations, although they may help to conceptualize these public frames of memory construction as a generational sequence insofar as the generation of eyewitnesses is gradually being replaced by the media generations of TV series and public debates – with Holocaust consciousness by now firmly enshrined in the moral standards of the nation.[44]

The moral conundrum of the 68ers in coming to terms with the past of their parents has often been overplayed in the long-standing debate about the German 'inability to mourn'. This 1967 formula was meant by Alexander and Margarete Mitscherlich to show the intimate relationship with the *Führer* as the internalized love object of the *Volksgemeinschaft* which could not be shed for fear of total self-delusion. Tilman Moser, in an act of alleged patricide, has rightly blamed it for some misapprehension about the moral dilemmas faced by the 'first generation' and has pointed his finger at the moral superiority complex of the 'second generation' that was fuelled by it.[45] More recently Christian Schneider has even claimed that the 68ers had somehow unconsciously found their 'generation object' in the Holocaust, that is, in the idealization of and identification with father figures such as Max Horkheimer and Theodor W. Adorno. They stood in, it is claimed in this psychoanalytic reading, for the victims as love objects who allowed the transfer of their students' obsessive self-hate to some proxy self-victimization and moral superiority.[46] Others, like Dan Diner, can see nothing of the sort, rather a glaring absence of the brutal reality of the Holocaust in the 68ers' idea of fascism, which together with their sometimes rather dubious support for the 'oppressed' Palestinian people allows him to speak of the metamorphosis of German anti-Semitism from the right to the left.[47] Both these readings of the 68 generation as a memory generation seem misplaced, simply because the options and choices under review cannot simply be read in terms of 'Holocaust functionality'.

There is clearly a danger in this kind of psychological shorthand for generational memory, particularly when it comes with a package of popular assumptions about German character traits or marketable sound bites as in Harald Welzer's recent best-seller on why *Grandpa Was No Nazi*.[48] A number of pieces of research have claimed that in three-generation family interviews a 'cumulative heroization' of the first generation is the paramount narrative of the second and eventually the third generation. The self-justification of such transgenerational projections is not unusual in family transitions, especially if this storyline can be sold to some outside member of the imagined family community. But it simply cannot explain the present boom in public soul-searching to be found in second- and third-generation family memoirs, which speak of the worst fears when it comes to the family secrets of the first generation.[49] Obviously, matters are more complicated. The 'generational imprinting' of collective memory also varies according to the period and the future viability of such memory.[50] Perhaps an often-forgotten piece of advice from Karl Mannheim can help us here. There is, Mannheim argues, a misleading temptation in reading generations into whatever cultural change we might want to explain. Most of the fundamental elements of historical change can only be detected, he argues, 'in the medium of the social and historical phenomena which constitute a secondary sphere above them'. Therefore, 'the student of the generation problem cannot try to specify the effects attributed to the factor of generations before he has separated all the effects due to the specific dynamism of the historical and social sphere. If this intermediary sphere is skipped, one will be tempted to resort immediately to naturalistic principles, such as generation, race, or geographical situation, in explaining phenomena due to environmental or temporal influences.'[51] This is why Mannheim insists that, since generational potentialities are always present in any situation, 'the particular features of a given process of modification cannot be explained by reference to them'.[52]

This is not to say that a very personal home in time (*Zeitheimat*) is everybody's individual anchor in his or her progression from a sense of origin to memory, a lifelong process attendant on the changing cultural patterns of historical transition and memory.[53] But nothing seems to indicate that this cultural adjustment is ruled by a recurring excess of youthful excitability (as in 'political generations') or by some parental substitution complex in collective emotions (as in 'memory generations'). It is time, it seems, to deconstruct the 'generational fallacy' in much of modern German history. Instead, we should look in more detail into the politics of self-generationalization, seeing this perhaps as a very German way of holding on to the model of male and bourgeois redemptive youth as a protagonist in the national drama or perhaps as a psychodynamic sequence of ever more reluctant or confessional memory generations, just as the case may be. 'Silent generations' should also be brought back into focus and checked against underlying European patterns and emotional codes which may sometimes be linked to very intense bodily experience (as, for example, in the 'generation of the pill'). This would help to deconstruct the 'manly' character of most of the generations discussed here and make room for the female side of shared experience, such as that of the generation of rising expectations after 1945, which in many ways predates the feminist movement.[54]

Obviously, the experience of violence and humiliation does have the potential to organize self-appointed generations in their self-styled mission and/or frustration. But violence is no automatic generational marker either. Rather it is the emotional framing of and craving for intense forms of belonging which flow from it, sometimes even in afterlife, as the most recent debate about the 'children of war' generation in Germany can show. Most of the emotional stories of loss and pain now told by senior citizens as belated 'Witnesses of War' are coming out of hiding as if they had previously been crowded out by the public acknowledgement of guilt.[55] In any case, it is symptomatic that it is usually fatherless sons who are presently seeking emotional relief as a 'generation' of troubled fathers now in retirement age after having had their vocal revolt against their suddenly very present fathers in 68, and having silently endured family misfortunes for which they now seek an explanation in their childhood deprivations. It is a telling legacy of the German generational model that even today, in this emotional debate, fatherless daughters and motherless sons apparently still have to go without that sense of victimization, which seems to nurture a longing for a belated generational communion in Germany as well as in other countries ravaged by war.

Notes

1. H.-U. Wehler, 'Wolfgang J. Mommsen 1930–2004', *Geschichte und Gesellschaft*, 31 (2005), 135–42.
2. H. Schelsky, *Die skeptische Generation. Eine Soziologie der deutschen Jugend* (Düsseldorf, 1957).
3. D. Moses, 'Die 45er. Eine Generation zwischen Faschismus und Demokratie', *Neue Sammlung*, 40 (2000), 233–64.
4. F. Illies, *Generation Golf. Eine Inspektion* (Berlin, 2000) and *Generation Golf 2* (Berlin, 2003); P. Nolte, *Generation Reform. Jenseits der blockierten Republik* (Munich, 2004). On Joschka Fischer, see *Der Spiegel*, 22 September 2005.
5. C. Leggewie, *Die 89er. Porträt einer Generation* (Hamburg, 1995); H. Bude, *Das Altern einer Generation. Die Jahrgänge 1938 bis 1948* (Frankfurt, 1995).
6. R. Wohl, *The Generation of 1914* (London, 1980).
7. U. Herbert, 'Drei politische Generationen im 20. Jahrhundert', in J. Reulecke (ed.), *Generationalität und Lebensgeschichte im 20. Jahrhundert* (Munich, 2003), pp. 95–114.
8. H. Fogt, *Politische Generationen. Empirische Bedeutung und theoretisches Modell* (Opladen, 1982).
9. R. Overmans, *Deutsche militärische Verluste im Zweiten Weltkrieg* (Munich, 1999).
10. K. Mannheim, 'The Problem of Generations', in Mannheim, *Essays on the Sociology of Knowledge* (Oxford, 1952), pp. 276–320.
11. Mannheim, 'The Problem', p. 310. For criticism, see: K. Matthes, 'Karl Mannheims "Das Problem der Generationen" neu gelesen. Generationen "gruppen" oder "gesellschaftliche Regelung von Zeitlichkeit"', *Zeitschrift für Soziologie*, 14 (1985), 363–472; J. Zinnecker, 'Das Deutungsmuster "Jugendgeneration". Fragen an Karl Mannheim', *Jahrbuch Jugendforschung*, 2 (2002), 61–89.
12. L. Niethammer, 'Generation und Geist. Eine Station Karl Mannheims auf dem Weg zur Wissenssoziologie', in R. Schmidt (ed.), *Systemumbruch und Generationswechsel. Mitteilungen des SFB 580: Gesellschaftliche Entwicklung und Systemumbruch* (Jena, 2003), no. 9, pp. 19–32; see also Niethammer, 'Die letzte Gemeinschaft. Über die Konstruierbarkeit von Generationen und ihre Grenzen' (Inaugural speech for the Göttingen graduate school on Generations in Modern History), at www.generationengeschichte.uni-goettingen.de.
13. G.E. Gründel, *Die Sendung der jungen Generation. Versuch einer umfassenden revolutionären Sinndeutung der Krise* (Munich, 1932).
14. My translation from: 'Wir haben hier die einzigartige Steigerung eines Pubertätsphänomens, das in keiner Zeit ganz fehlt, zu einer großen gesellschaftlichen und kulturellen Woge. Und da, wo die Erweckung nicht mit kirchlichen oder freien theologischen Sinngehalten in Verbindung steht, erscheint sie in der Form der immanenten Mystik, d.h. einer ganz säkularen Religiosität, die aus unausgeschöpften Lebenstiefen quillt.' E. Spranger, *Psychologie des Jugendalters* (Leipzig, 1924).
15. U. Herbert, Best. *Biographische Studien über Radikalismus, Weltanschauung und Vernunft 1903–1989* (Bonn, 1996).
16. U. Herbert, '"Generation der Sachlichkeit". Die völkische Studentenbewegung der frühen zwanziger Jahre in Deutschland', in F. Bajohr (ed.), *Zivilisation und*

Barbarei: Die widersprüchlichen Potentiale der Moderne. Detlev Peukert zum Gedenken (Hamburg, 1991), pp. 115–44.

17. H. Lethen, *Verhaltenslehren der Kälte. Lebensversuche zwischen den Kriegen* (Frankfurt, 1994).

18. M. Wildt, *Generation des Unbedingten. Das Führungskorps des Reichssicherheitshauptamtes* (Hamburg, 2002).

19. C.R. Browning, *Ordinary Men. Reserve Police Battalion 101 and the Final Solution in Poland* (New York, 1992).

20. H. Bude, *Deutsche Karrieren. Lebenskonstruktion sozialer Aufsteiger aus der Flakhelfer-Generation* (Frankfurt, 1987); P. Thane, 'Family Life and "Normality" in Postwar British Culture', in R. Bessel and D. Schumann (eds), *Life after Death: Approaches to a Cultural History of Europe during the 1940s and 1950s* (Washington DC, 2003), pp. 193–210.

21. For a reappraisal of the generation of 45 in their 'generational conflict' with the men of the past in German journalism, see C. von Hodenberg, *Konsens und Krise. Eine Geschichte der westdeutschen Medienöffentlichkeit 1945–1973* (Göttingen, 2006).

22. The 'official voice' of the BBC was no less 'consensual' in the fifties according to A. Briggs, *The History of Broadcasting in the United Kingdom*, vol. 5, *Competition* (Oxford, 1995); for the post-war 'conservative compromise', see K. O'Morgan, *The People's Peace: British History since 1945* (Oxford, 1999), chap. 4.

23. T. Mergel, 'Politischer Journalismus und Politik in der Bundesrepublik', in C. Zimmermann (ed.), *Politischer Journalismus. Öffentlichkeit und Medien im 19. und 20. Jahrhundert* (Oberfildern, 2006), pp. 193–212; see also K.C. Führer, '"Aufmerksamkeit" und "Vertrauen" als Kategorie der Mediengeschichte', in B. Weisbrod (ed.), *Die Politik der Öffentlichkeit – die Öffentlichkeit der Politik. Politische Medialisierung in der Geschichte der Bundesrepublik* (Göttingen, 2003), pp. 151–74.

24. W. Kraushaar, *1968 als Mythos, Chiffre und Zäsur* (Hamburg, 2000).

25. A. Marwick, *The Sixties. Cultural Revolution in Britain, France, Italy and the United States c. 1958–c. 1974* (Oxford, 1999).

26. L. Passerini, *Autobiography of a Generation: Italy 1968* (Hanover N.H., 1996); Passerini, *Autoritratto di Gruppo* (Firenze, 1988).

27. N. Elias, 'Der bundesdeutsche Terrorismus. Ausdruck eines sozialen Generationskonflikts' in Elias, *Studien über die Deutschen. Machtkämpfe und Habitusentwicklung im 19. und 20. Jahrhundert* (Frankfurt, 1989), pp. 300–89.

28. This is the shortcoming of a historical approach which lines up 68 as just another German youth revolt: M. Roseman (ed.), *Generations in Conflict. Youth Revolt and Generation Formation in Germany 1770–1968* (Cambridge, 1995).

29. B. Baumann, *Wie alles anfing* (1975) (Berlin, 1991); for Meinhoff texts see M. Hoffmann, *Rote Armee Fraktion. Texte und Materialien zur Geschichte der RAF* (Berlin, 1997).

30. B. Weisbrod, *Gewalt und Zivilität. Das "Peaceable Kingdom" und die Grenzen des zivilgesellschaftlichen Ansatzes* (Bochum, 2006).

31. H. Bude, '"Generationen im Kontext". Von den Kriegs- zu den Wohlfahrts-generationen', in U. Jureit and M. Wildt (eds), *Generationen. Zur Relevanz eines wissenschaftlichen Grundbegriffs* (Hamburg, 2005), pp. 28–44.

32. S. Arber and C. Attias-Donfut (eds), *The Myth of Generational Conflict. The Family and the State in Ageing Societies* (London, 2000); see also M. Kohli and H. Kühnemund (eds), *Die zweite Lebenshälfte. Gesellschaftliche Lage und Partizipation im Spiegel des Alters-Survey* (Opladen, 2000).

33. D. Wierling, *Geboren im Jahr Eins. Der Jahrgang 1949 in der DDR. Versuch einer Kollektivbiographie* (Berlin, 2002). On the construction of 'typical' GDR generations, see also A. Schüle, T. Ahbe and R.Gries (eds), *Die DDR aus generationsgeschichtlicher Perspektive. Eine Inventur* (Leipzig, 2006).

34. Schmidt, *Systemumbruch und Generationswechsel*.

35. J. Straub, 'Unverlierbare Zeit, verkennendes Wort. Nach der Shoah: Sekundäre Traumatisierung der "zweiten Generation"', in K. Platt (ed.), *Reden von der Gewalt* (Munich, 2002), pp. 271–302; see also A. von Friesen, *Der lange Abschied. Psychische Spätfolgen für die 2. Generation deutscher Vertriebener* (Gießen, 2000).

36. See D. Bar-On, *Fear and Hope. Three Generations of the Holocaust* (Cambridge, Mass., 1995). See also G. Rosenthal (ed.), *The Holocaust in Three Generations. Families of Victims and Perpetrators in the Nazi Regime* (London, 1998).

37. G. Rosenthal, 'Historische und familiale Generationenabfolge', in M. Kohli and M. Szydlik (eds), *Generationen in Familie und Gesellschaft* (Opladen, 2000), pp. 162–78.

38. E. Krejci, 'Innere Objekte. Über Generationenfolge und Subjektwerdung. Ein psychoanalytischer Beitrag', in Jureit and Wildt, *Generationen*, pp. 80–107.

39. P. Novick, *The Holocaust in American Life* (Boston, 1999).

40. R. Moeller, *War Stories. The Search for a Usable Past in the Federal Republic of Germany* (Berkeley, 2001); F. Biess, *Homecoming. Returning POWs and the Legacies of Defeat in Postwar Germany* (Princeton, 2006).

41. S. Goltermann, 'The Imagination of Disaster. Death and Survival in Postwar West Germany', in P. Betts, A. Confino and D. Schumann (eds), *Death in Modern Germany* (London, 2006).

42. H. Knoch, *Die Tat als Bild. Fotografien des Holocaust in der deutschen Erinnerungskultur* (Hamburg, 2001).

43. B.-O. Manig, *Die Politik der Ehre. Die Rehabilitierung der Berufssoldaten in der frühen Bundesrepublik* (Göttingen, 2004).

44. N. Frei, *1945 und wir. Das Dritte Reich im Bewusstsein der Deutschen* (Munich, 2005).

45. T. Moser, 'Die Unfähigkeit zu Trauern. Hält die These der Überprüfung stand? Zur psychischen Verarbeitung des Holocaust, in Moser, *Vorsicht Berührung* (Frankfurt, 1992), referring to: Alexander and Margarete Mitscherlich, *Die Unfähigkeit zu trauen. Grundlagen kollektiven Verhaltens* (Munich, 1967).

46. C. Schneider, 'Der Holocaust als Generationsobjekt. Generationsgeschichtliche Anmerkungen zu einer deutschen Identitätsproblematik', *Mittelweg*, 36 (2004), 56–73.

47. D. Diner, *Verkehrte Welten. Antiamerikanismus in Deutschland* (Frankfurt, 1993), pp. 117–67.

48. H. Welzer, S. Moller and K. Tschuggnall, *'Opa war kein Nazi'. Nationalsozialismus und Holocaust im Familiengedächtnis* (Frankfurt, 2002). For criticism, see the debate between H. Welzer, A. von Plato and N. Frei, 'Tradierung von Geschichtsbewußtsein: Thesen und Entgegnungen', *Werkstatt Geschichte*, 30 (2001), 61–72.

49. See already D. von Westernhagen, *Die Kinder der Täter. Das Dritte Reich und die Generation danach* (Munich, 1987), and more recently the successful family memoirs of Wibke Bruhns (*Meines Vaters Land. Geschichte einer deutschen Familie*), with 17 editions since 2004, or Uwe Timm (*Am Beispiel meines Bruders*), with seven editions since 2003.
50. See H. Schumann and J. Scott, 'Generations and Collective Memories', in *American Sociological Review*, 54 (1989), 359–81, on age-specific varieties of American collective memory.
51. Mannheim, 'The Problem', p. 311. In German: 'Der Forscher kann die dem Generationsfaktor zurechenbaren Wandlungen nur dann erfassen, wenn er zunächst alle der historischsozialen Dynamik zurechenbaren Veränderungen abgehoben hat. Überspringt man diese "mittlere Sphäre", so wird man alle jene Momente, die der sogenannten "Milieuentwicklung", der "Zeitsituation" zuzurechnen wären, unmittelbar einem naturalistischen Faktor (Generation, Rasse, geographische Lage usw.) zuzurechnen geneigt sein' 'Das Problem der Generationen', in Mannheim, *Wissenssoziologie. Auswahl aus dem Werk* (Berlin/Neuwied, 1964), p. 554.
52. Mannheim, 'The Problem', p. 312.
53. This concept was first used by the writer W.G. Sebald in an interview with Volker Hage, in *Akzente*, 50 (2003), 35–50 (quote on 36).
54. C. Benninghaus, 'Das Geschlecht der Generation. Zum Zusammenhang von Generationalität und Männlichkeit um 1930', in Jureit and Wildt, *Generationen*, pp. 127–58.
55. H. Schulz, H. Radebold and J. Reulecke (eds), *Söhne ohne Väter. Erfahrungen der Kriegsgeneration* (Berlin, 2004). For a less conclusive view of childhood deprivation in war, see N. Stargardt, *Witnesses of War. Children's Lives under the Nazis* (London, 2005).

3
Orphaned by History: French Youth in the Shadow of World War II

Richard Vinen

> But the numerical majority, in fact, is a matter of only secondary importance. It may even be deceptive, because when a doctrine conquers the crowd it starts to die in the eyes of philosophy ... We have not sought to draw the portrait of the average young man of 1912, but rather to sketch the features of the best and to describe the representatives of the new elite.
>
> Agathon, 1912[1]

> We christened the generation that preceded us, for generation it certainly was, that of the Exhibition of Decorative Arts [1925]. 'A funny way to mark out ages', Albert Thibaudet [1873–1946] remarked with some irony. 'You will therefore be the generation of the year when there was a nigger's head on the postage stamps, the year of the Colonial Exhibition [1931]'.
>
> Robert Brasillach, 1941[2]

In his essay on 'The Problem of Generations', Karl Mannheim distinguished between a French approach to the subject, which he believed to be marked by Comtian positivism with an emphasis on the biological realities of successive age cohorts, and the German approach, which he thought was characterized by a 'romantic historical' emphasis on the subjective way in which generations were perceived.[3] The examples of Agathon, the pseudonym under which Alfred de Tarde and Henri Massis published a study of French students in 1912, and Brasillach, who published his recollections of life in an elite Paris lycée and at the Ecole Normale Supérieure (ENS) in 1941, might raise all sorts of interesting questions for someone who wished to adopt a positivist approach to generations.[4] However, as the quotations above suggest, neither Agathon nor Brasillach – nor indeed the majority of French writers on the subject – were Comtian positivists.[5] Agathon specifically rejected the 'scientific' approach to generations, and Brasillach's remarks suggest a playful awareness that generations are highly subjective entities.

These quotations also suggest that French writers did not apply the word 'generation' to any age cohort, but that generational identity was closely tied to other political and social identities. Thinking about generations in France has (as elsewhere) been very much associated with thinking about youth. Agathon's study was concerned with people around 20 years old. Brasillach has been described by one of his biographers as the 'James Dean of French Fascism'. He was certainly too fast to live – he published his first novel at the age of 20 and his memoirs at the age of 30 – though he was not, as it turned out, too young to die, since he was shot for treason at the age of 35. Thinking about generation in France, as elsewhere, has also tended to revolve around men rather than women. Agathon's study was confined to men and evoked women only with reference to marriage and 'immorality'. Brasillach's autobiographical writings are almost entirely about male friendships, and his sister – who married his best friend Maurice Bardeche – is the only woman to receive more than a passing mention. The examples of Agathon and Brasillach suggest that the affirmation of a generational identity in France has been strongest on the political right. Elsewhere, and with some notable exceptions (Evelyn Waugh or Ernst Junger), the claims of youth have generally been associated with the political left. In France, however, the young men studied by Agathon were influenced by nationalism and religious revival, while Brasillach and his friends were almost all Maurrassians. Finally, thinking about generations in France has been closely bound up with reflections on a particular kind of educational elite that emerged from half a dozen Paris lycées and the *grandes écoles* to which their best students were sent. Agathon explicitly based their study on young men from this elite. Brasillach's milieu was made up of men he had met in *hypokhâgne* (the high-powered supplementary class that prepared students for entry to the ENS) at Louis-le-Grand. It is not surprising that Pierre Nora, who studied in the *khâgnes* of both Louis-le Grand and Henri IV in his ultimately fruitless efforts to gain admission to the ENS, should be so preoccupied by generation, nor that one of the most well-known French works to use generation as its central idea should be Jean-François Sirinelli's study of *normaliens* and *khâgneux* between the wars.[6]

Agathon (writing on the eve of World War I) and Brasillach (writing about the 'après-guerre' of the 1920s and the 'avant-guerre' of the 1930s) wrote on the explicit assumption that the generations they described were part of a continuous pattern and that they would be succeeded by younger generations. Their writings raise obvious questions in the minds of a contemporary reader. In the case of Agathon, those questions relate to one man. This man fitted in with everything that Agathon claimed to identify as characteristic of the new elite. He was born in 1890, attended a Paris school (Stanislas), was a Catholic and a nationalist: his name was Charles de Gaulle. In the case of Brasillach, questions are raised most forcibly by one of his last works (written when he was in cell 344 of Fresnes prison awaiting trial in 1944). This was 'Lettre à un jeune homme de la classe de 60'.[7] The imagined recipient of Brasillach's letter was a young man who would be called up for military service in 1960. The young man would have been born in 1940 (just as the Germans invaded Norway), and would have grown up in wartime France – never tasting chocolate or oranges or bananas. We know now that Brasillach's imagined boy would, in fact, have been called up for military service at the height of the Algerian War. We know too that Charles de Gaulle was the central figure in France's experience of both World War II and the Algerian War. We also know, however, that generation played remarkably little part in the ways in which the French discussed either Algeria or the World War. Indeed, generation, which has loomed so large in discussion of twentieth-century France generally, seems to be remarkably unimportant for discussion of the period overshadowed by de Gaulle, that is the period from 1940 to 1970. Why is this?

World War II

The World War did not produce a single clear expression of generational belonging in France. There was, for one thing, no single war generation and, in some ways, no single war. The conventional conflict of 1940 was different from the guerrilla war of 1943–4. Like all wartime armies in the twentieth century, the French army of 1940 took troops from a wide age range. The average French soldier was around 30 (substantially older than the men conscripted in peacetime), but this average concealed ages that ranged from 20 to over 50. There was no sharp generational divide between front line troops and reserve troops or staff officers. The whole French army shared the tedium of the phoney war until May 1940 (Brasillach wrote his memoirs during the free time accorded by his service on the Maginot Line) and then had the same experiences of chaos and retreat after the German invasion. Almost two million French soldiers were captured and over half of these were still in German camps at the end of the war. Experience of German imprisonment was not confined to any particular age group. If we confine our attention to just Brasillach's fellow *normaliens*, then we note that Brasillach himself (born 1909) was a prisoner of war as was Jean-Paul Sartre (born 1905). They were, however, accompanied by men as young as Louis Althusser (who was born in 1919 and who treated his time in Stalag X as a kind of extended gap year between the Lycée du Parc and the ENS), and men as old as the philosopher Jean Guitton (who had been born in 1902). The Germans tried to divide these prisoners in generational terms (they proposed to release veterans of World War I and fathers of large families). However, these efforts were not very successful. Generally, the release of prisoners cut across age groups as men were released because of their contacts and/or personal enterprise rather than because of their age. Sartre and Brasillach were released early, while Althusser and Guitton stayed in their camps until 1945.[8]

In some respects, it might be argued that the early stages of the Vichy regime in France produced a kind of reverse generational revolution. Instead of the young pushing aside the old, it was the young who were seen to have failed in 1940, and this increased the prestige of the old, who were seen to have succeeded in 1916 and 1917. It is significant that Henri Massis (who had co-written the influential study of the young cited above and who had himself been born in 1886) became a Vichy official with responsibility for 'youth'. Pétain was 84 years old when he became Head of State in 1940. The cult of the memory of Verdun flourished under Vichy. The Légion Française des Combattants was the closest thing that Vichy ever established to a mass organization and it was dominated by men of over 50 who were veterans of World War I.[9] Vichy was not, however, a regime based on a single generation. Pétain was 30 years older than the *anciens combattants* who were, supposedly, most loyal to him, and 11 years older than the second most senior member of his government (Maxime Weygand). A substantial minority of Vichy ministers were very young by the standards of the French political elite – Jean Bichelonne, who served as Minister of Industrial Production, had been born in 1904.

Even as the war turned against the Germans, and hence against Vichy, it was rare for anti-Vichy sentiment to take a particularly generational form – indeed, in some ways, the most important conflict brought by World War II in France was not one between generations but one within a generation. It was men in their twenties who made up a large part of those who fought for the Resistance in 1944, but men of the same age also made up the bulk of active fighters for collaborationist forces such as the Milice.

World War II also produced a more complicated and fragmented set of generational identities that were not directly to do with fighting. The rationing system carved the French population up by age cohorts. In particular, the J3 category (taking in those between the ages of 3 and 18) was adopted as a generational badge by some adolescents under Vichy. Of course, the whole notion of adolescence changed during the occupation.[10] The Sovietologist Alain Bescançon, who was born in 1932 and spent most of the war as a schoolboy at the Stanislas in Paris, pointed out that children, gentile children at least, were still protected from the worst horrors of war in a way that they would not have been in, say, Yugoslavia, and that, in this sense, childhood continued to exist.[11] On the other hand, poor food meant that children grew more slowly and that they often reached puberty later. Vichy literally kept part of the population in short trousers by insisting that textile shortages made it impossible for boys under 15 to wear long trousers. The group of people defined as children for administrative purposes (that is, the J3) also grew because people found it beneficial to remain in this category even when they passed the age of 18.

The *chantiers de jeunesse* (the youth camps to which Vichy sent men in their early twenties) also created a particular kind of generational experience – the *chantiers* fitted in neatly with Catholic youth organizations and scout troops that had existed before 1940, and created a sense of generational identity among some young men that persisted for years after the war (associations representing 'les anciens' of the *chantiers* were still in existence in the 1990s). However, the *chantiers* never brought a whole generation of French young men together. This was partly because they were a contested institution – strongly disliked by most men who went through them – but also because they never extended to the whole of France: the Germans forbade them in the northern zone.[12]

Compulsory labour service also produced a particular age category. In February 1943 all men born in 1920, 1921 and 1922 (that is, all of those who would normally have been eligible for military service) were required to make themselves available for labour service in Germany. Men who were deported to work in Germany often recalled their experience in generational terms and often assumed, unfairly as it happens, that older French men whom they met in Germany must have volunteered to work there. Once again, though, labour service was never a unifying experience for French men of a particular generation. On the contrary, compulsory labour service divided young men because some of them chose to hide or to join the Maquis rather than to go to Germany. After the war, these various groups of men of the same age had very different memories, which were often based on reproaching those of their contemporaries who had made different choices.[13]

Most of all, it should be stressed that the generational identities discussed above were all awkward and, to some extent, transient. People whose early life had been marked by the *chantiers*, labour service or rationing often knew that their experiences were not the same as those of all their contemporaries and sometimes felt too that their experiences were quickly forgotten by society as a whole. This forgetfulness was important because it made it difficult for those who had undergone such experiences to assert a particular generational identity in the eyes of generations who came later. René Limouzin initially entitled his wartime memoir *Le Temps des J 3*, but then changed the title for later editions on the grounds that readers would no longer know what the term J 3 meant.[14]

There was not even a single 'Resistance generation'. It is true that a large number of those who fought in the summer of 1944 had been born in the early 1920s (these were the men who had been faced with the choice of joining the Maquis or enduring compulsory labour service in Germany). However, the Maquis took in men from a wide age range, and very young men were never as numerically preponderant in it as they would have been in a peacetime conscript army. Furthermore, conventional warfare produces a clear separation between young men who endure the physical risks of combat and their elders who give the commands. There was no such division in the French Resistance. Marc Bloch was born in 1886, served as an officer throughout World War I, returned to service as, in his own words, the 'oldest captain in the French army' in 1940, and was finally shot as a Resistance activist in 1944. The most famous Resistance martyrs – Jean Moulin, born 1899; Jean Cavaillès, born 1903; Pierre Brossolette, born 1903 – were all over 40 by the time that they died. Some Resistance leaders were actively hostile to the young. Jacques Lecompte-Boinet, for example, had been born in 1905. He had been excused military service in 1939–40 on the grounds that he was the father of a large family, and only entered into combat at the age of 36 when he founded Ceux de la Résistance. He justified his Resistance activity by looking back to older generations (particularly to his father-in-law Marshal Mangin) rather than by looking to the young. Men such as Lecompte-Boinet often saw themselves as the real Resistance elite and were contemptuous of the large numbers of much younger men who flooded into the Maquis in 1943 and 1944. For middle-aged Resistance leaders, the concept of 'Resistance generations' often referred to the date at which people had joined the Resistance more than it referred to their age. In this context the 'anciens' of 1940 saw themselves as more authentic than the new men of 1944.

The absence of a specifically generational mobilization related to World War II was particularly striking in the decade or so that followed its end. Given that Vichy had been a gerontocratic regime focused on the cult of Verdun, one might have expected this to be the moment at which youth would acquire great prestige. In fact, politicians who had grown to prominence before the war remained influential. Even departmental liberation committees were often dominated by men who were, in fact, veterans of World War I rather than World War II.[15] People who did objectively belong to the generation of World War II were remarkably reluctant to present themselves in these terms. This can be seen in the Poujadist small business movement of the 1950s. Most Poujadists had been born between 1910 and 1920 – they belonged precisely to the generation that had fought World War II, and some of their discontent probably came from ways in which their careers had been interrupted by that war. However, Poujadist rhetoric looked back to the unifying, reassuring myth/memory of Verdun, not to the divisive recent past. When Poujade (born in 1920) attacked the modernizing prime minister Pierre Mendès France (born in 1909 and, like Poujade, a veteran of the Free French Air Force), he did so by saying that Mendès compared unfavourably with 'our fathers who were at Verdun'. Similarly, François Mitterrand had fought in the campaign of 1940, escaped from a German prisoner of war camp and, eventually, joined the French Resistance. After the war he became one of the few very young ministers in the Fourth Republic. Yet once again, he did not use his generation as a means of political mobilization. Indeed, as minister of *anciens combattants*, he did everything that he could to stress his association with World War I rather than World War II.

If there was no clear-cut sense of who belonged to the Resistance generation, there was, paradoxically, a clear sense of who was excluded from it. Those who grew up after 1945 were often painfully conscious that they had not lived through a crucial experience. Claude Nicolet (born in 1930) described his admiration for Pierre Mendès France thus: 'I have always envied those amongst my elders who were awakened by the political exaltation of the Resistance ... we [his own contemporaries] are a generation abandoned by history.'[16]

This curious sense of being a generation 'abandoned by history' on the part of those who grew up too late to participate directly in World War II was widely noted. In 1959, the journalist Françoise Giroud (born in 1916) published a book about the younger generation in which she specifically suggested that no cause mobilized them as Spain, Munich and the Resistance had mobilized her own generation.[17]

The sense that post-war generations were overshadowed by the experiences of their elders had an important impact on how France's most important military conflict after 1945 was perceived. Between 1954 and 1962, France fought a war to maintain her presence in Algeria. One might expect that this conflict, more than any other, would be remembered in generational terms. It was fought primarily by conscripts, and these conscripts, unlike those of 1914 or 1940, were drawn from a fairly narrow age range: men in their early twenties (that is, born in the period between 1934 and 1942).

Having said this, conscripts of the Algerian war rarely asserted their experience in strongly generational terms. Few conscripts deserted or protested against the war or, for that matter, expressed enthusiastic support for it.

There are some obvious reasons why the conscripts of the Algerian war did not develop a generational interpretation of their own experiences. It was difficult to present the conscript soldiers as either victims or heroes of the war. They were not victims because casualty rates were comparatively low, and because the Algerians suffered much more from the war than French soldiers. On the other hand, French conscripts were not, even in the eyes of those who supported French Algeria, heroes either – because, although conscripts made up the bulk of French troops present in Algeria, the most serious fighting was done by professionals. After the French departure from Algeria in 1962, the war was little discussed at all – Algeria was seen as a defeat by the right and as a crime by parts of the left. Conscript soldiers would probably not have found a ready audience even if they had tried to discuss their experiences in public. Furthermore, the conscripts returned to France at a time of rapid economic expansion. Most of them were soon absorbed in work and in family life.[18]

Young men who fought in Algeria felt that their experience of war was trivial by comparison with what their elders had endured. Not only were they overshadowed by their parents' memories of World War II but they often felt diminished by comparison with their grandfathers' experiences of World War I. In his great book on veterans of World War I, Antoine Prost (born in 1933) recalls how he, as a young conscript in

Algeria, was conscious that he was not enduring the 'real' war that had been endured by his elders.[19] Another historian, Alain Corbin (born in 1936), recalls trying to elicit the clemency of a lycée inspector by telling him that he was about to be posted to Algeria. The inspector looked at him contemptuously and said 'Moi, monsieur, j'étais à Verdun.'[20]

Most importantly, a group of people whose primary experience was World War II remained very powerful during the Algerian war and often defined the terms in which Algeria was discussed. Both those professional soldiers who fought hardest to keep Algeria French and those left-wingers who protested most vigorously against French conduct in Algeria were often veterans of the Free French or the Resistance. Often their discussion of Algeria was conducted with reference back to World War II. Thus, for example, when Jacques Massu (born in 1908), the French commander during the battle of Algiers and a veteran of Free French forces, published his memoirs in 1971 he was almost obsessively concerned to defend himself against allegations by Resistance veterans – such as Paul Teitgen, who had been arrested by the Gestapo during the occupation and worked as a French civilian administrator during the Algerian war – that the French army had used 'Nazi' methods.[21]

This sense of having missed out on the great political drama of recent times produced a curious generational deference, which was most marked among the most self-consciously left-wing young people in France. This deference can be seen in the attitudes to Sartre. Ever since his days as a lycée teacher, Sartre had exercised a remarkable hold over his juniors. The cult of Sartre (which reached a peak in the early 1960s and then underwent a revival in 1968) was most powerful among the young. Sartre's disciples – such as Claude Lanzmann (born in 1925) or Benny Levi (born 1945) – were young enough to be his children. Eventually, indeed, Sartre adopted his mistress and admirer Arlette Elkaim (born in 1938) as his daughter. It is notable that the most vigorous opponent of Sartre's hegemony over French intellectual life was not one of his juniors but his exact contemporary, a man whom he had known since they attended the ENS together: Raymond Aron.

As the example of Sartre and Aron suggests, the generational deference that influenced post-war France may have had something to do with the fact that this was also a period when elite educational institutions (particularly the ENS) exercised a particular power. The very fact that a larger part of the French population was becoming educated during the 1950s and 1960s (particularly the fact that a larger proportion of that population were going to university) only heightened the prestige of those who could claim special access to the sacred heights of philosophical tradition. Nothing illustrates the importance of formal academic study in France more than the fate of Camus. Camus (born in 1913) was a few years younger than Sartre. He also possessed the very qualities that mattered for post-war youth culture in Anglo-Saxon countries (qualities that Sartre conspicuously lacked): physical beauty and working-class origins. Camus did indeed became an icon for fashionably alienated youth in England, an inspiration for everything from Colin Wilson's *The Outsider* to the early songs of The Cure.[22] But he almost withdrew from French intellectual life in 1952, after a devastating review of his *L'Homme révolté* in *Les Temps modernes* by Sartre's protégé Francis Jeanson (born in 1922). Camus had committed several crimes in the eyes of the Sartrean establishment: he had attacked Stalinism and asked for mercy for collaborators (among them Robert Brasillach). Most of all, however, he had committed one unforgivable crime: failing to understand Kant.

The democratization of the younger generation?

Nora has suggested that the period from 1959 to 1965 saw a 'democratization' of generational ideas as the standard-bearers for youth ceased to be novelists and philosophers and became, instead, pop stars. He sees this process as starting in 1959 (the year in which the 'blousons noirs' first began to attract attention), and he sees it exemplified in the 'Salut les Copains' radio programme that broadcasted pop music in France in the early 1960s. Nora's interpretation is odd in three respects. First, it places an emphasis on the early and mid-1960s as a turning point, when normally Nora's work revolves around a 'crisis of memory' that occurs in the 1970s. Secondly, Nora describes a generational revolution that preceded the student protests of 1968 – though, in the same essay, Nora suggest that 1968 acquired its significance largely through commemoration after the event. Thirdly, Nora's approach is normally resolutely Francocentric, but his essay on generations draws much of its evidence from England and America.

In fact, the cult of youth in England and America in the 1960s was very different from that in France. In particular, rock music never assumed the importance in France that it had in Britain or America. It is true that many French teenagers listened to rock music – 52 per cent of all French schoolchildren were said to listen to 'Salut les Copains'. But listening was a relatively passive experience. Unlike their Anglo-Saxon counterparts, French teenagers rarely attended rock music concerts or wore clothes that associated them with particular bands. Most of all, French teenagers knew that the most exciting of the bands that they listened to came from outside their own national culture. Indeed, the most striking example of 'generational rock' that Nora cites (it is one of his very rare references to an Englishman) is The Who's 'My Generation' sung by Roger Daltrey with what Nora rather strangely describes as his 'regard bleu du prolo Londonien'.[23] The Who do indeed encapsulate important changes in youth culture during the 1960s. Members of the band were young (Daltrey was born in 1944, and Townsend, who actually wrote 'My Generation', was born in May 1945), and they addressed their songs to people even younger than themselves (childhood is a big theme in their songs). The Who illustrated rock music's propensity to both mock and flirt with consumer culture: the album *The Who Sell Out* included 'commercial breaks' advertising products in the style of American radio. The band also illustrated the fact that 'youth culture' in England was increasingly taken to mean working-class culture. The Who themselves cultivated a working-class image, and it is indicative of the way in which upper-middle-class figures deferred to symbols of the working class in the Britain of the 1960s that the Who's manager should have been Kit Lambert – a member of a minor aristocratic family and son of the composer Constant Lambert (said to be the model for Moreland in Anthony Powell's *A Dance to the Music of Time*).[24]

The Who, however, were quintessentially Anglo-Saxon (it is no accident that their fans often decorated their clothing with Union Jacks). French people may have listened to The Who, but a band such as this could never have existed in France. Such deference of the upper middle class towards working-class music would have been inconceivable in France: it is hard to imagine the editor of *Le Monde* in solemn conversation with Johnny Hallyday, though the editor of *The Times* endured a well-reported meeting with Mick Jagger in 1967. When French people talked about youth leaders in the late 1960s, they still meant overwhelmingly students rather than singers. The Who's flirtation with consumerism would have meant nothing in France – the bourgeois left despised consumption, and the working classes were still, in large measure, too poor to indulge in such conspicuous spending. Most importantly, France still had military service. Almost all Frenchmen were polishing their boots at an age when Pete Townsend was smashing guitars.

The generation that produced the first rock stars in Britain and America was also the generation that had been born around the time of World War II. In Anglo-Saxon countries this fact did not arouse much comment – very few people knew or cared that the middle name of

John Lennon (born in 1940) was Winston. In France, by contrast, the generation born around the time of World War II were haunted by the sense that they had missed out on the great event of modern times. Not surprisingly, this obsession could become particularly marked among French Jews.[25] Pierre Goldman was born on 22 June 1944 (just at the end of the occupation). His father was a heroic leader of the Jewish Resistance in France. Goldman grew up convinced that it was his 'duty' to die before he was thirty. He became involved in left-wing violence, was convicted of killing two women during a bank raid, released and finally assassinated in mysterious circumstances in 1979. Goldman's funeral was a great political event, attended by Sartre and de Beauvoir. Pierre Goldman was a bigger star than his half-brother Jean-Jacques, a pop singer.[26]

1968

All discussion of generations in France in the 1960s ultimately leads to the 'events' of 1968. If we judge things in objective terms (positivist terms, as Mannheim would put it), then 1968 was undoubtedly a generational rebellion. It involved people who were drawn from a very distinct generation (born during the baby boom that immediately followed World War II). This was a period when just over 16 per cent of the French population was aged between 16 and 24.[27] The baby boom generation had been formed by particular experiences – the rapid economic growth of the 1950s and 1960s and the rapid expansion in educational opportunities that went with it. The student population of France was much larger in 1968 than it had been even just five years previously. It had specific grievances relating to overcrowded universities and declining job opportunities.

However, 1968 has rarely been understood, least of all by its participants, in purely positivist terms. Certainly, there was much talk of youth in 1968, and many participants may well have understood the events of that year primarily in these terms. However, not all of them did so. Indeed, if we look at 1968 in what Mannheim would define as 'romantic historical' terms, then it might be argued that 1968 saw an inversion of the normal pattern of generational leadership. On previous occasions (1848 is the obvious example), a small group of vocal, articulate and privileged young men had managed to persuade the world that they represented 'youth'. In 1968 a small group of vocal, articulate and privileged young people put themselves at the head of a real youth movement and persuaded the world (or at least themselves) that they represented the working class, the Third World peasantry and almost every entity *other* than French youth.

In any case, the student movement was not homogeneous. The majority of people who turned up to demonstrations in that year were what some historians have labelled the 'pedestrians' of the revolution. These people were indeed drawn from the post-war baby boom and probably did think in generational terms (though it is hard to know precisely what they thought because relatively few of them have left accounts of their experience and because many of them seem to have been remarkably apolitical before 1968).

However, three general observations can be made about the profile of the most prominent leaders of 1968. First, some of them were much more ideologically committed than other students. Members of Trotskyite, Anarchist and Maoist groups provided much of the rhetoric behind 1968 – though only a tiny proportion of French students were Trotskyites, Anarchists or Maoists. The most ideologically committed students were often, initially at least, hostile to the student demonstrations, which they regarded as trivial and parochial. Maoists, in particular, believed that real revolutionary agitation was to be undertaken in the factories rather than in the universities, and they were disconcerted when it seemed that workers themselves might sympathize with the student protests.

Secondly, the great bulk of French students attended universities, and their experience there was different from that of previous generations. Universities had expanded rapidly, new universities (notably Paris X at Nanterre) had been established, new subjects (notably sociology) had taken in great numbers of students. However, some of the most articulate and forceful students did not go to university but to the grandest of all French *grandes écoles*: the ENS. Students at the ENS were much more politicized than their contemporaries at universities and, in particular, *normaliens* seem to have provided a disconcertingly large proportion of the Gauche Prolétarienne, which probably explains why this minuscule Maoist group was taken so seriously. *Normalien* Maoists were particularly likely to volunteer as 'établis' who worked in factories and attempted to make contact with the working class.

Normaliens did not, however, have much sympathy with the purely generational grievances of their own contemporaries in the universities. The ENS had barely expanded at all. Its size, location, culture and even curriculum were still very much what they had been when Brasillach studied there in the early 1930s. *Normaliens* were cut off from the material concerns of ordinary students – they did not have to worry about jobs (they were salaried servants of the state from the moment they entered the school) or exams (no one who had got into the school was likely to be frightened of exams) or facilities (the school was much better provided than other institutions in France). However, if *normaliens* were cut off from their contemporaries, they were in close touch with their elders. The small-group teaching of the school put *normaliens* in touch with a certain number of men from an earlier generation and particularly, of course, with Althusser, who was *répétiteur* (or exam coach) at the rue d'Ulm. *Normaliens* also had an obvious association with earlier generations of students at the same institution. They had their own cult of the dead (particularly revolving around the *normalien* philosopher and Resistance martyr Jean Cavaillès) and some of them had (or soon acquired) personal association with the most eminent of former *normaliens* – Sartre.

Thirdly, leaders of the student movement were generally rather older than the average. Some had been born not during the baby boom but during the demographic depression that preceded World War II. Alain Geismar, for example, was born in 1939. In fact, the central political event for most student leaders was World War II – not because they had any personal memories of it, but simply because they had grown up in its shadow. It is notable that the very youngest student leaders had been born in the last year of the war. Daniel Cohn-Bendit was born in 1945 of German Jewish parents who had taken refuge in Montauban. Gerand Filoche, who was to become an activist with the Jeunesse Communiste Révolutionnaire and the Ligue Communiste Révolutionnaire, was born on Christmas Eve 1945. He must have been conceived pretty much on the day that his father returned from five years in a German prison camp. Not surprisingly, he recalled that the memory of the war was 'obsessional' during his childhood.[28]

The leaders of this rebellion very often took their rhetoric from references to World War II ('CRS/SS', 'we are all German Jews') and often also admired leaders who had been active in the Resistance, or who had managed to present themselves as having been active in the Resistance. The great idols of 1968 were mainly relatively old men. Among politicians, Mendès France (born in 1909) and Mitterrand (born in 1917) were the two figures who seemed most respected. Oddest of all was the position of Charles de Gaulle (born in 1890). Students attacked the Gaullist regime but they did so by subsuming it into some wider 'capitalist' or 'imperialist' structure. Student leaders were reluctant to take on the General or his historical legacy directly. Olivier Rolin's autobiographical novel *Tigre en papier* (2002) recalls the horror of Maoist guerrillas when they realize that the defence company boss that they have kidnapped had in fact been a hero of the Free French. The ambiguity towards de Gaulle was most strikingly illustrated by Régis Debray (born in 1940). Debray left France entirely before 1968 because he argued that it was only in the jungles of South America that he could hope to relive the heroism of the French Resistance.

At times, young left-wingers' fascination with the Resistance and with other anti-fascist mobilizations of the mid-twentieth century went with a more general renunciation of generational identity. When young Maoists went to work in factories during the late 1960s and early 1970s they often met young workers who were fascinated by contemporary Anglo-Saxon youth culture. As soon as the workers left the factory, they scrubbed the grime from their faces, put on flared jeans, untied their long hair and went out to dance to the music of T Rex. The bourgeois Maoists by contrast were almost deliberately middle-aged. They dressed 'like Jean Gabin' and smoked Gaullois (the 'authentically proletarian cigarette'). One young woman recalled that her earnest bespectacled manner amused her fellow workers so much that they named her Nana (a reference to the very unhip Greek singer Nana Mouskouri, not to Zola).[29]

Part of the Maoist distaste for the youth culture of the late 1960s sprang of course from the perception that such a culture was commercial, Americanized and depoliticized. There is, however, more to it than that. The association between admiration for the working class and distaste for youth culture also had specific historical roots. The French working class had experienced a moment of particular strength in the late 1940s and early 1950s. The industrialization brought about by World War II and the Monnet Plan meant that industrial workers were more numerous than ever before and also that they were more concentrated than before or afterwards in those large-scale heavy industrial enterprises that were most likely to produce a particular kind of class consciousness (and most likely to be regarded as 'authentically proletarian' by middle-class observers). The economic effects of the war tied in with its political effects as first the Popular Front and then the Resistance produced a particularly politically engaged group of workers, and also a group of workers who were particularly likely to elicit the admiration of the left more generally. This was the period during which what Gérard Noiriel has labelled the 'unique generation' of workers emerged. This was the first and last generation of workers who were themselves the sons of workers (rather than being the sons of peasants), who remained in single enterprises for long periods of time, who were unionized for most of their careers and who were recognized as having high levels of skill. This unique generation was undermined during the 1960s by new consumer industries that made increasing use of unskilled workers (often women), by the deliberate relocation of factories away from centres of working-class strength, and by the increasing prominence of immigrants (especially immigrants from Africa and Algeria who did not fit easily into French working-class organizations).[30]

The result of all this was that by the late 1960s, when young middle-class people most ardently wanted to make contact with the working class, 'true workers' were often seen as old or middle-aged and that celebration of the 'real working class' went with a kind of nostalgia. The generation of students who became politically active in the late 1960s were fascinated by a generation of workers who had been most active 20 or more years earlier.

The return of generation in French life

If, as this chapter has suggested, the years after World War II saw notions of generation eclipsed in French public discussion, then this eclipse certainly did not last. In the late 1970s and 1980s, references to the notion of generation became almost ubiquitous in France. How then did the circumstances described above change? The first answer relates to France's relationship with her recent past. Curiously, Nora's argument that French fascination with generation dates from the early 1960s means that he separates this fascination from the central argument of his own book: that there was a 'crisis of memory' during the early 1970s. Yet this crisis of memory actually did much to revive notions of generation in France. In the first place, discussion of Vichy and/or collaboration became much more common in the aftermath of academic books (notably by Robert Paxton) and of films (such as *Lacombe Lucien* or *The Sorrow and the Pity*). If France had been a nation of collaborators rather than a nation of resisters, then the young were less likely to defer to their elders. Indeed, a whole school of literature has been produced by writers such as Marie Chaix (born 1942), Patrick Modiano (born 1945), Dominique Jamet (born 1936) and Alexandre Jardin (born 1965), who write about the discreditable things that their fathers (in Jardin's case his grandfather) did during the occupation.[31] Secondly, the sharp decline of Marxism in France meant a decline in the class identities that had formerly overshadowed identities based on generation. It is no accident that the Socialist campaign slogan in the 1988 presidential elections was 'Generation Mitterrand' – the left had nothing other than generations left to believe in. Perhaps because of the collapse of faith in Marxism – or left-wing politics or, indeed, politics *tout court* – young people in France during the past decade or so have often been very conscious of the gap between themselves and their parents. Indeed, while the *soixante-huitard* generation sought to minimize the gulf between themselves and what they imagined to be the 'Resistance generation', the children of the *soixante-huitards* have often seemed to revel in drawing attention to the gulf between themselves and their parents.

Social change in France has also affected ideas of generation. The French education system has internationalized. The *normaliens* who exercised such influence during the late 1960s had an intensely Francocentric view of the world (one thinks of Régis Debray looking at de Gaulle through the prism of Chateaubriand's view of Napoleon, or of Olivier Rolin's evocation of Victor Hugo's description of the French revolutionary past). These days, students at *grandes écoles* are encouraged (and, in the case of the Institut d'Etudes Politiques, compelled) to spend part of their educational career abroad. Attitudes to generation and youth culture are now likely to owe as much to Berkeley as to the Boulevard St Michel. France is richer now than it was at the height of the *trente glorieuses*, and consumerism gained a very firm hold in France during the 1980s (1968 frequently appears as a motif in advertisements).

Nothing illustrates the transition in attitudes to generation in France better than the history of the newspaper *Libération*. *Libération* was founded in 1973. Its origins lay in the student protests of 1968, but at first it did not embrace an identity based on generation. Its presiding eminence was Sartre. The newspaper rejected the consumerism that went with youth culture in Anglo-Saxon countries (at first it took no paid advertising). Most importantly, as its name suggests, *Libération* was based on piety towards the Resistance. The founders of the newspaper wrote to the widow of the Resistance leader Emmanuel d'Astier de la Vigérie asking her permission to use the name that had originally belonged to the newspaper that he edited in the 1940s.

In the early 1980s, *Libération* changed. Serge July (born in 1942) staged a coup that placed him at the head of what had previously been an editorial cooperative. The paper began to take paid advertising – indeed its format often seemed devised primarily as a vehicle for advertising. It became increasingly preoccupied with American popular culture (July regarded the American magazine *Rolling Stone* as a model) and increasingly explicit in its role as the newspaper of French youth (of course, youth is a moving target, and many of those who read

Libération today would not have been born in 1973). Most of all, *Libération* had become, more than any other French newspaper, the vehicle for an aggressive reexamination of the war years and the Resistance. It regularly carried pieces by the historian Henry Rousso (born in 1954), the most celebrated writer on the construction of French myths about the occupation. Rousso was a member of the 'jury' convoked under the aegis of *Libération* in May 1997 that examined the cases of Claude and Lucie Aubrac and handled these two Resistance veterans with a notable lack of respect. When d'Astier de la Vigérie's widow first became worried about the direction that the newspaper was taking, she wrote asking them to cease using the name of her husband's paper. The editors pointed out that they, unlike her, had taken the precaution of copyrighting it.

Conclusion

This chapter has sought to make certain general points. First, it has argued, in opposition to Mannheim, that attitudes to generation in France have rarely been characterized by a Comtian emphasis on precise definitions of generational cycles but rather by a looser emphasis on the 'spirit' of generations, which sometimes bears only a tangential relation to the biological generation to which people actually belong. Secondly, it has argued, in opposition to Nora, that the key changes in French discourse about generations did not happen in the early 1960s. On the contrary, there was a conflict in the middle part of the twentieth century between the objective reality of generations in France and their 'romantic historical' construction. On the one hand, some very distinct generational cohorts emerged out of World War II. The birth rate increased during the 1940s (in France, it increased during the war as well as after it). The people born during this period had experiences that were very specific to their generation. The first memories of the youngest of them involved rationing and deprivation. Their adolescence was marked by post-war economic growth and, perhaps more significantly, expansion of educational opportunities. The youth of people born during this period intersected with two important events. Those born in 1940 were called up during the last stages of the Algerian war, while those born five or six years later were at university during the student protests of 1968. Everyone, from Brasillach writing to his imaginary 'young soldier of 1960' in 1944 to the demographer Alfred Sauvy writing in 1958, imagined that the generation born in the 1940s would have its own particular identity and ideas.[32] Yet, to a remarkably large extent, this was a suppressed generation: an age cohort that was remarkably disinclined to assert itself in generational terms. A great deal of this can be explained with reference to World War II. The war produced a variety of experiences that were specific to particular age cohorts. However, perhaps because those experiences were so complicated, contradictory and mutually exclusive, there was never a sense that any particular generation could be described as the war generation. Curiously, however, the war did produce a clear sense of generational exclusion. That is to say, people who reached adulthood after 1945 often felt that they had, in some way, been orphaned by history and that their own experiences were overshadowed by those of their elders.

The final contention of this chapter is that the return of generation to French political life marks the closing of a particular era in French political life – an era dominated by a strong political left, a self-conscious and confident intellectual elite, and a sense of connection with World War II.

Notes

1. Agathon, *Les Jeunes gens d'aujourd'hui* (Paris, 1912), p. 11.
2. R. Brasillach, *Notre Avant guerre*, first published in 1941, republished in *Une Génération dans l'orage* (Paris, 1968), p. 91.
3. K. Mannheim, *Essays on the Sociology of Knowledge* (London, 1952), pp. 276–320.
4. A study of the French educational elite in the early twentieth century would, first of all, raise questions about the 'natural' span of a generation. Traditionally, French army officers, such as Brasillach's father, tended to marry late and consequently to be much older than their children (often a mother would be closer in age to her children than to her husband). Agathon suggested that increasing numbers of young men were adopting a military career, but also that these young men (inspired by a revived Catholicism) were increasingly likely to marry young. The two world wars would have an effect on the 'natural' span of generations. Many of the men studied by Agathon would have been dead by 1918. Many boys grew up without natural fathers in the interwar period (Brasillach's own father died, though not in combat, in 1915). Boys such as this encountered key members of the 'older generation' as men who had been frozen into perpetual youth by death rather than as ageing representatives of paternal authority. The intense life of elite Paris schools (in which many boys were boarders) and of the *grandes écoles* might have affected attitudes to generation. Many young men had filial feelings towards their teachers. Alain (Emile Chartier), who taught philosophy at Henri IV, was particularly influential, and even young men who did not go to this school, such as Brasillach, often contrived to attend his classes. Alain's generational identity was particularly complicated. He had been born in 1868, but had volunteered to

fight in World War I and was consequently an honorary member of the 'génération du feu', as well as being a pacifist whose writings particularly appealed to the anti-war generation of Sartre and Aron. A large proportion of men entering the ENS (about a fifth in the 1920s) were the children of *instituteurs* (primary school teachers). This had particular implications for generational relations. Sexual equality was more common among this group than in almost any other section of French society. Primary school teachers often married other primary school teachers, and women often continued to work after marriage. Clearly, children growing up in such households had different relations with the 'older generation' than those that a child born to a 50-year-old army officer and his 25-year-old wife might be expected to have. Putting grandparents into the picture makes things even more complicated. Mannheim suggests that generational differences only really matter among the urban and educated, and that the peasantry was marked by lack of change from one generation to another. In fact, however, it was common in France for *instituteurs* to be the children of peasants and the parents of children who entered higher education and the *grande bourgeoisie.* Fernand Braudel (the son of *instituteurs* and the grandson of peasants) suggested that children reared by peasant grandparents grew up to be conservative, but Braudel's own close relations with his grandparents seem to have inspired an innovatory interest in long-term social currents rather than conservatism. Maurice Agulhon (a Communist-turned-Socialist historian), Georges Pompidou (a literary scholar-turned-Gaullist politician), Georges Pelorson (a friend of Samuel Beckett who became a Fascist official) all seem to have been affected in equally complicated ways by the good relations that they enjoyed with their peasant grandparents.

5. Oddly, Mannheim cites Agathon and the Maurrassians Georges Valois and Jacques Bainville in a footnote, as though their work would support his thesis.
6. Jean-François Sirinelli, *Génération intellectuelle. Khâgneux et normaliens dans l'entre-deux guerres* (Paris, 1986).
7. This work circulated in clandestine editions between 1945 and 1948 and then in various legal collections from 1948 onwards.
8. Althusser, Guitton and Brasillach all describe their captivity in diaries and autobiographical works. Yves Durand gives an overview of French experiences of captivity in Yves Durand, *La Captivité: Histoire des prisonniers de guerre. Français, 1939–1945* (Paris, 1980).
9. J.-P. Cointet, *La Légion Française des Combattants. La Tentation du fascisme* (Paris, 1995).
10. See the play of 1943 by Roger Ferdinand, *Les J 3*; a variety of magazines were targeted at the J3 immediately after the war.
11. A. Besançon, *Une Génération* (Paris, 1982).
12. A. Huan, F. Chantepie and J.-R. Obeix, *Les Chantiers de la jeunesse* (Paris, 1998).
13. B. Garnier and J. Queilllien (eds), *La Main d'oeuvre française exploitée par la Troisième Reich* (Caen, 2003).
14. R. Limouzin, *Le Temps des J 3* (Paris, 1983), republished as *Le Temps des vérités* (Paris, 1991).
15. L. Capdevilla, *Les Bretons au lendemain de l'occupation. Imaginaire et comportement d'une sortie de guerre, 1944–1945* (Rennes, 1999).

16. C. Nicolet, *Pierre Mendès France ou le Métier de Cassandra* (Paris, 1959), p. 37.
17. F. Giroud, *La Nouvelle vague* (Paris, 1958), p. 328.
18. C. Mauss Copeaux, *Appelés en Algérie, la parole confisquée* (Paris, 1999).
19. A. Prost, *Les Anciens combatttants et la société française, 1914–1939* (Paris, 1977).
20. A. Corbin, *Un Historien du sensible* (Paris, 2000).
21. J. Massu, *La Vraie bataille d'Alger* (Paris, 1971).
22. The Cure's 1978 song 'Killing an Arab' is an obvious reference to a Camus novel.
23. P. Nora, 'La Génération' in Nora (ed), *Les Lieux de Mémoire, III, Les Frances* (Paris, 1997), pp. 931–71.
24. A. Motion, *The Lamberts. George, Consant and Kit* (London, 1986), p. 943.
25. Y. Auron, *Les Juifs d'extrême gauche en mai 68: Cohn-Bendit, Krivine, Geismar. Une Génération révolutionnaire marquée par la Shoah* (Paris, 1998).
26. P. Goldman, *Souvenirs obscurs d'un juif polonais né en France* (Paris, 2005); M. Prazan, *Pierre Goldman, le frère de l'ombre* (Paris, 2005).
27. J.-F. Sirinelli, *Les Baby-Boomers. Une génération, 1945–1969* (Paris, 2003), p. 263.
28. G. Filoche, *1968–1998. Une Histoire sans fin,* (Paris, 1989), p. 9.
29. M. Dressen, *De l'Ampi à l'Etabli. Les étudiants maoistes a l'usine, 1967–1989* (Paris, 1999), p. 115.
30. G. Noiriel, *Workers in French Society in the 19th and 20th Centuries* (1990).
31. Note that all but one of these writers belonged to the same generation as those who had deferred to the Resistance during the 1960s, but their work began to be published from the 1970s onwards.
32. A. Sauvy, *La Montée des jeunes* (Paris, 1959).

4

'Generation' as a Political Argument in West European Protest Movements during the 1960s

Holger Nehring

In almost all European countries (with the possible exception of Britain), historians, journalists and commentators have identified a 'generation of 68'. This chapter seeks to redefine the parameters of the debate by showing how 'generation' served protesters at the time as a political argument.[1] The focus is on the West German, Italian, French and British movements in the second half of the 1960s that developed in opposition to nuclear weapons and educational policies, and drew further momentum from domestic political fallout from the war in Vietnam. By appealing to a generational community, the protesters sought to communicate their much more complex aims succinctly and effectively.[2] Discussions of 'generation' in general and 'the young' in particular served as placeholders for fundamental debates about the nature of political movements and social groups.[3]

The aim of this chapter is to historicize the use of generational arguments and place them in their political and social contexts. Its focus is the question of how and why generational arguments emerged during the 1960s. The chapter thus highlights the synthetic character of the concept 'generation'. The retrospective insertion of biographies into larger historical contexts is part of making sense of the self.[4] Talking about 'generation' is a device that enables historical actors to make sense of their biographies and connect their lives with history.[5] Guido Viale's recollections of his involvement in the Italian movement capture this process well: 'Everyone stakes his own experience in struggle. [...] I am with them because we are struggling against the same enemy, but with respect to the problem of my liberation.'[6]

This interpretation does not mean that generations were merely invented to serve as political arguments. Generational arguments cannot be split into 'real' and 'invented' elements: the main purpose of talking about generations is to transcend the individual space of experiences – construction and political reality have to match each other. Generational arguments serve to construct a homogeneous version of the past in the present and offer solutions for the society of the future.[7]

This argument is based on the assumption that generational experiences are not merely generational or social facts, but have to be actively created on the basis of structural determinants. Although most of the recent writing on generations pays lip service to this problem, many authors have failed to come to terms with its implications. Instead, they either unquestioningly reproduce the actors' arguments,[8] or they use 'generation' as a tool which endows the narrative with an almost biological necessity.[9] They forget, however, that it took individual and personal effort to make sense of one's own biography; individual experiences had, in a process of self-socialization, to be 'generationalized'.[10] Expressing political, social and cultural developments in generational terms offered activists a key which served two functions: it opened up common experiences and it mobilized them.[11]

The creation of collective identities is especially important for social movements, as they do not possess the organization of parties and more formal pressure groups. Merging the many different views of the activists into political aims is one of the key factors in social mobilization: people can only be mobilized if their social actions can be directed towards certain aims and common assessments of the social situation, that is, if the main groups which make up a social movement have found a cognitive identity. Such an identity helped the protesters of '1968' to present their aims more effectively to an external audience and to the political system as a whole.[12] The term 'generation' was particularly useful for such identities as it communicated strong feelings of belonging. It evoked biological certainties that seemed to transcend social, political and cultural differences between the different groups and thus led to an artificial 'naturalization of social classifications'.[13] Generational arguments, therefore, have a strong potential for binary coding, which simplifies political communication.[14] This chapter first develops some general themes in discussions about 'generations' in four West European countries (West Germany, Britain, France, Italy) before highlighting the specificities of each case.

The 'generationalization' of politics in Western Europe

None of the protest movements in West Germany, Italy, France and Great Britain were merely a student or youth movement. Yet one element characterized the use of 'generation' as political argument in all four countries: it was linked to metaphors of life and spiritual–cultural renewal. Despite many differences of detail, the movements shared common experiences that were due to the transnational convergence of the underlying ideas and of socio-economic developments in the four countries at the time. New Left ideas formed the transnational ideological cornerstones of generational arguments, as they highlighted the importance of the younger generations for social change. What was 'new' about the New Left was its novel cognitive orientation, which its supporters contrasted with that of the traditional labour movements. New Left movements criticized both the self-imposed restrictions of democratic socialism in welfare societies after an alleged 'end of ideology' and the perversion of communism in the Stalinist system. They sought to promote a new kind of socialism which stressed the importance of friendship and community. This entailed a new interpretation of social transformation. According to the New Left, social change was to be driven by the liberation of the individual from collective constraints in society at large, primarily through new forms of life, new ideals of culture and the arts, particularly grouped around experimental forms of living for young people. New Left ideas also stressed new forms of organization. Activists argued against hierarchies and in favour of both direct action and what they conceived as a more direct form of democracy.[15]

Most explicitly, 'generation' became a political argument in the ways in which West European New Left groups sought to promote social change. While the old left had endowed the 'proletariat', however defined, with that role, the New Left regarded a 'new' and more broadly defined set of groups, such as the young and educated, the working class, students and social pariahs, as the promoters of social change. It is precisely this uncoupling of the connection between proletariat and emancipatory struggle that made New Left ideas so attractive to the various protest movements. The 'young intelligentsia' was now endowed with the mandate to intervene in social struggles as one of the main 'revolutionary subjects'. Many came, with Herbert Marcuse, to regard youth 'as the new carriers of revolutionary infection'.[16]

Such ideas could only gain widespread acceptance among West European protesters because they appeared to relate to the socio-economic changes at the time. Contemporary commentators agreed that young people emerged as historical actors in their own right across West European societies in the decade before 1968. They were at first characterized by the classic attributes of 'youth' – dynamism, progress and optimism – while more sceptical assessments came to dominate towards the end of the decade.[17] Indeed, even in Britain, where generational arguments among protesters were the least widespread, 'youth' became one of the central markers of debate on societal change.[18] Young West European activists were also helped to develop shared perspectives by the fact that the lifestyles of the young in West European countries were converging in this era. Protesters listened to the same kind of music, wore similar clothes and engaged in similar activities, and they became increasingly aware of this.[19]

Political and socio-economic developments in Western Europe during the 1950s and 1960s further bolstered the trend of ideological and cultural convergence. Boom years and affluence had brought experiences around Europe closer together during the 1950s and 1960s. Convergence could also be seen at the level of political systems. A specific kind of consensual model of democracy emerged, based on the negotiation of conflicts and on widely held notions about central features of post-war societies such as the welfare state. During the 1960s, this consensus often found an expression in Grand Coalitions, such as in the Federal Republic and in Italy.[20] Many commentators expected a 'breach' with these structures,[21] but it was not yet clear who would open it. In this context, 'generation' offered itself to younger activists as a term to differentiate one's own experiences from those of previous age groups and thus explain one's own political stance.[22]

But converging ideas and socio-economic developments were not sufficient to create a common discourse about 'generations' among West European protesters. The protesters' mutual observation at the time and their participation in common protests enabled them to read their individual biographies into a generational matrix, a process which occurred mainly after the events.[23] These processes not only took place in a national framework, but coincided with common emotional identifications on a transnational level.[24]

It is these experiences that explain the frequency with which activists themselves have, in retrospect, referred to '1968' as a generational rebellion. But it is important to bear in mind that this kind of generational expression had more to do with creating group identifications than with the social structure of a generational cohort. The age groups among the protesters and their biographies were too diverse to classify them straightforwardly as a generation. This means that the use of 'generation' as a political argument varied across West European societies.

West Germany: Generation and the National Socialist past

The distinctive feature of the political relevance of generational arguments in the West German context was that, rather than identifying
their 'generation' *ex post*, the movements employed the term 'generation' at the time to signify their opposition to the government's policies
in a variety of areas much more effectively than the movements in
other countries did. This not only reflected the strong collective identity of the West German movement, but also some broader elements of
West German political culture. Making use of 'generation' as an argument allowed West German protesters to evoke three areas which were
under dispute – Germany's position in the Cold War in general and the
anti-communism of its political culture in particular, as well as the
alleged National Socialist past of some government ministers and political decision-makers. Likewise, commentators framed student protesters
by referring to the last days of the Weimar Republic: the street battles
between communists and the SA were still in people's minds – and both
groups had appealed to the population primarily as young and dynamic
movements.

This discourse about the young generation and its relationship with
National Socialism and Communism was particularly resonant in the
Federal Republic as a frontline state in the Cold War, since the GDR government sought to present itself as a young, dynamic, anti-fascist and,
therefore, peaceful state. It is thus no coincidence that the journalistic
slogan 'Don't trust anyone over 30!' was coined in the West German
context.[25]

In the Federal Republic, generational arguments came primarily from
the young and were less frequently used the other way round. In the
course of the 1950s and 1960s, adults developed increasingly positive
attitudes towards the young: in 1950, only 24 per cent of those polled
said that they had a positive impression of the young; in 1956, 38 per
cent answered positively; in 1960, 44 per cent; and in 1975, 62 per
cent.[26] The familial relationships between young people and their parents were often better than the motto 'Don't trust anyone over 30' suggests, even if they were not in entire harmony.[27] Many participants only
stated with hindsight that they 'did not want to be like their parents'.[28]
What distinguished the West German protesters from protesters in
other countries was not only the importance of National Socialism. It
was that many of the ideas which the student and young protesters
adopted were not bequeathed to them directly, but had to be completely reassembled from the experiences of Weimar.[29]

The West German protesters used generational arguments in order to obtain political influence in a society which was in a process of diversification and which offered the young a high level of influence on the cultural level, but still barred them from mainstream politics.[30] Only in 1970 was the voting age lowered from 21 to 18. There is countercultural evidence for the radicalization of generational arguments in the late 1960s. A song of the Cologne underground rock band Floh de Cologne ran: 'The old folks live from their past, / we live from our future, / old folks dream of the moon, / shoot them up.'[31]

It was in the movements against the Vietnam War, against the Emergency Laws and for educational reforms that these discourses were turned into political arguments, especially during the Grand Coalition government from 1966 onwards.[32] The student activists' memoirs and reminiscences illustrate how powerful such arguments against the Vietnam War were in post-war West German society: 'For years I'd had nightmares about the terrible bombing of Dresden at the end of the Second World War. I could see the houses burning still. And that's what I identified with the Vietnamese – the campaign against the war was a kind of working through my personal history.'[33] Another activist echoed these feelings in his writings during the 1970s: 'Children of ruins [...]: Rubble, houses which were torn apart, lumps of concrete, phosphor fire bombs and blue scars on the body of a friend [...] that is what we experienced as the first background to our lives, under the [...] pressure and threat of annihilation – that is our generation, a junk generation [...].'[34]

Especially the National Socialist past became a crucial marker for generational identity.[35] Gudrun Ensslin, later member of the Red Army Faction, explained: 'You cannot talk to the people who made Auschwitz.'[36] Anti-National Socialism and, more generally, anti-fascism, had drawn large numbers into student activism from early on; these political stances were perceived as central aspects of the generational division of West German society.[37] It was thus that the West German protesters came to perceive themselves as the 'young intelligentsia'.[38] Such arguments came to be intimately linked to the protesters' politics of the past. By identifying themselves as the young generation, they also sought to disentangle themselves from the residual guilt that connected them to National Socialism.[39]

'Generation' even became a political argument in debates among the activists and supporters themselves. Especially 'Cold War Liberals' (Uta Poiger), born in the late 1920s and early 1930s, who assumed that an 'end of ideology' had arrived, came to disagree with the more radical generational arguments of the protesters and, indirectly, accused the protesters of reinjecting into politics ideologies which had long gone: 'The difference [...] between your generation and the generation of those who are today between 40 and 50', the TV presenter Günter Gaus told the student leader Rudi Dutschke, 'seems to lie in the fact that you, the younger ones, do not possess the understanding of the redundancy of ideologies that we have gained over the past decades.'[40]

The conservative press conglomerate owned by the publishing tycoon Axel Springer and attacked by the students for its political stance was especially assiduous in drawing direct lines from the 1960s to the 1920s and evoking traditional fears of mass society.[41] Following the Socialist German Student Federation's Springer tribunal, the mass-market *Bild* announced 'End of the Twenties, Beginning of the Thirties'.[42] Even more explicitly, a leader in June 1967 argued that 'the Germans want no brown and no red SA, no columns of toughs, but peace' and simultaneously caricatured the student leader Rudi Dutschke as a psychopath with a disembodied head.[43] For those critical of the protests, the *protesters* were the ones who had not yet grown up and faced the reality of democracy. The protests were 'child play' and the problems they addressed mere 'infantile illnesses'.[44] According to this view, the protesters' emotionality was an expression not of genuine political concerns but of a lack of self-control and normality. The protesters thus became part of a threat to the democratic order of the young West German state.[45]

Helmut Schelsky's influential interpretation of a calm and 'sceptical generation' provided the foil for these debates. In the mid-1950s, the sociologist had predicted that the generation which grew up during the 1950s would never react in a revolutionary manner to the developments of the time. Schelsky had studied and worked with the conservative sociologists Hans Freyer and Arnold Gehlen during the 1930s and had, since the late 1930s, been a member of the National Socialist Party. He distinguished young people in the 1950s from the 'youth movement generation' of the 1900s and the highly ideological 'generation of political youth' of the 1920s and 1930s.[46] Such arguments struck a chord with a West German society eager to distance itself from the National Socialist past and, simultaneously, from the GDR which, at the time, appeared to many in the West as a state belonging to the socialist youth movement. Like many non-academic commentators, Schelsky took a scornful attitude to the protesters. In the preface to the 1975 edition of his *Sceptical Generation* he argued that the role of the activist Benno Ohnesorg, shot dead by a policeman in June 1967, 'resembled in macabre detail that of the National Socialist "martyr" Horst Wessel'.[47]

Conversely, the protesters used generational arguments to justify the concept of 'democracy from below', which went beyond the liberal consensus. The older generation, so the argument ran, was not yet ready for this since it was still under the influence of its authoritarian upbringing.[48] As the conservative columnist Armin Mohler noted, 'young West Germans wrap themselves in the bodies of Jews [...] to gain an advantage'.[49] Generational arguments were thus used not only as moral accusations, but also to discredit political opponents: 'We only needed to say Dachau, and they became insecure.'[50] Thus, in July 1967, Berlin student leaders replied publicly to the new Berlin mayor Klaus Schütz's characterizations of student methods as 'fascist': 'Today pogrom and propaganda, tomorrow the final solution, Herr Schütz.'[51] The lifestyles and habits of the young embodied this distance from the National Socialist past: the preferred music styles, the clothing and the hairstyle associated with the young and their pronouncedly civilian habits symbolized this move away from what they called the militarist past.[52]

Yet, the generational arguments used by some West German protesters against the allegedly 'fascist' generation of their parents was much more complicated than the generational rhetoric suggests. By defining themselves as biologically disconnected from the National Socialist past, the protesters sought to disentangle themselves from the web of German history. Rather ironically, their rhetoric of pathos and determination was not dissimilar from the one used by the right-wing student movement of the 1920s. Their rhetoric of remembering was, on an individual emotional level, an act of forgetting.[53] It was also highly gendered. Although women participated in the protests, the kinds of argument to which they tied 'generation' were those of the determined male fighter. This gendering was replicated in newspaper reports, most famously in the *Spiegel*'s famous cover photo with a fierce-looking Rudi Dutschke.[54] 'Generation' as a political argument could only obtain resonance because it struck a chord with the scientific and media discourses about West German youth which had formed in the mid-1950s. Due to the National Socialist experience, this discourse about generations assumed a salience it could not achieve in other West European societies.[55] It was, in the end, the reporting in the media, especially the TV footage, which turned the student protests into a generational revolt.[56] In discussions about educational reforms in the early 1960s, the analytical category 'youth' offered itself as a historical actor that embraced the need for progress, however defined, across the whole of society, while at the same time eschewing precise class affiliation. Youth had become the central foil for debates on social and political problems, much more so than in France, Italy or Britain.[57]

Italy: The young generation as the new *Resistenza* and the centrality of state power

Generational arguments played a role for the Italian student protesters, but never achieved the central importance they had in the Federal Republic. The co-operation between the syndicalist trade unions and the students is an indication of this. Generation could apparently not be used as easily in Italy to encapsulate other social issues. The main debate concerned the legitimacy of state power and the perennial Italian problem of the nature of government. The students, accordingly, were not shy to stage themselves as new kinds of brigands, thus taking on the mantle of the brigand protests in the south of Italy in the nineteenth century.[58]

As in the Federal Republic, the Italian student movement gained its initial impetus from generational conflict in the universities, in this case those of the northern industrial triangle. It emerged in opposition to status-quo-orientated proposals for university and educational reform. This conflict also had a significant religious dimension in Italy. The pontificate of John XXIII had opened the Italian Church to a new ferment of ideas and activities and, more than before, attention was paid to issues of social justice. This is one of the reasons why the first rebellions broke out in Catholic universities during the academic year 1967–8: at Trento, which had only been founded in 1962, and in the Catholic university at Milan.[59] The revolt spread to Turin at the end of November and then throughout the country, even to some secondary schools in the major urban areas.

In the students' opinion, planned legislation only offered half measures against overcrowding, inadequate funding, outdated teaching styles and the hegemony of the professoriate. The Moro government's support for the colonels' regime in Greece and the Vietnam War were further points of contention. Many contemporary publications talked of 'giving youth a voice'. But they highlighted mostly problems in school and university education that were said to be apolitical, and put forward what the protesters regarded as prescriptive political norms that suppressed real democracy.[60]

With the escalation of protests after the death, allegedly caused by fascist violence, of the Rome architecture student Paolo Rossi, the students switched the conflict to one over the legitimacy of state power.[61] Between March and May 1968, students left the campuses and also campaigned in the city streets. New Left ideas in Italy centred primarily on the revitalization of Gramsci's ideas, Raniero Panzieri's *Operaismo* and

Herbert Marcuse's writings, and offered a bridge between the different movements that also disagreed with the role of the Catholic Church in Italian public life.[62] Thus, the political debate around these issues was not conducted in terms of 'generations', but primarily in terms of the country's troubled past and its untested democracy.[63] Age thus became an argument in the debates about antifascism and the shape of Italian post-World War II democracy.[64]

This does not mean that arguments of a generational kind did not matter. To use one's own youth to confront the authoritarian past of one's parents was an extremely powerful discursive move. As in other countries, it allowed very different familial experiences to be read into a single generational matrix which could, in turn, be used to produce political arguments. In retrospect, many students said that they rejected the family in favour of greater commitment to their peer group and to collectivist ideals. Fiorella Farinelli recalled: 'By far the best of the graffiti on the walls of my faculty at the university [...] was this one: "I want to be an orphan". I agreed with it, I photographed it, I took a poster of it back to my home; it was the slogan I liked most.'[65]

The Italian press often linked the student demonstrations to the fascist period and defended the policies of its centre-left government in Rome. Italian students raised concerns about the past and the stability of democracy. Thus the paper *La Stampa* wrote about the student protests not in generational terms, but primarily in terms of 'disorders' and 'grave episodes', thus initially lacking the harsh rhetoric of the German Springer press.[66] Some letters to the editors of newspapers raised generational issues indirectly: 'I am a father who works ten hours a day so that my son may study at a university [...] I do not believe that there is a big difference between the March on Rome and the occupation of the university.'[67] Pictures linking students to Chinese communism (by depicting them as 'filocinesi') and communism in general were used increasingly, although again without being directly linked to generational issues.[68] In February 1968, a newspaper portrayed Turin students as 'left-wing fascists' by showing pictures of students raising their arms in fascist salute and shouting 'Mao! Mao!'[69] The dominant preoccupation remained not generational conflict but state order. Papers and critics portrayed activists as dangerous, left wing and a fascist threat to civil order, while depicting the school administration, police and government as defenders of democracy and order.[70] As in the Federal Republic, by linking leftist students with the fascist era the press played on the majority population's fear of disorder, fascism and communism. Correspondingly, student leaders used the terms 'fascista' and 'nazi' in an effort to mobilize against what they regarded as a repressive establishment and thus opened a debate that had been closed during the immediate post-war years. Discourses about moral panic, violence and hooliganism further underlined this interpretation. Oral history evidence suggests, however, that debates at the time were, like in the Federal Republic, far less coherent and far more fractured than they might appear in retrospect.[71]

But, whereas in West Germany conjuring up the Weimar past meant eliciting fears of dictatorship, Italian students used generational arguments primarily to criticize ancient hierarchies reinforced by Mussolini. Also, communism played less of a role in Italian debates, primarily because of its association with wartime resistance and the reformist posture of the Italian Communist Party (PCI).

France: A generation *ex post*

Although 'génération' is part of Pierre Nora's massive assembly of French sites of memory,[72] and although generational arguments were used in French debates to highlight the different experiences of students and other groups, generational arguments never came centre stage.[73] Generational arguments only came to dominate in the 1970s and 1980s, when the political meanings of the 1960s campaign were pushed aside.[74] A social movement which spanned the various burning issues of the time (peace in Vietnam, the practice of presidential rule in the Fifth Republic, the conduct of educational policy) only emerged during the first half of 1968 and came to include workers as well when the revolt spread across the country. It was, therefore, much more difficult at the time to make sense of the revolt purely in generational terms, although certain elements of this kind could be found here as well.

The main focus in France was what the students regarded as their battle against authoritarianism: that of the state, the schools, the universities and the factories.[75] In the memoir literature, these aims were then 'generationalized': 'Everything I had ever dreamt of since childhood [...] now became real. People were saying, fuck hierarchy, authority, this society with its cold rational elitist logic! [...] Suddenly, the French were showing they understood that they had to refuse the state's authority because it was malevolent, evil, just as I'd always thought as a child. Suddenly they realised that they had to find a new sort of solidarity.'[76]

Although generational arguments initially did play a role, they became less important as the protests developed. Student activism had played a more important part in France than in other Western countries, but was, until the mid-1960s, primarily contained within the National Student's Union (*Union Nationale des Etudiants de France*, UNEF), which had a particular impact on the campaign against the war in Algeria in the early 1960s.[77] Generation conflict was not, however, the mobilizing factor. Protesters and their opponents discussed the state of the education system primarily in terms of authoritarianism and the opposition between communism and anti-communism.[78] As in the Federal Republic, there was a growing awareness among French youth that they had been excluded from the political system. A drawing on a university wall illustrates this. The message, painted below a paving stone, the students' main weapon, read: 'under twenty-ones, your ballot paper'.[79] The protests started as the revolt of a relatively small group of students at the suburban university Nanterre against bad housing and living conditions, overcrowded lectures and bleak job opportunities. Due to a lack of support, the student strike at the beginning of the academic year 1967–8 against the reforms of the university system began to ebb after a few weeks.[80]

These events had been preceded by the unconventional actions of small student groups such as the 'Enragés' and the 'Mouvement 22 Mars', which had still been structured by generational arguments.[81] While the 'Enragés' wanted to abolish universities altogether, the 'Mouvement' had plans to create a 'critical university'. Both groups were based on specific lifestyles associated with the young, but they never managed to establish the link between their lifestyle and their 'generation' as such. The individualistic subcultures in which they tried to achieve progress through individual acts of transgression never went beyond a small circle.[82]

These protests spread to the Sorbonne, whose administration dealt with the disciplinary proceedings against eight Nanterre students. Then, however, the generational coding of the protests was replaced by an antagonism between state and protester as student actions met with stiff state resistance, in particular a police deployment on the central quadrangle of the Sorbonne. It was this coding, rather than the generational one, that led to the building of solidarity between other students and the protesting groups.

Much more than in other countries, one key 'critical event' led to the escalation of protests and synchronized the several protests into one movement.[83] The event in question was the so-called night of the barricades on 10–11 May 1968, when pupils and students occupied an enclave within Paris's Quartier Latin after a peaceful demonstration. Through media reports, particularly television, these events made an impact beyond Paris and led to solidarity campaigns elsewhere: the interplay between media reporting, student protest and governmental reactions synchronized the perceptions of heterogeneous social groups, establishing a common and public time frame for all participants and observers. But the synchronizing factor was not the concept of generation but rather the issue of the legitimacy of state power and force.[84] Unlike in other countries, French protesters and their governments drew on the same points of reference, albeit from different perspectives. By evoking the 'barricades', they tapped not only the heritage of the French Revolution, but also memories of the Paris Commune in 1871 and of the liberation of Paris from German occupation in 1944.[85] For many activists, the experience of police reaction to demonstrations first against the Algerian war and then against conditions at universities made them 'discover fascism'.[86]

But neither the students nor the observing media used this event primarily to highlight the generational dimension, for example, by offering an interpretation that linked the students directly to the *Résistance*. Also, at the time, commentators and activists alike conceptualized the protests rather as a 'commune étudiante' than as a clash between generations.[87] Only *a posteriori* were these protests reinterpreted as a generational revolt when the participants had been resocialized by taking part in the protest activities of the French May.[88]

It was this non-generational coding which made the co-operation between trade unions and students possible. When Prime Minister George Pompidou fulfilled the students' demands only 14 hours after the violent evacuation of the Quartier Latin, the protesters' success served to raise the expectations of other social groups.[89] They transferred the students' arguments about the legitimacy of state power to their workplaces by protesting against the 'état patron' in the factories. 'Generation' did not play a dominant role in these arguments. Instead, what mattered was the debate about legitimacy which united workers and student movements in a 'community of aspirations': 'We have to replace the industrial and administrative monarchy with democratic structures of self rule.'[90] What mattered in this 'democracy from below' was not the biological certainty that generational arguments appeared to suggest. Instead, it was the feeling of disparity. By chanting 'We are all German Jews', the French students allied themselves with the Other by refusing to identify with a biological self.[91]

Britain: The absence of generations

In Britain, student protests congealed into one coherent social movement much less than in the other countries under discussion. Much more than in the other West European countries, these events remained isolated protests at different universities against specific measures of the university administrations.[92] They thus maintained their character as student protests much more than in other countries and did not develop into an extra-parliamentary opposition. The initial spark for these student protests was the appointment of a new Director to the London School of Economics and Political Science. This was the white Rhodesian Walter Adams, who was revealed to have close links with Ian Smith, the hard-line Prime Minister of Rhodesia who wished to maintain a system of white supremacy in the country. The protests escalated and led to disciplinary action against some of the protesters during 1966.[93] Other higher-education institutions were also disrupted during 1968: at Edinburgh, Leicester and Aston, and at the art colleges of Guildford, Croydon and Hornsey, students demanded greater representation on governing committees. Protests against specific speakers further radicalized the students' demands: such provocations included a lecture by a US Embassy official at Sussex, Enoch Powell's 'Rivers of Blood' speech at Birmingham, and a lecture by a biological weapons researcher at Essex.

The main focus of student radicalism, however, became the opposition to the Vietnam War. The peak of protests came in 1968, when several marches on the US Embassy in Grosvenor Square ended in violent battles between the students and the police. Once again, the LSE became the hub of the conflict when the School's board of governors threatened to close the institution down if there was any occupation coinciding with the anti-Vietnam march in October 1968. As in France, the main focus of the debates in Britain was legitimacy. But, unlike their French counterparts, British students expressed their concerns primarily in terms of 'race' and the university administrations' power, not with reference to generations.

While these protests created a network of activists who interpreted their experiences in generational terms, 'generation' never achieved the importance as political argument that it had in West Germany or even in France and Italy. This does not mean that such arguments were entirely lacking. In his 1960 essay 'Outside the Whale', Edward P. Thompson argued along generational lines in order to explain and show the need to overcome the apathy within affluent society in Britain and break through the thought-barrier of what he called 'Natopolitan' ideology.[94]

While the protesters themselves did not use 'generation' as a political argument, some contemporary observers and commentators identified what they regarded as the underlying cultural forms and patterns of protest in generational terms. These commentators connected the student protests especially to the lifestyle of the young and to specific youth subcultures that created 'moral panics'.[95] Edward Thompson's fatherly advice to Sheila Rowbotham encapsulates this quite well: Thompson talked of the protest movement as belonging to 'a culture so excessively self-absorbed, self-inflating and self-dramatising'.[96]

Yet commentators (and some activists) described youth subculture in terms of opposition to 'the Establishment', and in class terms, rather than along generational lines.[97] Especially at the beginning of the decade, assessments tended not to accord any major importance to youth, while bringing resentment at class distinctions to the fore. Schelsky's 'sceptical generation' was the 'generation X' in Britain. Unlike Schelsky's interpretation, however, this definition of an essentially non-political group remained dominant in public and social-scientific discourses even after 1968.[98]

Conclusion

Generational experiences have formed powerful political arguments. Their use in political debates has driven historical developments more than their social-structural existence, a fact that has not yet been properly acknowledged.[99] The political use-value of 'generation' varied across the societies under consideration. In Britain, the student protests could never achieve the status they had in other West European societies, partly because 'generation' did not suffice to create a collective identity for the movement. There was no major political issue that could be simplified by drawing attention to the generational element. In France and Italy, 'generation' had far more potency as a political argument than in Britain. Here it could be used to draw attention to the needs of the young; it could also serve to denounce political opponents as tainted with a fascist past. The arguments at the time were, however, only read into a generational matrix after the events.

The Federal Republic was a special case, mainly because the National Socialist past and the Cold War background interacted with the political system in ways that, more than elsewhere, pushed the protesters outside the boundaries of respectable politics and thus enhanced their need for alternative group identities. Here, generation worked particularly well as a political argument. It enabled protesters to draw a line between past collaboration with National Socialism and the emergency legislation and police intervention of the present. The protagonists could also draw on a longer-standing tradition of generational discourse. The political use of the generation concept in the Federal Republic was, in itself, nothing new. During the 1920s, 'generation' and 'generational community' had taken a central place in political debates on the advent of a 'people's community' or the 'end of class society'.[100]

This trope explains the revival of generational arguments in the Western world during the 1970s. Once the political aims of the protesters were overshadowed by political violence and apparently trumped by the reformist agendas of governments, 'generation' helped turn the protests into relatively harmless and playful events which had more to do with lifestyle and psychological predispositions than with politics.[101] The 'generationalization' of experiences during the 1960s was not limited by national boundaries but assumed an increasingly transnational character as activists observed each other. Yet generation as a political argument remained embedded in specific national interpretive contexts at the time. It was only through memorialization of 'the movement' from the 1970s onwards that the '1968 generation' became a (West) European phenomenon.

Notes

I should like to thank the participants at the conference 'Generations in Europe', in particular Christoph Conrad and Bernd Weisbrod, as well as J. M. Moses, for their helpful suggestions on an earlier version of this paper.

1. See the sceptical remarks in B. Weisbrod, 'Generation und Generationalität in der Neueren Geschichte', *Aus Politik und Zeitgeschichte*, 8 (2005), 3–9 and U. Jureit and M. Wildt (eds), *Generationen. Zur Relevanz eines wissenschaftlichen Grundbegriffs* (Hamburg, 2005), p. 9.
2. P. Abrams, 'Rites de Passage: The Conflict of Generations in Industrial Society', *Journal of Contemporary History*, 5 (1970), 175–90, here 178.
3. J. Reulecke, 'Zornige junge Männer – Jugendprotest als Kennzeichen des 20. Jahrhunderts?', in idem, *'Ich möchte einer werden so wie die ...' Männerbünde im 20. Jahrhundert* (Frankfurt am Main, 2001), pp. 19–34, here 33.
4. H. Schumann and J. Scott, 'Generations and Collective Memories', *American Sociological Review*, 54 (1989), 359–81; M. Corsten, 'Biographie, Lebenslauf und das "Problem der Generation"', *BIOS. Zeitschrift für Biographieforschung, Oral History und Lebensverlaufsanalysen*, 14/2 (2002), 32–59.
5. J. Kristeva, 'Eine Erinnerung', *Schreibheft*, 26 (1985), 134–43; L. Passerini, *Autobiography of a Generation. Italy, 1968* (Hanover, NH, 1997). Passerini's original title *Autoritratto di Gruppo* captures this much better.

6. Quoted in Passerini, *Autobiography*, p. 94.

7. For a general overview of different approaches, see A. Schulz and G. Grebner, 'Generation und Geschichte. Zur Renaissance eines umstrittenen Forschungskonzepts', in idem (eds), *Generationswechsel und historischer Wandel* (Munich, 2003), pp. 1–23, here 4.

8. See, for example, U. Herbert, *Best. Biographische Studien über Radikalismus, Weltanschauung und Vernunft 1903–1989* (Bonn, 1996).

9. See, for example, C. von Hodenberg, *Konsens und Krise. Eine Geschichte der westdeutschen Medienöffentlichkeit 1945–1973* (Göttingen, 2006).

10. U. Daniel, *Kompendium Kulturgeschichte. Theorien, Praxis, Schlüsselwörter* (Frankfurt am Main, 2001), p. 331; N. Luhmann, *Soziale Systeme. Grundriß einer allgemeinen Theorie* (Frankfurt am Main, 1984), pp. 326–7.

11. J.P. Azéma, 'La Clef Générationelle', *Vingtième Siècle*, 22 (1989), 3–10.

12. R. Eyerman and A. Jamison, *Social Movements. A Cognitive Approach* (Cambridge, 1991).

13. M. Douglas, *How Institutions Think* (London, 1987), p. 48.

14. For the general theoretical context, see Luhmann, *Soziale Systeme*, pp. 197–8 and 602–3.

15. K.A. Otto, *Vom Ostermarsch zur APO. Geschichte der außerparlamentarischen Opposition in der Bundesrepublik* (Frankfurt am Main, 1977); I. Gilcher-Holtey, *'Die Phantasie an die Macht'. Mai 68 in Frankreich* (Frankfurt am Main, 1995), pp. 44–104; Lin Chun, *The British New Left* (Edinburgh, 1993); P. Ginsborg, *A History of Contemporary Italy 1943–1980* (Harmondsworth, 1990), pp. 304–7.

16. R. Viénet, *Enragés et situationistes dans le mouvement des occupations* (Paris, 1968), pp. 219–43. For a very short summary of Marcuse's ideas, see S. Lönnendonker, B. Rabehl and J. Staadt, *Die antiautoritäre Revolte. Der Sozialistische Deutsche Studentenbund nach der Trennung von der SPD, vol. 1: 1960–1967* (Wiesbaden, 2002), pp. 278–9.

17. A. Gestrich, 'Kindheit und Jugend – Individuelle Entfaltung im 20. Jahrhundert', in R. van Dülmen (ed.), *Entdeckung des Ich. Die Geschichte der Individualisierung vom Mittelalter bis zur Gegenwart* (Cologne et al., 2001), pp. 465–87, especially 466.

18. See, for example, P. Abrams and A. Little, 'The Young Activist in British Politics', *The British Journal of Sociology*, 16 (1965), 315–33; F. Musgrave, *Youth and the Social Order* (London, 1964); Catherine Ellis, 'No Hammock for the Idle: The Conservative Party, "Youth" and the Welfare State in the 1960s', *Twentieth Century British History*, 16 (2005), 441–70; S. Fielding, *Labour and Cultural Change* (Manchester, 2003), pp. 165–86; E. Janes Yeo, '"The Boy is the Father of the Man": Moral Panic over Working-Class Youth, 1850 to the Present', *Labour History Review*, 69 (2004), 185–99.

19. M. Winock, *Chronique des Années Soixante* (Paris, 1987), p. 103; A. Marwick, *The Sixties: Cultural Revolution in Britain, France, Italy, and the United States, c.1958–c.1974* (Oxford, 1999); U.G. Poiger, 'Amerikanisierung oder Internationalisierung? Populärkultur in beiden deutschen Staaten', *Aus Politik und Zeitgeschichte*, 45 (2003), 17–24.

20. M. Conway, 'The Rise and Fall of Western Europe's Democratic Age, 1945–1973', *Contemporary European History*, 13 (2004), 67–88; H. Kaelble

(ed.), *Der Boom 1948–1973. Gesellschaftliche und wirtschaftliche Folgen in der Bundesrepublik Deutschland und in Europa* (Opladen, 1992).

21. E. Morin, C. Lefort and J.-M. Coudray, *La Brèche. Premières réflexions sur les événements* (Paris, 1968).

22. J.-P. LeGoff, *Mai 68. L'héritage impossible* (Paris, 1998), pp. 34–7.

23. See, for example, Tariq Ali, *Streetfighting Years. An Autobiography of the Sixties* (London, 1987), p. 169 and Daniel Cohn-Bendit on the 'night of the barricades', 10–11 May 1968, quoted in R. Fraser, *1968. A Student Generation in Revolt* (London, 1988), p. 7.

24. Ali, *Street Fighting Years*, 172; S. Rowbotham, *Promise of a Dream. Remembering the Sixties* (Harmondsworth, 2001), p. 172.

25. Note the perceptive remarks in J. Varon, *Bringing the War Home. The Weather Underground, the Red Army Faction, and Revolutionary Violence in the Sixties and Seventies* (Berkeley, 2004), 20–73.

26. E. Noelle and P. Neumann (eds), *Jahrbuch der öffentlichen Meinung 1958–1964* (Allensbach and Bonn, 1965), p. 200; E. Noelle-Neumann (ed.), *The Germans. Public Opinion Polls, 1967–1980* (London, 1981), p. 53. On the general context, see D. Siegfried, '"Don't trust anyone older than 30?" Voices of Conflict and Consensus between Generations in 1960s West Germany', *Journal of Contemporary History*, 40 (2005), 727–44.

27. F.H. Tenbruck, 'Väter und Söhne. Das Generationsproblem in neuer Perspektive', in G. Böse (ed.), *Unsere Freiheit morgen. Gefahren und Chancen der modernen Gesellschaft* (Düsseldorf and Cologne, 1963), pp. 125–39, here 136; K. Allerbeck, *Soziologie radikaler Studentenbewegungen. Eine vergleichende Untersuchung in der Bundesrepublik und in den Vereinigten Staaten* (Munich, 1973), p. 108.

28. See, for example, U. Kätzel (ed.), *Die '68erinnen. Porträt einer rebellischen Frauengeneration* (Berlin, 2002), p. 59.

29. C.-D. Krohn, 'Die westdeutsche Studentenbewegung und das "andere Deutschland"', in A. Schildt, D. Siegfried and K.-C. Lammers (eds), *Dynamische Zeiten, Die 60er Jahre in den beiden deutschen Gesellschaften* (Hamburg, 2000), pp. 695–718.

30. U.G. Poiger, *Jazz, Rock, and Rebels. Cold War Politics and American Culture in a Divided Germany* (Berkeley, 2000).

31. Ana & Bela, *Kölnisches Volksblatt* (1 November 1969).

32. M. Schneider, *Demokratie in Gefahr? Der Konflikt um die Notstandsgesetze. Sozialdemokratie, Gewerkschaften und intellektueller Protest 1958–1968* (Bonn, 1986).

33. Karin Kerner, student at the Free University, Berlin, quoted in Fraser, *1968*, p. 88.

34. R.D. Brinkmann, *Rom, Blicke* (Reinbek, 1979), p. 356. See also P.A. Richter, 'Die Außerparlamentarische Opposition in der Bundesrepublik Deutschland 1966 bis 1968', in I. Gilcher-Holtey (ed.), *1968. Vom Ereignis zum Gegenstand in der Geschichtswissenschaft* (Göttingen, 1998), pp. 35–55, here 48–9.

35. For a more general overview of this aspect, see B. Davis, 'New Leftists and West Germany: Fascism, Violence, and the Public Sphere, 1967–1974', in P. Gassert and A. Steinweis (eds), *Coming to Terms with the Past in West Germany: The 1960s* (New York, 2006) and C. Kohser-Spohn, *Mouvement*

étudiant et critique du fascisme en Allemagne dans les années soixante (Paris, 1999).

36. Quoted from K. Briegleb, 'Vergangenheit in der Gegenwart', in idem and S. Weigel (eds), *Gegenwartsliteratur seit 1968* (Munich, 1992), pp. 73–115, here 91. This attitude, however, was not universal. Cf. the evidence in W. Jaide, *Das Verhältnis der Jugend zur Politik. Empirische Untersuchungen zur politischen Anteilnahme und Meinungsbildung junger Menschen der Geburtsjahrgänge 1940–46* (Darmstadt, 1963), p. 100. For the general backgrund, see A. Schildt, 'Die Eltern auf der Anklagebank? Zur Thematisierung der NS-Vergangenheit im Generationenkonflikt der bundesrepublikanischen 1960er Jahre', in C. Cornelißen, L. Klinkhammer and W. Schwentker (eds), *Erinnerungskulturen. Deutschland, Italien und Japan seit 1945* (Frankfurt am Main, 2003), pp. 317–32.

37. H.-U. Thamer, 'Die NS-Vergangenheit im politischen Diskurs der 68er Bewegung', *Westfälische Forschungen*, 48 (1998), 39–53.

38. M. Schmidtke, *Der Aufbruch der jungen Intelligenz. Die 68er Jahre in der Bundesrepublik und den USA* (Frankfurt am Main, 2003), pp. 284–87.

39. U. Jureit, 'Generationen als Erinnerungsgemeinschaften. Das "Denkmal für die ermordeten Juden Europas" als Generationsobjekt', in Jureit and Wildt (eds), *Generationen*, pp. 244–65, here 256.

40. 'Rudi Dutschke zu Protokoll. Fernsehinterview von Günter Gaus', in G. Dutschke, H. Gollwitzer and J. Miermeister (eds), *Rudi Dutschke. Mein langer Marsch. Reden, Schriften und Tagebücher aus zwanzig Jahren* (Reinbek, 1980), pp. 42–57, here 49. See also R. Löwenthal, *Der Romantische Rückfall* (Stuttgart, 1970). For the background, see A.D. Moses, 'The Forty-Fivers. A Generation between Fascism and Democracy', *German Politics and Society*, 17 (1999), 94–126, here 119.

41. On the background, see P. Nolte, *Die Ordnung der deutschen Gesellschaft. Selbstentwurf und Selbstbeschreibung im 20. Jahrhundert* (Munich, 2000), pp. 273–318.

42. *Bild*, 5 February 1968, reprinted in Otto (ed.), *APO: Außerparlamentarische Opposition in Quellen und Dokumenten (1960 – 1970)* (Cologne, 1989), no. 125, 259–61.

43. *Bild*, 3 June 1967, reprinted in Otto (ed.), *APO*, no. 236. For the disembodied head, see *Die Welt*, 21 February 1968, 2; 'Sie wollen Berlin ruinieren', *Berliner Morgenpost*, 7 April 1968. On the historical background to these fearful attitudes towards youth movements, see D. Linton, *Who Has the Youth, Has the Future* (Princeton, 1991). On the response of the police, see K. Weinhauer, *Schutzpolizei in der Bundesrepublik. Zwischen Bürgerkrieg und Innerer Sicherheit: Die turbulenten sechziger Jahre* (Paderborn et al., 2003), pp. 273–332.

44. Marion Countess Dönhoff, *Im Wartesaal der Geschichte. Vom Kalten Krieg zur Wiedervereinigung. Beiträge und Kommentare aus fünf Jahrzehnten* (Stuttgart, 1993), p. 193; R. Schörken, *Die Niederlage als Generationserfahrung. Jugendliche nach dem Zusammenbruch der NS-Herrschaft* (Weinheim and Munich, 2004), p. 186.

45. F.-W. Kersting, '"Unruhediskurs". Zeitgenössische Deutungen der 68er-Bewegung', in M. Frese, J. Paulus and K. Teppe (eds), *Demokratisierung und*

gesellschaftlicher Aufbruch. Die sechziger Jahre als Wendezeit in der Bundesrepublik (Paderborn et al., 2003), 715–40.

46. Schelsky, *Die skeptische Generation. Eine Soziologie der deutschen Jugend* (new edition, Frankfurt am Main et al., 1975), pp. 82 and 488–9. On the background, see F.-W. Kersting, 'Helmut Schelskys "Skeptische Generation" von 1957', *Vierteljahrshefte für Zeitgeschichte* 50 (2002), 465–95.

47. Schelsky, *Die skeptische Generation*, ix and xviii.

48. D. Baacke, *Jugend und Subkultur* (Munich, 1972), p. 36.

49. *Die Zeit*, 10 March 1967.

50. A contemporary looking back, quoted in Kaspar Maase, BRAVO *Amerika. Erkundungen zur Jugendkultur der Bundesrepublik in den fünfziger Jahren* (Hamburg, 1992), p. 82 and E. Wisselinck, *Volk ohne Traum. Das Lebensgefühl der jungen Generation in Selbstzeugnissen* (Munich, 1964), p. 49.

51. APO-Archive, Free University Berlin, File 'FU Allgemeines', 1-9.67.

52. K. Maase, 'Körper, Konsum, Genuss – Jugendkultur und mentaler Wandel in den beiden deutschen Gesellschaften', *Aus Politik und Zeitgeschichte*, 45 (2003), 9–16.

53. H. Welzer, S. Moller and K. Tschugnall, *'Opa war kein Nazi.' Nationalsozialismus und Holocaust im Familiengedächtnis* (Frankfurt am Main, 2002); L. Niethammer, 'Sind Generationen identisch?', in J. Reulecke (ed.), *Generationalität und Lebensgeschichte im 20. Jahrhundert* (Munich, 2003), pp. 1–16, here 13–14. On the 1920s, see H. Mommsen, 'Generationskonflikt und politische Entwicklung in der Weimarer Republik', in ibid., 114–26 and the classic exposition by Karl Mannheim, 'The Problem of Generations' (1927), in *From Karl Mannheim*, ed. K.H. Wolff (New Brunswick and London, 2nd edn, 1993), pp. 351–95, here 355–61.

54. *Der Spiegel*, 11 December 1967, front cover.

55. Schelsky, Die skeptische Generation.

56. See, for example, the series in the weekly *Die Zeit* which was subsequently published as a book: Kai Hermann, *Die Revolte der Studenten* (Hamburg, 1967).

57. Typical for the 1950s: Schelsky, *Die skeptische Generation*. Typical for thinking in the late 1960s: L. Rosenmayr, 'Jugend als Faktor sozialen Wandels (Versuch einer theoretischen Exploration der Jugendrevolten)', in F. Neidhardt et al. (eds), *Jugend im Spektrum der Wissenschaften* (Munich, 1970), pp. 203–28.

58. See, in general, J. Kurz, *Die Universität auf der Piazza. Entstehung und Zerfall der Studentenbewegung in Italien 1966–1968* (Cologne, 2000).

59. R. Lumley, 'Social Movements in Italy 1968–78' (unpublished Ph.D. thesis, Centre for Contemporary Cultural Studies, University of Birmingham, 1983), p. 189.

60. Marwick, *The Sixties*, pp. 551–2.

61. S. Tarrow, *Democracy and Disorder. Protest and Politics in Italy, 1967–75* (Oxford, 1989); A. Agosti, L. Passerini and N. Tranfaglia (eds), *La cultura e i luoghi del '68* (Milan, 1991).

62. S. Hellman, 'The "New Left" in Italy', in M. Kolinsky and W.E. Patterson (eds), *Social and Political Movements in Western Europe* (London, 1976), pp. 243–73; R. Lumley, *States of Emergency. Cultures of Revolt in Italy from 1968 to 1978* (London, 1990), pp. 63–7.

63. On the debate in the press more generally, see S.J. Hilwig, 'The Revolt against the Establishment. Students versus the Press in West Germany and Italy', in

C. Fink, P. Gassert and D. Junker (eds), *1968. The World Transformed* (Cambridge, 1998), pp. 321–49.

64. L. Paggi, 'Antifascism and the Reshaping of Democratic Consensus in Post-1945 Italy', *New German Critique*, 67 (1996), 101–10; G. de Luna and M. Revelli, *Fascismo/Anti-fascismo. Le idee, le identitá* (Florence, 1995), p. 146.

65. Quoted in Passerini, *Autobiography*, p. 48.

66. See, for example, 'Cronica Cittadina', *La Stampa*, 11, 17, 18 January 1968.

67. Quoted in G. De Luna, 'Aspetti dei movimenti del '68 a Torino', in A. Agosti et al., *La Cultura e i luoghi del '68*, p. 198. See also M. Degl'Innocenti, *L'epoca giovane. Generazioni, fascismo e antifascismo* (Manduria et al., 2002).

68. Lumley, *States of Emergency*, 73.

69. *La Stampa*, 21 February 1968, p. 2.

70. *La Stampa*, 7 February 1968, p. 2.

71. S.J. Hillwig, '"Are You Calling Me a Fascist?" A Contribution to the Oral History of the 1968 Italian Student Rebellion', *Journal of Contemporary History*, 36 (2001), 581–97, here 596; A. Portelli, *The Battle of the Valle Guilia: Oral History and the Art of Dialogue* (Madison, WI, 1997), pp. 183–4; J.M. Foot, 'Words, Songs and Books. Oral History in Italy. A Review and Discussion', *Journal of Modern Italian Studies*, 3/2 (1998), 164–74.

72. P. Nora, 'La Génération', in idem (ed.), *Les Lieux de mémoire* (Paris, 1997), vol. 2/4, pp. 2975–3015.

73. On these developments, see L. Joffrin, *Mai 68. Histoire des événements* (Paris, 1988). See, on the various interpretations: M. Zancarini, 'Les Interprétations de mai 68', in *Les années 68: événements, cultures politiques et modes de vie. Lettre d'information*, 10 (February 1996), ed. IHTP, 4–23; M. Mead, *Le Fossé des générations. Les nouvelles relations entre les générations dans les années soixante-dix* (Paris, 1970), pp. 78 and 91.

74. K. Ross, *May '68 and its Afterlives* (Chicago, 2002), pp. 182–215. A good example for this kind of history writing is J.-F. Sirinelli, *Les Baby-boomers. Une génération 1945–1969* (Paris, 2003); idem, 'Die Babyboomer und der Mai 1968 in Frankreich', *Vierteljahrshefte für Zeitgeschichte*, 53 (2005), 527–45; and D. Bertraux et al., 'Mai 68 et la formation de générations politiques en France', *Le Mouvement Social*, 143 (April/June 1988), 75–95.

75. Gilcher-Holtey, *Phantasie an die Macht*, 133, 303, 323.

76. Nelly Finkielsztejn, student at Nanterre University, quoted in Fraser et al., *1968*, p. 8.

77. A. Belden Fields, *Student Politics in France: A Study of the Union Nationale des Etudiants de France* (New York, 1970).

78. Marwick, *The Sixties*, 100–1.

79. Marwick, *The Sixties*, plate after p. 428.

80. See, for example, D. and G. Cohn-Bendit, *Linksradikalismus. Gewaltkur gegen die Alterskrankheit des Kommunismus* (Hamburg, 1968); H. Hamon and P. Rotman, *Génération, vol. 1: Les années de rêve, vol. 2: Les années de poudre* (Paris, 1987–88).

81. R. Viénet, *Wütende und Situationisten in der Bewegungen der Besetzungen* (Hamburg, 1977).

82. B. Lacroix, *L'Utopie communautaire* (Paris, 1981).

83. P. Bourdieu, *Homo academicus* (Frankfurt am Main, 1988), p. 276 and I. Gilcher-Holtey, 'Die Nacht der Barrikaden. Eine Fallstudie zur Dynamik

sozialen Protests', in F. Neidhardt (ed.), *Öffentlichkeit, öffentliche Meinung, soziale Bewegungen* (Opladen, 1994), pp. 375–92.

84. Marwick, *The Sixties*, 602–3.

85. R. Gildea, *The Past in French History* (Oxford, 1994).

86. P. Goldman, *Souvenirs obscures d'un juif polonais né en France* (Paris, 1975), p. 33.

87. E. Morin, C. Lefort and C. Castoriadis, *Mai 68: La brèche suivi de vingt ans après* (Paris, 1988), pp. 20–1, 28–9.

88. Morin et al., *Mai 68*, p. 186 and J. Jousselin, *Les Révoltes des Jeunes* (Paris, 1968).

89. See, for example, P. Gavi, 'Des ouvriers parlent', *Les Temps Modernes*, 265 (1968), 82–3.

90. Albert Detraz, et les militants de la CFDT, 'Positions et action de la CFDT en mai 1968', *Syndicalisme*, special issue, 1969. On the background, see R. Kedward, *La Vie en Bleu. France and the French since 1900* (London, 2005), 448–52.

91. J. Rancière, 'La cause de l'autre', in idem, *Aux bords du politique* (Paris, 1998), 148–64.

92. A useful summary from the perspective of value change is offered by Nick Thomas, 'Challenging Myths of the 1960s: The Case of Student Protest', *Twentieth Century British History*, 13 (2002), 277–97.

93. R. Dahrendorf, *LSE: A history of the London School of Economics and Political Science, 1895–1995* (Oxford, 1995).

94. E.P. Thompson, 'Outside the Whale' (1960), in idem, *The Poverty of Theory and Other Essays* (London, 1978), pp. 1–33.

95. S. Cohen, *Folk Devils and Moral Panics* (Bungay, 1972), pp. 177–204; B. Osgerby, *Youth in Britain since 1945* (Oxford, 1998), pp. 26–8 and 82–103.

96. Rowbotham, *Promise of a Dream*, p. 168.

97. Marwick, *The Sixties*, 55–6.

98. See C. Hamblett and J. Dverson, *Generation X* (London, 1965), 26–7; A. Bicât, 'Fifties Children, Sixties People', in V. Bogdanor and R. Skidelsky (eds), *The Age of Affluence 1951–1964* (London, 1970), p. 325.

99. For words of caution, see R. Koselleck, 'Erinnerungsschleusen und Erfahrungsschichten. Der Einfluß der beiden Weltkriege auf das soziale Bewußtsein', in idem, *Zeitschichten. Studien zur Historik* (Frankfurt am Main, 2000), 265–84.

100. Werner Kindt (ed.), *Die deutsche Jugendbewegung 1920 bis 1933. Die bündische Zeit* (Cologne, 1974), pp. 247–8. For a right-wing example, see Kurt Sontheimer, 'Der Tatkreis', *Vierteljahrshefte für Zeitgeschichte*, 7 (1959), 230–61. For a very rough sketch, see A. Schildt, *Ankunft im Westen. Ein Essay zur Erfolgsgeschichte der Bundesrepublik* (Frankfurt am Main, 1999), 181–9.

101. Cf. L.S. Feuer, *The Conflict of Generations: The Character and Significance of Student Movements* (New York, 1969); M. Levitt and B. Rubenstein, 'The Student Revolt: Totem and Taboo Revisited', *Psychiatry*, 34 (1971), 156–67; C. Levitt, *Children of Privilege: Student Revolt in the Sixties* (Buffalo, NY, 1984); R. Inglehart, 'The Silent Revolution in Europe: Intergenerational Change in Post-Industrial Societies', *American Political Science Review*, 65 (1971), 991; H. Bude, *Das Altern einer Generation. Die Jahrgänge 1938–1948* (Frankfurt am Main, 1995), pp. 40–1.

5
The First Soviet Generation: Children and Religious Belief in Soviet Russia, 1917–41

S. A. Smith

The Soviet state, in the words of William Husband, 'became the first modern government ... to promote the rejection of all religious deities as a sustaining national ideal'.[1] The Bolsheviks stood in an Enlightenment tradition that championed reason as the source of progress in society, and saw the application of scientific knowledge to nature and society as the key to human advance. When they seized power in October 1917 a central element in their vision of socialism was the transformation of a population steeped in religion and superstition into one governed in its thinking and action by the norms of science and rationality. Bolshevik hopes for a society based on science and rationality were pinned on youth: children must be fashioned to become enlightened, rational, class-conscious members of the collective. However, their parents, especially their mothers, could potentially derail this project; for as Stalin put it in 1923, 'working and peasant women can cripple the soul of the child or give us a youth who is healthy in spirit ... according to whether the mother sympathizes with the Soviet system or trails behind the priest, kulak and bourgeoisie'.[2]

The burden of anti-religious work, particularly among children, fell on three organizations: on schools, the Communist Youth League (Komsomol) and the Union of Godless. Schools are the main focus of this chapter and their activities in this sphere are examined in the next section. Of the other two organizations, the Komsomol was the more vigorous, and though it had responsibility for mobilizing youth in support of state tasks along a broad front, anti-religious work was always high on its agenda.[3] Its influence was limited, however, by the fact that in 1925 it had only 1.5 million members, only a fifth of them women, which represented a mere 6 per cent of the age-cohort eligible for membership.[4] The Union of Godless, founded in 1925, was, in theory, a non-state organization set up to propagate mass atheism. In 1926, it had only about 87,000 members in a population of 147 million, of whom 120.7 million lived in the countryside. Its membership grew rapidly during Stalin's 'revolution from above', from about half a million in mid-1929 to five million in 1932, but it fell to perhaps as few as 300,000 by 1935.[5] Despite occupying a 'prominent and even noisy position within the Bolshevik propaganda apparatus', it was in almost constant organizational crisis, and its obsession with recruitment, training cadres and selling magazines left it little time to engage seriously with countering religious belief.[6]

If the Bolsheviks were loud in their denunciations of religion, they never came close to fashioning a coherent and consistent strategy for anti-religious work. Much of their energies went into trying to bring the Orthodox Church to heel, frontal attacks on the Church between 1922 and 1925 and again, more violently, during the 'cultural revolution' (1928–31), being followed by periods of standoff between state and church. Behind the twists and turns of policy lay fundamental disagreements on strategic questions such as the relative importance of the struggle against religion as a policy objective; whether religion would wither away as the social conditions of the masses improved during the construction of socialism; whether the struggle against religion was a matter of long-term education or whether it could be advanced through 'administrative methods'. Disagreements on tactics followed. Initially, the Union of Godless advocated the use of persuasive methods of propaganda and education in respect of religion in opposition to the so-called priest eaters of the Komsomol, who favoured a confrontational approach, revelling in antics such as setting pigs loose in church or staging 'anti-festivals' at Easter and Christmas. However, the Union itself was split between a majority of *Kulturträger* and a minority who favoured a 'class struggle' approach to religion. During the 'cultural revolution', the Union assumed a more combative stance, accusing both the Komsomol – which was by this stage pursuing a relatively moderate approach to anti-religious work – and the Commissariat of Enlightenment of excessive compromise with religion.

It was to schools that the regime looked principally to carry out anti-religious work among children. Soviet Russia was a youthful society. In 1926, two-thirds of the 100.9 million population of the RSFSR was under the age of 30. Those aged 14 or under comprised almost 37 per cent of the population; those aged from 15 to 29 almost 30 per cent. By contrast, only 6.5 per cent of the population was in its 50s and only 6.7 per cent over 60.[7] Between 1914 and 1923, Russia had undergone a demographic collapse, brought about by war, revolution, epidemic disease and famine. One careful analysis reckons that between 1917 and 1922 the population within the 1926 borders of the Soviet Union fell by 10 to 11 million, excluding emigration, and that if one includes the birth deficit, then the population loss was of the order of 20 to 25 million.[8] Yet Soviet society recovered rapidly. Between 1922 and 1926, no fewer than 19.2 million babies were born, and it is on this age-cohort born after the revolution, especially during the 'baby boom' years of the early 1920s, that this chapter concentrates.[9]

Karl Mannheim argued that a generation becomes an 'actuality' by 'being exposed to the social and intellectual symptoms of a process of dynamic destabilization'.[10] This 'first socialist generation' was not unscathed by processes of 'dynamic destabilization' – above all, by the massive upheaval and violence unleashed by forced collectivization of agriculture and crash industrialization (1928–31) – but its most striking characteristics were, first, that its formation took place entirely within Soviet society and, second, that the Soviet state sought consciously to mould its world view through schooling, propaganda and the mass youth organizations. If one thinks of a generation as an 'an age cohort that comes to have social significance by virtue of constituting itself as cultural identity',[11] then this generation may represent the first instance in history in which the state itself endeavoured to transform an age-cohort into a generation by consciously elaborating an identity for it.

Schools and anti-religious education

In 1919, N.I. Bukharin and E.A. Preobrazhenskii proclaimed in the *ABC of Communism*: 'We must not rest content with the expulsion of religious propaganda from the school. We must see to it that the school assumes the offensive against religious propaganda in the home so that from the very outset the children's minds shall be rendered immune to all those religious fairy tales which many grown-ups continue to regard as truth.'[12] In practice, the school never 'assumed the offensive' as these leftists hoped. In accordance with the decree of January 1918 separating church and state, the Commissariat of Enlightenment forbade religious instruction in schools and ordered the removal of religious objects from classrooms, but it did not replace Orthodox with atheistic proselytizing.[13] In the countryside resistance to the abolition of religious instruction proved strong.[14] In 1924–5, a survey of 32,730 households in Penza province revealed that villagers were dissatisfied that religion was no longer taught in schools because they fretted that 'their children will no longer be god-fearing'.[15] However, opposition faded with time. In 1925, in the town of Ves'egonsk in Tver' province 72 per cent of grandparents were dissatisfied with the new school, 56 per cent of them because of the absence of religious instruction, compared with 48 per cent of parents, of whom only 24 per cent cited absence of religious instruction as the cause of dissatisfaction.[16]

Through the 1920s, the Commissariat of Enlightenment gave little attention to 'non-religious' education, overwhelmed as it was with implementing its radical vision of the 'unified labour school', where individual subjects were replaced by the 'complex method', i.e. integrated study of a particular theme under the headings of nature, labour and society. In mid-1925 it issued a letter 'On Non-Religious Education in the Primary School', which declared that knowledge of science and technology would gradually render religious belief obsolete, and pronounced: 'A special inculcation of anti-religiosity in the soul of the child is absolutely not necessary', a statement that would come back to haunt it during bouts of militant anti-religious struggle in 1928–31 and 1937–8.[17] From 1927, the Commissariat came under attack for its refusal to engage in anti-religious education. A conference organized by Union of Godless and the State Academic Council of the Commissariat on 25 November 1927 exposed sharp disagreements as to whether a non-religious or an anti-religious education was appropriate and whether anti-religious education should be taught as a separate subject or be integrated into the teaching of 'complex' themes. N. Amosov, on behalf of the Union, accused teachers of 'desertion from the anti-religious front', but M.M. Pistrak, on behalf of the State Academic Council, condemned sloganeering and the replacement of religion with 'anti-religious belief' (*verovanie*).[18] The question of when anti-religious education should start in school also proved contentious, some arguing that it was inappropriate for first-graders, since the school had not yet won the confidence of the children, others arguing that first-graders could be encouraged to discuss such topics as dreams, the (non-) existence of angels and demons, why they should not fear the dead and why it is useless to pray.[19] The advocates of anti-religious education came out on top, but at this stage they still saw the promotion of atheism as a long-term matter of 'enlightenment'.

This all changed with the onset of 'cultural revolution' in 1928, which unleashed a class war on 'social aliens' and an assault on old values, practices and hierarchies of every kind.[20] The Law on Religious Associations of 8 April 1929 banned public worship, closed places of worship, removed church bells, authorized the mass arrest of clergy and imposed burdensome taxes and insurance fees on functioning congregations.[21] The notion that the 'class enemy' was 'carrying out its work under the cover of religion' now became the leitmotif of anti-religious propaganda.[22] On 2 October 1928, the Union of Godless called for the school to be turned into a key centre of anti-religious struggle, a view characterized by N.K. Krupskaia, deputy commissar of enlightenment, as wholly misguided. As the campaign against the 'right opposition' stepped up in the following year, the Commissariat was accused of downgrading the struggle against religion, of a lack of confidence in the masses, of fearing to provoke 'kulak uprisings' and of unprincipled compromises such as tolerating fir trees at Christmas and birch trees at Trinity.[23] Although the new militant line paid lip service to the danger of reducing anti-religious policy to a 'struggle against priests and sectarian preachers, the closure of churches and the cutting down of bells', in practice it was the 'right-opportunist deviation' as represented by the Commissariat – and even by the Anti-Religious Commission – that bore the brunt of the zealots' wrath.

Serious efforts were made to mobilize children in the campaign. The Young Pioneers, the nursery organization of the Komsomol, which catered for 10- to 16-year-olds, was now summoned to become 'organizer of the children's godless movement'. On 22 June 1929, the Union of Godless issued a directive to 'make Pioneers conscious of the class essence of religion ... and of the necessity of uncompromising struggle with religion'. Bonfire discussions were to be held on such topics as why religious holidays are harmful and how religion helps the rich. Excursions to monasteries were to be organized in order to expose their role as exploiters of the people.[24] Teachers were encouraged to organize tableaux in which pupils dressed up as priests carrying bottles of vodka bearing labels such as 'Vodka helps drug the people with religion'; or to get their pupils to build a sleigh bearing a scarecrow figure of Capital, to be pulled by pupils dressed as priests, mullahs and rabbis. There was even talk of a 'godless five-year plan' and of organizing 'shock brigades' of anti-religious activists.[25]

In summer 1931, the party central committee, tired of the disorder in schools, threw its weight behind a new curriculum that emphasized subject-based teaching, the acquisition of reading, writing and arithmetic, and discipline and order in the classroom. Teachers now looked to the Commissariat of Enlightenment to provide standardized syllabi, textbooks and teaching manuals.[26] Although the Commissariat did issue a detailed directive on anti-religious education in December 1934 and circulated a model syllabus, the turn to subject teaching meant that anti-religious education retreated once again to the margins of the curriculum. The All-Russian Conference on Antireligious Propaganda, called in June 1935 by the Union of Militant Godless (the adjective had been added to their name during the cultural revolution), bemoaned the fact that anti-religious education in schools was taught either badly or not at all.[27] A survey of Tosnenskii district in Leningrad oblast' in November of that year revealed that 'no antireligious work is being conducted' in schools in spite of the strength of sectarians in the area.[28] A survey in 1936 of Amosovskii rural soviet near Pskov concluded that anti-religious work in schools was 'weak' and that teachers – 'many from socially alien milieux' – were unaware of the aforementioned directive of the Commissariat.[29] The period of the Great Terror saw militant anti-religious education again sputter into life. In May 1937, *Pravda* demanded that the 'teaching of academic subjects ... be thoroughly steeped in anti-religious propaganda'.[30] The Commissariat of Enlightenment once more went through the motions of toeing a militant line. But little changed in practice. In August 1939 the lead article in *Antireligioznik*, journal of the Union of Militant Godless, complained for the umpteenth time that the 'majority of schools do not carry out anti-religious work' and sourly noted that at its most recent conference, the Commissariat of Enlightenment had not even mentioned anti-religious education.[31]

Larry Holmes is broadly, if not completely, correct to conclude: 'From 1917 to 1941, Soviet Russia's schools contributed almost nothing to a direct assault on religion. The educational system, like society itself, proved more tradition-bound and inert than expected'.[32] The key reasons were as follows. First, primary education only became near universal in the course of this period. In 1925, only about half of the school-age population was in elementary school, the average time spent at school being 2.3 years for girls and 2.5 years for boys; 2.3 years for rural children and 3.1 years for urban children.[33] Between 1928 and 1930, enrolment in primary grades grew by 48 per cent, so that education for children aged from 8 to 11 became near universal in urban areas and about 90 per cent in rural regions.[34] Nevertheless, the impact of school on those children who were only in education for three years remained limited. Second, schools remained chronically under-funded and teachers were overworked, underpaid and subject to abuse by local officials. In particular, teachers were ill-equipped and poorly motivated to carry out the grandiose schemes for anti-religious education dreamed up by the Union of Godless. E.I. Perovskii cited the opinion of a teacher of first-graders in a primary school outside Moscow who, when asked in

1934 what she did by way of anti-religious education, simply replied that she admonished any pupil who came to school wearing a cross. When asked what her programme was she looked blank, but explained that children now rarely attended church. Perovskii fumed that this 'overestimates our successes and underestimates the forces of the enemy – the religiosity of the environment that surrounds the school'.[35]

Perovskii had a point; and it relates to the third and most important factor limiting the impact of anti-religious education. This is that family and local community continued to be more influential in the socialization of young children than the school. For the rural community, Orthodox Christianity had always been central to social identity. The agricultural cycle was intertwined with the liturgical cycle, so that key activities such as ploughing, sowing or reaping coincided with major festivals in the church calendar; the sense of local community was intimately bound up with the veneration of particular saints or representations of the Virgin Mary; Christian rituals marked the key rites of passage of birth, marriage and death; and these same rituals provided a rich resource which individuals and communities could draw upon to cope with tribulations of all kinds such as drought, disease, old age or infertility. If the principal Christian rituals were performed by the priest in church, it was nevertheless in the family that children learned a basic knowledge of the Christian faith, if only through such simple means as the veneration of icons, the teaching of prayers or visits with their parents to church on high feast days. Even in Leningrad in 1929, 73 per cent of 1696 school students said that icons were displayed in their homes and 71 per cent said that their families observed religious holidays.[36] Consequently, notwithstanding the clarion call of Bukharin and Preobrazhenskii to ensure that 'children's minds shall be rendered immune to all those religious fairy tales which many grown-ups continue to regard as truth', the family continued for millions of children to be more influential in transmitting the cherished values of tradition than the school in propagating norms of science and rationality.

Yet this was a period when the hallowed patterns of rural life were violently shattered by collectivization and pell-mell urbanization. By 1937, over 90 per cent of peasant households had been thrust into collective farms.[37] If the frontal assault on the Orthodox Church failed to destroy it, its institutional presence in the village was greatly weakened. The number of churches in the RSFSR fell from 39,530 in 1914 to 19,212 in 1936, and the number of clergy from 79,000 in 1926 to 31,000 in 1937.[38] If only a minority of rural youth ardently embraced 'godlessness', the commitment to religion of probably a majority of families weakened. Few sought to bring up their children as non-believers, but many neglected to educate them in the faith with the same commitment that their own parents had shown. As rural communities were forcibly severed from their customary way of life, parents came to feel less confident that the old beliefs and values could equip their children for the socialist future.[39] A common compromise was for parents to take children to church while they were young but to cease to do so once they started school. A survey in 1936 of Amosovskii rural soviet near Pskov found that 80 per cent of pre-school children went to church with their parents, compared with only 35 per cent of school children.[40] And the same survey of Kingiseppskii circuit in Leningrad oblast' found that 50 per cent to 60 per cent of preschool children went to church with their parents, compared with just 25 per cent to 30 per cent of schoolchildren.[41] The daughter of a kolkhoz farmer declared: 'My mama forces me to go to church, but I won't once I start school.' And a worker's daughter explained: 'I've been to church once. But when I go to school I shall become a Young Pioneer.'[42] Generally, however, girls went to church more willingly than boys.

Schools alone cannot change society, but they can give support to social change that is already underway. The impact of anti-religious education on children may have been slight, given its marginality to the curriculum, but the school nevertheless exercised a secularizing influence: one that came not from formal anti-religious elements in the curriculum but from the ambient culture – the so-called hidden curriculum. Pioneers, for example, who numbered 13.9 million by 1940, set an anti-religious tone in schools, and children quickly learned to conform to the informal hostility to religion displayed by Pioneers, teachers and other opinion-formers. The fact that many children associated starting school with stopping going to church suggests they were well aware of this. Following the upheavals of Stalin's 'revolution from above', especially, the school became a place where the verities of village life were directly challenged and, if home continued to be more important in the socialization of children than the school, the latter's influence was nevertheless growing.

Surveying religious belief

Given the grandiose ambition to create the world's first atheist society, it is hardly surprising that the regime regularly surveyed the population to measure the extent to which citizens were abandoning religion.

Attention focused particularly on the 'first socialist generation'. A number of surveys sought to measure the beliefs of Soviet children about the supernatural, which raise a number of theoretical and methodological problems. The very attempt to measure such beliefs may be misguided in societies where belief is internal to social practice, where it permeates the whole of social life, galvanizing feeling as well as thinking, rather than being articulated as intellectual propositions that can be held up to scrutiny. And in the case of Orthodox Christianity this may be particularly misguided, since faith had always been expressed more through the performance of ritual than through knowledge of a corpus of doctrine, ritual being the social drama through which the meaning of Christian doctrine was enacted. More obviously, we must assume that these surveys exaggerate the level of non-belief since the surveyors were under ideological pressure to achieve a 'good' result and some children may have felt pressure to give what they sensed to be a 'correct' answer. Nevertheless a couple of the surveys offer children relatively open-ended opportunities to express their beliefs, and the less open-ended questionnaires are sufficiently numerous to allow one to discard surveys based on small samples or dubious methodology (e.g. where results are organized by social class). Even in the best of the surveys, however – that undertaken by L.O. Azarevich – comparison of some of the original *ankety* (the completed questionnaires for each respondent) with her statistical tabulation of findings suggests she exaggerates the extent of non-belief by including in the category of non-believers children who, for example, equated God with the priest.

The only statistical source that purports to gauge the extent of religious belief across the entire population is the census of 1937, the first and last Soviet census to ask about religious belief (see Table 5.1). This revealed that 42.9 per cent of adults in the USSR – 55 per cent of men and 33 per cent of women – were non-believers.[43] This certainly underestimated the extent of religious belief, possibly by a substantial margin, for we know that many were reluctant or afraid to admit that they were believers.[44] Nevertheless, the pattern revealed by the census of a decline in religious belief across generations is plausible, especially if we assume that the margin of error caused by under-reporting of belief is consistent across the population. If that is the case, the census figures suggest that the percentage of believers almost halved between the generation which lived through the revolution – roughly, those in the 30–34 and 35–39 age groups – and the 'first Soviet generation' (those in the 16–17 and 18–19 age groups).

Table 5.1 The percentage of the age group who stated they were believers (1937 Soviet census)

16–17 years	18–19 years	20–24 years	25–29 years	30–34 years	35–39 years	Over sixties
8.8%	13.9%	17.0%	20.0%	25.3%	26.8%	47.8%

Source: Lebina, *Povsednevnaia zhizn' sovetskogo goroda: normy i anomalii 1920–1930 gody* (St Petersburg, 1999), p. 142.

The extent to which the 1937 census under-reports religious belief becomes apparent when one examines surveys of religious belief among schoolchildren, since these show a consistently higher proportion of believers among children and youth than the low percentages of the census. In 1927, a survey of over 3000 schoolchildren in ten provinces revealed that 51 per cent considered it 'not necessary' to believe in God, 60.3 per cent of boys and 41 per cent of girls assenting to this proposition, with the proportion rising from 47 per cent among ten-year-olds, to 52 per cent among 14-year-olds, to 88 per cent among 16-year-olds.[45] All surveys show that boys were less religious than girls and all show that religiosity was greater in the countryside than the towns. In Moscow and Leningrad, according to surveys in 1925–6 and 1929 respectively, the proportion of schoolchildren who described themselves as unbelievers was around one-third, compared with one-quarter who described themselves as believers; the largest group, however, were the 'don't knows'.[46] In sharp contrast, a survey of 875 pre-teen children in the small town of Sergiev Posad in Moscow province revealed that 37 per cent of boys and 67 per cent of girls said that they were believers and that only a tiny 3.7 per cent said they did not believe in God.[47] This, however, was equally untypical, since Sergiev Posad was a major religious centre, the seat of the monastery of St Sergius of Radonezh.

Levels of religious belief were higher among young children. In 1933–4, E. Perovskii conducted a survey of 129 seven- and eight-year-olds who were about to start school. They comprised 67 urban children in the preparatory class of the No.19 middle school in Saratov and 62 rural children drawn from one village in Saratov and two villages in Moscow province. One half (64) of the children said they believed in God. Of these only 31 prayed at home; but of these only 13 said they prayed without parental pressure. Forty-two in this group said they had visited or went regularly to church, of whom 18 said they enjoyed doing so. The majority of those who said they believed in God knew that he 'lives in the sky', 'we can't see him', 'he is good', 'he gives us health', 'is angry' and – a theme that came up fairly regularly – 'he punishes those who do not obey their parents'. An eight-year-old son of a workersaid: 'Mama has told me about God. He is good, and sometimes flies here. He's in the sky. I'm not afraid of him. I love him because he's good.' An eight-year-old daughter of a worker said: 'My grandma talks about God, how he lived and fed off roots. When you die, you suffer torments. I'm afraid of him.' As in Azarevich's survey discussed below, some children confused God with the local priest. A seven-year-old daughter of a worker said: 'God is the priest (*batiushka*). He prays to God and when someone dies he buries them.' Others confused God with his representation in icons. 'I know all about God. He hangs on our wall in a silver frame. There is a God. I'm not afraid of him. I love him. He prays like the people pray in church.' The answers of those who said they did not believe in God were less confused. An eight-year-old daughter of a *sluzhashchii* (white-collar employee) said: 'My grandma talks about God all the time. But I don't believe in him.' The seven-year-old son of a kolkhoz farmer said: 'We don't have any old folk. And I don't believe in God, I've never seen him. I don't pray and they don't force me to. I've never been to church.' Some hedged their bets. The eight-year-old daughter of a kolkhoz farmer said: 'Papa says there is no God, but Mama says there is – in heaven. But I've never seen him.'[48]

By far the richest study of children's religious beliefs was undertaken by L.D. Azarevich, who headed a network of kindergartens in Kaluga province that formed part of the first experimental educational station of the Commissariat of Enlightenment.[49] Between 1929 and 1931, she interviewed 72 children, ranging in age from six-and-a-half to seven-and-a-half, 27 from families of collective farmers and 45 from families of individual farmers. The great value of the survey is that it recorded the responses of each child to each question. The results come out remarkably close to those of Perovskii, with 35 (49.3 per cent) of the 72 children professing belief in God, 33 (45.8 per cent) professing disbelief and four uncertain.[50] However, it appears that Azarevich inflated the percentage of non-believers by including children who showed uncertainty or confusion as to whether God exists.[51] Few children were as informed as seven-year-old Serezha Kargin, son of a middle peasant, who confidently replied: 'There is a God. He is in heaven and holds the sky and earth in his hands. He made icons and people.'[52] Ten children in the sample (30 per cent) equated God with priests. 'The priest is God. He lives in church. God does not work. He locks up the church. He has sons'. 'No. I don't believe in God because they sent him away somewhere.'[53] Moreover, if a plurality believed in God, only a minority believed this entailed praying to him. Twelve out of 27 said there was no need to pray, and several more were uncertain. Seven-year-old Vania Korgin believed in God: 'Yes. He goes about on a cloud in the heavens, watches and lights up everything [*zazhigaet vse*].' But he did not approve of prayer: 'The Komsomol don't pray. I like those who don't pray.' Several children explained their disapproval of prayer by reference to official policy. 'No. Because the colonists [i.e. Communists] have forbidden it'. 'No, because we now live under a different government. Before you could.'[54] Even among children who had not started school, then, there was awareness that belief in God was frowned on in Soviet society.

Contrary to Azarevich's own statistics, if one includes the responses of the confused, up to four-fifths of the children may be said to have entertained a belief in God in some form or other. That the general conception of God was highly anthropomorphic is not surprising in children so young. In general, the children had a poor grasp of Orthodox doctrine: almost all, for example, equated the soul with animation and claimed that animals and even plants had souls. Only eight of the 33 believed that the soul lives on after death. Six-year-old Zina Ivanovna opined: 'The soul lives in the stomach. I think it exists. What do *you* think? Only people have souls. Cats or pine trees don't. Your soul dies when you die.'[55] This ignorance of doctrine may reflect the fact that Christianity was no longer taught in school and that churches had been closed. Yet complaints about the theological ignorance of children had been legion in the latter years of the nineteenth century, so the level of religious education may not have deteriorated so much since 1917.[56]

Children's belief in the supernatural

In the mid-1930s, it came as something of a shock to anti-religious educators to discover that many apparently 'godless' children continued to adhere to folk beliefs about the supernatural. Perovskii observed:

We have conducted a broad and organized struggle (in the press, in schools, clubs etc.) against god and the emotions associated with him, religious morality and rituals … and systematically or piecemeal this has influenced the children. But we have conducted almost no struggle against beliefs in house sprites, wood sprites etc., the remnants of the ancient religion of clan society, since they have no defined cult, no worshippers of the cult, and languish in the remote corners. These are not mere trifles. They continue to live on through grandmothers, grandfathers and mothers, servants and the like. And they are transmitted to children, infecting their weak consciousness and burdening their emotions with heavy, oppressive fear.[57]

Similarly, A. Trachevskii noted that 'if the official religion of the priests is in decline, then the religiosity of daily life (*bytovaia religiia*) in all its manifestations – belief in omens, spells, house sprites – still has a firm hold on peasant life'.[58]

This 'religiosity of daily life' was of particular interest to the teachers at the first experimental station. In her survey Azarevich asked her seven-year-olds a number of questions about folk beliefs in the 'unclean force' (*nechistaia sila*), which by the second half of the nineteenth century had become increasingly synonymous with the Christian devil, but which even in the twentieth century could still encompass household spirits, spirits of the fields, woods, rivers or spirits causing illness.[59] Interestingly, her respondents displayed greater unanimity in their responses to these questions than they did in answering the question about God. Forty-one (57 per cent) out of 72 children believed in spirits, compared with 24 (33 per cent) who did not, and four who were unsure. My reworked sample suggests that as many as 25 out of 33 recognized the existence of a devil – more commonly, of 'devils' in the plural – and other supernatural creatures. Moreover, the answers were more vivid and colourful than those to questions about God, some respondents revealing gifts of fantasy of almost baroque proportions. 'Yes. They live in water, in the blue sea, they live. I saw a little black devil [*shutik*] in Moscow. For a ruble. They ride on little steamships. I was on a steamship and looked through the window and there on the beach was one combing its hair. If you bathe in the river it will annoy you, it will bite your foot.' 'Yes, yes, they exist. They live abroad in big houses. But I don't know. I've not seen them myself. My grandma came from Moscow and told me about them.'[60] Interestingly, the children talked mainly about wood sprites (*leshie*) and water nymphs (*rusalki*) rather than about house sprites (*domovye*), although the free compositions discussed below do feature tales about house sprites. 'There is a demon. He lives in the river … He can punish you by drowning so not many bathe in the river.' 'The devil gnaws on birch trees, eats grass and if he catches a person will eat him. The devil works hard. He seeks bread for himself. He takes away babies. He can punish you. But if you don't tease him he won't punish you.'[61] Many respondents, while expressing belief in devils and sprites, made clear that they had not actually seen them. 'There is a devil and a house sprite. They live in the dark forest, in meadows and nowhere else. That is what people say. I don't know. I don't know what they are like.' References to Moscow, to steamships and to big houses abroad, moreover, suggest these beliefs reflect not some pristine oral tradition but a tradition recycled through books, book illustrations and plays. 'In the school play children performed as water nymphs'. 'I've read about water nymphs in books, how they swim about with golden hair. In fact, I don't believe they exist.'[62]

Perovskii also asked his children about belief in sprites of different kinds, although his survey showed a lower level of belief in them than Azarevich's. This is probably due to the inclusion in his sample of children from the city of Saratov, who were much less likely to believe than those in the villages. Out of 125 children, 48 (38 per cent) said they believed in house sprites. The son of a kolkhoz farmer fantasized: 'I know all about the house sprite. He climbs through the window and turns the spinning wheel with his foot. He took the belt off the spinning wheel and crawled all over me under the sheepskin one night. My father fired his rifle at him and he ran away. He tangles the horse's mane. He's terrifying. He has a beard and big fat legs like this (he extends his arms to show how big) and he talks like the Germans. He's also sly. I really fear the house sprite.' Thirty-six out of 68 rural children when asked about witches said they believed in them. A daughter of a worker divulged: 'My grandma has told me about witches. They ride about on oven forks.' And a son of a worker's boasted: 'I know about witches. They are hairy [*shakhratye* – dialect] and tousled. I'm not afraid of them. If they wanted to play with me, I wouldn't be afraid. But if they wanted to eat me, then I would be afraid.' Finally, 21 out of 62 confessed they were afraid of the dead: they 'walk about', 'rise at night', can 'grab' one.[63]

Clearly, fear was an emotion galvanizing these children's responses, but it was not necessarily as predominant as Soviet educationalists and psychologists liked to claim. They insisted that fear lay at the heart of children's belief in the supernatural.

> Fear of the dark is encouraged by terrifying tales told in the family in the evening gloom: how the dead rise from their graves, how the house sprite will strangle you, how the water nymph will grab you by the leg and drag you off to its underwater kingdom ... Reading lives of the saints instils in the child a sense of himself as a sinner.[64]

Educationalists reminded parents and teachers that the 'frightened child begins to believe in man's dependence on secret forces' and recommended that they discuss gently and rationally with their children fear of the dark or of death.[65] Perovskii drew the politically correct conclusion from his survey to the effect that children feared God as a punitive father figure. But Azarevich, more frankly, concluded: 'We did not find that adults' assertions that God was almighty, or that he would punish children for bad behaviour, made much impression on the psyche or behaviour of the children.'[66]

The head of the first experimental educational station in Kaluga was the radical educationalist, S.T. Shatskii, who theorized that the child is subject to the 'minor pedagogical process' of the school and to the 'major pedagogical process' of its surroundings; and that for school to be effective it must coordinate the major and minor pedagogical processes. 'For this to happen, the school and the teacher must encounter the life surrounding the child, must intently study the pedagogy of the environment, its methods of education, so that by means of careful analysis of all educational factors, the positive factors can be identified and supported and the negative ones fought against.'[67] As part of her survey, therefore, Azarevich investigated the social environment of the villages of Kaluga. Literacy levels were rather high: 84 per cent of fathers of her pupils and 76 per cent of mothers could read. Yet the villages were small communities of no more than 40 to 50 households, where limited availability of land forced adult males to leave in search of work. This meant that village life was dominated by women and by the elderly, and this, she argued, produced a classic split between the 'generation of fathers' and the 'generation of sons'.

> To the former belong old people and, alas, the majority of women; alas, because ... what is new in contemporary life has relatively little influence on them; they live very much as in the past, only tending to their material needs, gossiping about everyone and about events such as funerals, weddings etc. They are the bearers of the traditions of everyday life, of religion etc. and they preserve belief in omens and superstitions of all kinds.

To the generation of sons, she opined:

> belong the majority of middle-aged men who do not live at home and who are familiar with urban life and who accept soviet government and communist ideals not out of submissiveness, but fully consciously; and one should add to this group young males and a section of young females who have remained in the countryside because of the impossibility of finding work in the towns.[68]

As a way of identifying the positive and negative factors in the 'major pedagogical process', Azarevich encouraged pupils to write free compositions about different aspects of their lives. In 1922–3, and again in 1929, they were asked to write on the theme 'What I heard in the village'. Most wrote essays that reproduced verbatim tales they had heard from their grandparents, mothers or others. Almost all concerned supernatural phenomena, and it is not clear whether this is because the teachers required the children to write on this theme or whether it reflected a childish fascination with the uncanny. Typical was 'A tale my grandfather told me', which was written as though in the grandfather's words:

> One night we went fishing and got the horse to drag the boat, as the water level had fallen sharply. We had almost got to the fishing spot when suddenly on the other side of the river we saw by a bird-cherry tree a white church, stretching up into the air. My friend who was worldly-wise said: 'Don't go any further or something bad will happen'. We stopped the horse and as we waited, the church suddenly vanished, crashing into the water. We made the sign of the cross and went off. 'You see, Maksim, if we had continued, not even our bones would have remained'.[69]

Most stories were of this type, a neutral exposition of a tale told to the child. Some stories involved the child, but only as a passive observer, and these were generally written in a confusing mixture of direct and indirect speech, which I have simplified for the sake of clarity:

> I arrived home one evening from the school colony and my mother and several other women I didn't know were talking about house sprites. One said: 'Granny Kulikova went out one night into her yard and began to call her horse. "Kobchik, ko-obchik, koo-ob-chik". And the house sprite answered back: "Kobchik, ko-obchik, koo-obchik". The old lady looked up and saw someone white sitting there, mimicking her words, and fled inside'. I listened to everything. And then my mother spoke. 'In one village a woman came out into her yard at night with a light. She could hear a terrible clatter of hoofs, and saw her horse tearing round the yard in a lather, and there on the horse was someone thrashing it with a cudgel. It was likely the house sprite was whipping the horse because he didn't like it.'[70]

In a few essays the narrator assumes the stance of rational sceptic:

> In the village of Kabitsino the following happened. On the eve of St John's Day everyone tells fortunes. They say that if you go to the hemp field with a black cat you'll find treasure. But no one goes, because they believe that that is the night that witches fly about. But once two men and a woman were driving their horses to the night pasture around midnight when they saw above the rye field a ball with fiery tails, crackling. They fled and the woman lost her shawl. But this was not a witch. Some big lads had brought to the field poles hung with birch branches that they set alight and started waving. But in the village they thought it was a witch.[71]

One can only speculate as to what motivated this fascination with the uncanny. Freud's classic conception of the *Unheimlich* suggests that what is most eerie or frightening derives not from what is far from our experience but from what is close to home but rendered secret through repression. The concept refers broadly to those objects and experiences, once very familiar, that return out of time and place to challenge the boundaries between subject and object, between interior and exterior. This may be particularly relevant to children, whose boundaries of the self are notoriously permeable. Freud contends that 'an uncanny experience occurs either when infantile complexes which have been repressed are once more revived by some impression, or when primitive beliefs which have been surmounted seem once more to be confirmed'.[72] In a rather surprising sociological twist, he links beliefs in the 'omnipotence of thoughts', 'the prompt fulfilment of wishes', 'secret injurious powers' and the 'return of the dead' to 'primitive' or 'animistic' societies. Rural Russia, of course, was far from being a 'primitive' society. Nevertheless, after 1917, it was subject to wrenching change that generated those conditions of uncertainty and danger that, according to Freud, can revive 'primitive beliefs which have been surmounted'. In such situations: 'We do not feel quite sure of our new beliefs, and the old ones still exist within us ready to seize upon any confirmation. As soon as something *actually happens* in our lives which seems to confirm the old, discarded beliefs, we get a feeling of the uncanny; it is as though we were making a judgement something like this: "So the dead *do* live on and appear on the scene of their former activities!"'[73] Freud's perspective is compatible with one developed more recently by ethnographers interested in the ways in which modernity appears to breathe new life into what they call 'occult cosmologies'. Whereas for Azarevich the telling by old folk and women of supernatural tales was proof that 'what is new in contemporary life has relatively little influence on them', these ethnographers contend that the idiom of the supernatural is utilized precisely to respond to modern challenges. Harry West and Todd Saunders argue that many experience modernity as 'fragmented, contradictory and disquieting' and believe power lies beyond their grasp. In an effort to put meaning on this situation, they turn to 'occult cosmologies' that perceive the world to be animated by secret, unseen or mysterious powers.[74] There is empirical evidence that this was true of Soviet Russia, especially in the wake of forced collectivization, when many peasants seized on occult idioms such as those of the Antichrist, of letters sent from heaven or of female apparitions foretelling doom, in an effort to make sense of the disasters that had befallen them.[75] It is thus plausible to suppose that even as the Soviet state was striving to promote science and rationality in the countryside, the secondary effects of its policies of brutal social and economic transformation were to revitalize idioms of the supernatural, thus creating a potent mix of old and new ideas and intensifying the conflict between generations.

Conclusion

The 'first Soviet generation', insofar as it was still predominantly rural, grew up in a world that was still enchanted. Following our sources, we have distinguished between religious belief and folk belief in entities with supernatural powers. Some children appear to have registered this distinction in that they seem to recognize that it was, above all, the Church and Christian teaching that were disparaged by the regime. But for many, especially the very young, it is doubtful that the distinction had much salience; indeed it is doubtful whether they perceived a distinction between the natural and the supernatural worlds at all, seeing God, the devil, water sprites and the like as being as real as the fields and forests in which they romped. Moreover, as some educationalists admitted, once in school, the scientific explanations of natural phenomena to which children were exposed could serve to supplement rather than to supplant supernatural understandings of the social world, producing what I. Flerov called a 'duality of views' (*dvoistvennost' vo vzgliadakh*).[76] It was thus possible for children – like many adults – to hedge their bets, to allow the new to sit – more or less comfortably – alongside the old.[77]

That said, and notwithstanding the revitalization of 'occult cosmologies' that occurred during the 1930s, the generational trend was clear. Religious belief was in rather rapid decline among the young, even if it was expressed more in terms of doubt and indifference than in terms of committed disbelief. The 'first Soviet generation' grew up in an environment in which belief in the supernatural was challenged even as it was learned. Even if we assume that the percentage of children who believed in God was much higher than the 49 per cent suggested by Azarevich and Perovskii, this still left a growing minority who were outright sceptical about the claims of religion. Even some seven- and eight-year-olds could articulate a robust rationalism – God was 'an old invention', 'imagined by the people', 'a false notion' – that must have warmed the hearts of the Union of Godless.[78] Moreover, those who expressed belief in sprites often made the point that this was not based on first-hand experience. The neutral, somewhat distanced way in which they wrote their stories – 'my mother's story', 'my aunt's tale' – suggests less than wholehearted endorsement. Indeed the very fact that seven- and eight-year-olds could articulate conflicting views testifies to the fact that they no longer lived in a world where 'tradition' went unchallenged, to the fact, as Azaverich put it, that they grew up in a world where the 'generation of fathers' was already being challenged by the 'generation of sons'. And once in school, the verities of family and community were challenged by the 'hidden curriculum', even if antireligious education was largely ineffective.

The limits on Bolshevik success in disseminating science and rationality sprang, ultimately, from their limited understanding of how cultural change is engendered. They conceived of culture as something attained through enlightenment rather than experienced through community. 'One achieved a level of enlightenment and behaviour and tried to impart it to the "dark masses".'[79] This essentially Enlightenment view of science and rationality steadily conquering territory from religion and superstition proved to be a poor guide to understanding the complexities of cultural change. Sociologists contend that the intrinsic merits of an idea rarely play a major part in its success or failure: it is the social relationships in which the idea is embedded that make it more or less persuasive. Most sociologists of religion consider change in social structure and culture as far more consequential for secularization than the ideological contest between science and religion; and insofar as they see science as a variable determining secularization – and many do not – they see its effects as being mediated through technology (which brings about a reduction in vulnerability to the vagaries of nature) or the embodiment of rationality in bureaucratic organizations.[80] The most potent challenges to the religious beliefs of the 'first Soviet generation' came, therefore, not from the direct efforts of the regime to disseminate science and rationality through education and propaganda, but from the secondary consequences of the massive and violent rending of the traditional relationships of the village which served to oust religion from its pivotal place in social life.

Notes

This paper arises out of my project, 'Struggling against "Superstition": Communism versus Popular Culture in the Soviet Union, 1917–41 and the People's Republic of China, 1949–76', which is generously funded by the Arts and Humanities Research Council. I thank Marina Loskutova for her invaluable research assistance and Isabel Tirado for her thoughtful comments.

1. W.B. Husband, *'Godless Communists': Atheism and Society in Soviet Russia, 1917–1932* (DeKalb, 2000), p. xii.
2. A. Chernykh, *Stanovlenie Rossii sovetskoi: 20-gody v zerkale sotsiologii* (Moscow, 1998), p. 185.
3. I.A. Tirado, 'The Revolution, Young Peasants, and the Komsomol's Anti-Religious Campaigns (1920–1928)', *Canadian-American Slavic Studies*, 26 (1999), 97–117.
4. A.E. Gorsuch, *Youth in Revolutionary Russia: Enthusiasts, Bohemians and Delinquents* (Bloomington, 2000), p. 188.
5. V.A. Alekseev, *'Shturm nebes' otmeniaetsia? Kriticheskie ocherki po istorii bor'by s religiei v SSSR* (Moscow, 1992), pp. 74, 87.
6. D. Peris, *Storming the Heavens: The Soviet League of the Militant Godless* (Ithaca, 1998), p. 226.
7. *Naselenie Rossii v XX veke: istoricheskie ocherki*, vol. 1, 1900–1939 gg. (Moscow, 2000), pp. 143, 154.
8. *Naselenie*, p. 95.
9. V.P. Danilov, *Rural Russia under the New Regime* (trans. and ed. O. Figes) (London, 1988), p. 41.
10. K. Mannheim, 'The Problem of Generations', in *Collected Works of Karl Mannheim*, vol. 5 (London, 1997), p. 303.
11. J. Edmunds and B.S. Turner, *Generations, Culture and Society* (Buckingham, 2002), p. 7.
12. N.I. Bukharin and E.A. Preobrazhenskii, *The ABC of Communism*, ed. E.H. Carr, (Harmondsworth, 1969), p. 305.
13. Husband, *'Godless Communists'*, p. 80.
14. E.M. Balashov, *Shkola v rossiiskom obshchestve 1917–1927 gg. Stanovlenie 'novogo cheloveka'* (St Petersburg, 2003), p. 145.
15. N. Rosnitskii, *Litso derevni* (Moscow, 1926), p. 94.
16. Balashov, *Shkola*, p. 70.

17. L.E. Holmes, 'Fear no Evil: Schools and Religion in Soviet Russia, 1917–1941', in S.P. Ramet (ed.), *Religious Policy in the Soviet Union* (Cambridge, 1993), p. 129.

18. 'Stenogramma disputa v Tsentral'nom dome rabotnikov prosveshcheniia', *Antireligioznik*, 1 (1928), 112–28.

19. I. Flerov, 'Antireligioznaia rabota v shkole', *Antireligioznik*, 6 (1928), 74–81; V. Fomichev, 'Tezisy po antireligioznomu vospitaniiu v shkole', Antireligioznik, 4 (1928), 58–64.

20. S. Fitzpatrick, *The Cultural Front: Power and Culture in Revolutionary Russia* (Ithaca, 1992); M. David-Fox, 'What is Cultural Revolution?', *Russian Review*, 58 (1999), 181–201.

21. A. Luukkanen, *The Religious Policy of the Stalinist State* (Tampere, 1997), pp. 66–7.

22. S. Khudiakov, 'Itogi Ispolbiuro TsS SVB, 28–30 marta 1932', *Antireligioznik*, 9 (1932), 28–32.

23. P. Zarin, 'Pravyi i levyi uklon v antireligioznoi propagande', *Antireligioznik*, 1 (1930), 5–11.

24. 'Direktivy Tsentral'nogo Sovet Soiuza Voinstvuiushchikh Bezbozhnikov SSSR', Gosudarstvennyi Arkhiv Rossiiskoi Federatsii, f. R-5407, op. 1, d. 38, l. 61.

25. Alekseev, *'Shturm nebes'*, pp. 112–13; S. Kopyrina, A. Chernes, 'Opyt antireligioznoi raboty detskoi biblioteki', *Antireligioznik*, 7 (1930), 87–9.

26. L.E. Holmes, *Stalin's School: Moscow's Model School No.25, 1931–1937* (Pittsburgh, 1999), pp. 10–11.

27. Alekseev, *'Shturm nebes'*, p. 144.

28. Tsentral'nyi gosudarstvennyi arkhiv istoriko-politicheskikh dokumentov Sankt- Peterburga (TsGA IPD SPb), f. 24, op. 8, d. 293, ll. 1–4.

29. TsGA IPD SPb, f. 24, op. 8, d. 293, ll. 31–7.

30. Holmes, 'Fear no Evil', p. 146.

31. Uluchshit' antireligioznoi raboty v shkole', *Antireligioznik*, 8 (1939), 1–5.

32. Holmes, 'Fear no Evil', p. 125.

33. L.E. Holmes, *The Kremlin and the Schoolhouse: Reforming Education in Soviet Russia, 1917–1931* (Bloomington, 1991), p. 94; Balashov, *Shkola*, p. 72.

34. Holmes, 'Fear no Evil', pp. 142–3.

35. E. Perovskii, 'Antireligioznoe vospitanie v shkole: ob ateisticheskikh i religioznykh predstaveleniiakh detei', *Antireligioznik*, 1 (1935), 26–31.

36. 'Antireligioznoe vospitanie v leningradskikh shkolakh', *Antireligioznik*, 2 (1930), 72–6.

37. S. Fitzpatrick, *Stalin's Peasants: Resistance and Survival in the Russian Village after Collectivization* (Oxford, 1994), p. 110.

38. Luukkanen, *Religious Policy*, p. 139; Husband, *'Godless Communists'*, p. 160.

39. These generalizations are based on the surveys discussed below.

40. TsGA IPD SPb, f. 24, op. 8, d. 293, l. 34.

41. TsGA IPD SPb, f. 24, op. 8, d. 293, l. 40.

42. Perovskii, 'Antireligioznoe vospitanie', 28.

43. *Naselenie*, p. 184.

44. C. Merridale, 'The 1937 Census and the Limits of Stalinist Rule', *Historical Journal*, 39 (1996), 233; Luukkanen, *Religious Policy*, p. 147.

45. *Deti i oktiabr'skaia revoliutsiia* (Moscow, 1928), p. 10.

46. See, respectively, *Antireligioznik*, 1 (1928), 123–4; *Antireligioznik*, 2 (1930), 72–6.

47. L. Sutulov, *Komsomol v bor'be s religiei* (Moscow, 1929), p. 67.
48. Perovskii, 'Antireligioznoe vospitanie', 27–8.
49. W. Partlett, 'Breaching Cultural Worlds with the Village School: Educational Visions, Local Initiative, and Rural Experience at S. T. Shatskii's Kaluga School System 1919–32', *Slavonic and East European Review*, 82 (2004), 847–85.
50. Arkhiv Rossiiskoi Akademii Obrazovaniia (ARAO), f. 1, op. 1, d. 294, ll. 187–8.
51. This is based on a reanalysis by Dr Marina Loskotova of 33 ankety, although these may not have formed part of the 72 collated by Azarevich.
52. ARAO, f. 1, op. 1, d. 294, l. 199.
53. ARAO, f. 1, op. 1, d. 294, ll. 68, 79.
54. ARAO, f. 1, op. 1, d. 294, ll. 68, 95.
55. ARAO, f. 1, op. 1, d. 294, l. 7.
56. G. Freeze, *Parish Clergy in Nineteenth-Century Russia: Crisis, Reform, Counter-Reform* (Princeton, 1983).
57. Perovksii, 'Antireligioznoe vospitanie', 30.
58. A. Trachevskii, 'Sueveriia krest'ian TsChO i bor'ba s nim', *Antireligioznik*, 8–9 (1930), 29.
59. L. Ivanits, *Russian Folk Belief* (Armonk, NY, 1989), Chap. 3.
60. ARAO, f. 1, op. 1, d. 294, l. 41, l. 87, l. 91.
61. ARAO, f. 1, op. 1, d. 294, ll. 155, 95.
62. ARAO, f. 1, op. 1, d. 294, l. 68.
63. Perovskii, 'Antireligioznoe vospitanie', 28–9.
64. G. Struchkov, 'Sem'ia, shkola, religiia', *Antireligioznik*, 3 (1941), 22–3.
65. T. Chuguev, 'Antireligioznoe vospitanie doshkol'nikov', *Antireligioznik*, 7 (1940) 30–7.
66. ARAO, f. 1, op. 1, d. 286, l. 12.
67. ARAO, f. 1, op. 1, d. 315, ll. 57–8.
68. ARAO, f. 1, op. 1, d. 286, ll.109–13.
69. ARAO, f. 1, op. 1, d. 241, l. 30.
70. ARAO, f. 1, op. 1, d. 241, l. 29.
71. ARAO, f. 1, op. 1, d. 315, l. 56 ob.
72. S. Freud, 'The "Uncanny"' (1919). The *Standard Edition of the Complete Psychological Works of Sigmund Freud*, vol. 17, trans. James Strachey (London, 1955), p. 249.
73. Freud, 'The "Uncanny"', pp. 247–8.
74. T. Sanders and H.G. West, 'Power Revealed and Concealed in the New World Order', in H.G. West and T.Sanders (eds), *Transparency and Conspiracy: Ethnographies of Suspicion in the New World Order* (Durham, NC, 2003), pp. 1–37.
75. L. Viola, *Peasant Rebels under Stalin* (Oxford, 1996), Chap. 2; S.A. Smith, 'Nebesnye pis'ma i rasskazy o lese: "sueveriia" protiv bol'shevizma', *Antropologicheskii forum*, 3 (2005), 280–306.
76. I. Flerov, 'Antireligioznaia rabota v shkole', *Antireligioznik*, 5 (1928), 52.
77. Husband, 'Godless Communists', p. 118.
78. Balashov, *Shkola*, p. 146.
79. Husband, 'Godless Communists', p. 35.
80. S. Bruce, *God is Dead: Secularization in the West* (Oxford, 2002), p. 107.

6
Identity, Agency, and the 'First Soviet Generation'

Anna Krylova

Introducing 'generation' into the debate on Stalinist identity

The Stalinist person, subject, or citizen, male or female, is an enigma in Western scholarship. A subject of academic research since the founding of Soviet and Russian studies, he, she or it has persistently raised historical and ethical questions about individual agency and autonomy in history in general and about the relationships between Soviet individuals and the Stalinist society they inhabited. How did Soviet citizens who lived in Russia in the 1920s and 1930s come to think about themselves? Whose terms did they use when they thought, wrote, talked, dreamed? Did they mean what they said in their letters and diaries? To what degree was the Stalinist ideological project successful in installing itself in the everyday lives and thoughts of its citizens? Did individuals manage to secure some distance between themselves and Stalinist ideology and official culture? And if they thought and spoke the Party line, did they mean it?

Tirelessly asked, these questions have generated in Russian studies stable sets of interpretative responses that have not lessened the enigmatic nature of individual life in Stalinist Russia, where repression and enthusiasm, opportunity and horror were all combined in one historical moment. Since the 1950s, the conceptual tools to answer these questions have been drawn from two opposing images of subjectivity: on the one hand, an estranged and resisting 'disbeliever' and, on the other, an indoctrinated 'believer' incapable of finding any critical space between himself and the system.[1]

The recent decade of the 1990s saw a continuing conversation between these two positions. The character of the disbeliever or dissident, an internal émigré who resists and subverts the system by manipulating it or playing with it, dominated the scholarship of the early 1990s. By the end of the decade, Jochen Hellbeck and Igal Halfin had enriched the discussion on Stalinist subjectivity with explorations of the inner worlds of Stalinist individuals. In their treatments, the word 'indoctrinated' began to mean not simply the passive dissolution of an individual into Stalinist ways of thinking but the individual's active quest to emulate in deed and thought the prescribed type of a Bolshevik–Stalinist personality. In other words, these two scholars created the option for historical subjects who did not oppose the Stalinist system to be emotionally charged and complex historical subjects. Especially in Hellbeck's work, the early Soviet subject is not a static indoctrinated self but a hard-working, feeling, and suffering individual who strives to become a Stalinist self. Even as he or she 'struggles' and 'becomes', this Stalinist person still acts exclusively on the terms of Stalinist ideology. He or she is an agent whose agency consists of the uncritical pursuit of a prescribed personality, or a portion of it.[2]

Philosophically and theoretically, the Western ideal of autonomous individuals, those freely willing and acting agents independent of the social and cultural structures into which they are born, has been under systematic critical investigation for more than a century. This uncomplicated notion of a critically minded and independently thinking human being does not easily fit the complex ways in which individuals relate to their sociocultural surroundings and become conscious of themselves. The other extreme, which implies the disappearance of individuals into their historical and cultural circumstances without a murmur of protest, makes the question about historical agency irrelevant altogether and leaves us with the simple assertion that the Stalinist self equals Stalinist ideology. Questions that such narratives of capitulation of self in history raise are not specific to historians of Stalinist Russia alone. They have long haunted cultural historians whose work posits subjectivities and identities as 'constructed' entities without seriously addressing the place and role of historical agency in such human contracts. Existing theories – all too frequently invoked – concerning the death of the author or the impossibility of thinking outside of discourse can hardly be considered satisfying answers. Instead of engaging with the complex relationship between individuals and their sociocultural surroundings, such approaches preclude any investigation by dismissing the problem altogether.

With this chapter on the first post-revolutionary generation – which, in pre-war Stalinist ideology, culture, and society, was referred to as the generation of 'new Soviet people' – I want to join the debate about the construction of Stalinist identity. My agenda is to consider the possibility of a Stalinist individual for whom the internalization of key terms of Stalinist official culture did not automatically lead to his disappearance as an active agent in his self-imagination. I make this argument in relation to the generation of young people who, in 1917, were either too young or not yet alive to participate in the Revolution, but who, in the 1930s, had to operate in the context of an official discourse that Stalinist society had launched on their behalf. I argue that the nature of the discussion about the first post-revolutionary generation in Stalinist official culture made it possible for the members of this generation to exercise agency when they engaged with questions about who they were.

One way to begin to make this argument is to complicate the relationship that we envision having existed between individuals and Stalinist official culture in the 1930s. The first point that we must question is the assumption that Stalinist official culture was an ideological formation whose core values were coherent, clearly articulated and free of contradiction. The 1930s discourse on the post-revolutionary generation of new Soviet people is a good starting point for exploring the ambiguities of Stalinist culture. On the one hand, the graduation of well-educated young people from schools and universities and their entry into the labour force was one of the defining social events of the decade. Systematically educated, cultured, and destined for white-collar jobs, they were the first results of the Stalinist expanded education system and a prime indicator of Soviet modernity. These young people were in the centre of official, cultural, and social discussion.

On the other hand, despite their centrality in Stalinist culture, young people were resistant to coherence and consensus. Discussion of their place in society was full of conflict and contradiction – more an ideological work in progress than a coherent and fixed story. These new Soviet people had multiple faces and provoked many conflicting emotions. On the one hand, they were celebrated as new and unprecedented, the incarnation of the proletarian future itself. On the other hand, they provoked recurrent waves of anxiety in Party and Komsomol circles and in society at large, since they were observed to look, talk, and handle themselves more like 'the bourgeoisie' than the standard-bearers of the proletarian revolution. From the point of view of the revolutionary generation, the generation of new people lacked crucial and familiar social identifiers – working-class experiences and a working-class past. Even worse, the category of class as it had been imagined and used in the Bolshevik ideological project turned out not to be easily applicable to these young people. The difficulty of projecting class identity on to a generation of well-educated young people without working-class experiences was, I argue, the source of much anxiety in workplaces and in Party and Komsomol organizations.

A critical point in my overall argument is that the contradictory attitude towards the new generation was never resolved in the pre-war era. Publicly, young people were continuously and simultaneously celebrated and castigated while an agreed sense of who exactly they were remained elusive. This generation was a social phenomenon that challenged the Bolshevik class-based categories of self-perception and represented a real ideological challenge for Soviet society.

Interpreted in the context of social and cultural conflicts of the 1930s, Stalinist ideology thus quickly loses the coherence implied by habitual narratives and concepts such as 'new Soviet person'. It is this reinterpretation of the Stalinist discourse on the generation of new people that allows me to bring agency into my understanding of Stalinist subject and not to ostracize the subject from its culture. I conclude my chapter with an analysis of young people who responded to the conflicted public discourse in letters to the popular Soviet writer Vera Ketlinskaia, whose 1938 novel *Courage* was one the first books about the post-revolutionary generation. Reading through the letters in relation to Stalinist culture, I trace how young individuals placed themselves against the backdrop of a culture that spoke on their behalf. I argue that, though they did internalize the conflicted perceptions of themselves, they nevertheless had to answer questions about their identity (who they really were) on their own, since the official discourse failed them in this respect.

The generation of new Soviet people in Stalinist official culture: Contradictions without resolutions

The Russian twentieth century easily breaks down into generational narratives. Especially during its first 50 years, it was rich in watershed historical events. Nor did dramatic social and cultural transformations bypass Russian society. The pace at which Russia's agrarian society was pushed towards industrialized, mass educated, mass cultured, and urbanized modernity in the 1930s was unprecedented in modern European history. By the end of the 1930s, Soviet Russia was a multigenerational society in the most conflicted meaning of the word, since it encompassed social groups not only scarred by revolutions, wars, and famines but also separated by major social and cultural divides. Having compressed a major industrialization effort into one decade, the Stalinist regime created a social body whose generational cohorts had cultural, educational, and career profiles that belonged to different historical stages of Russia's development. The pre-1917 class structure that informed Bolshevik ideology was in the process of transition towards a more complex social organization in which white-collar workers were to play a more and more defining role.[3]

Understandably, in Soviet Russia of the 1920s and 1930s, generational discourses carried much weight in official culture and made a lot of sense to contemporaries. On the one hand, the notion of generation was a perfect explanatory tool to account for a society so acutely divided by historical and social developments. On the other hand, it also enjoyed a prehistory among Bolshevik intellectuals and traditionally served as a useful trope in their thinking about society. In Bolshevik ideology before and after 1917, the generation of new people, which did not yet exist but was to be created in the future, was a goal in no way less revolutionary than the liberation of the working class in the present. The generational discourses of the 1920s were much concerned with theorizing about and waiting for a generation that, being untainted by the capitalist mode of production and thought, would constitute a historical breakthrough into a new and different mode of organizing human nature socially, culturally, and psychologically. The 1920s discussion about the ideal new people in the Soviet press and in literary and philosophical journals spotlighted an educated worker who enjoyed all types of labour – physical, manual, and mental. This idealized image, as we will see, was grossly out of step with the industrial, social, and cultural transformations that were just about to be launched by the Stalinist government. It was destined to come into conflict with the generation of young people produced by the industrial remaking of Russian society in the 1930s.

Much awaited and talked about, the 'new people' did indeed begin entering Stalinist society in the early 1930s. At least, this is when Soviet public discourse recognized the coming of age of the young generation that was born too late to participate in the Revolution and the Civil War. Leaving school, they began entering the workforce, which was in the throes of the most ambitious and demanding industrializing efforts ever, known at the time as 'building Socialism'. Their path first led to institutes and universities where they continued their education to become the first cohort of systematically trained specialists or white-collar workers – the managerial and cultural elite that the Stalinist state and its expanding economy were in great need of. Over the decade of the 1930s, these young people announced their presence through the growing memberships of Komsomol organizations, sports, and paramilitary clubs and associations. Just between 1938 and 1940, for example, the Communist Youth League (the Komsomol) grew by five million members; all were young men and women born after 1917 who joined Komsomol organizations primarily while in secondary school.

In the press, Party theory, and literature, these young people received special attention. Their arrival in the workforce and in universities, as well as their impact on the tastes and expectations of the Russian reading audience, were exciting topics. When Stalinist journalists, Party leaders and activists, and writers and literary critics surveyed young people from a lofty historical perspective, this generation of graduates, students, specialists, and white-collar workers appeared to be the incarnation of the revolutionary promise of 1917 and the symbol of Russia's victory over the cultural and industrial backwardness of its past. According to the highly abstract terms of this discourse, these well-educated young people without any working-class experience were new, different, and unique, or, as a *Pravda* editorial put it: 'These are new people indeed. They are made out of new material. They are pieces of the communist future.'[4]

Yet the excited celebration of this unique generation of new people represented only the surface level of the public discussion and social reality of the 1930s. Easily recognizable as different, the young people were not easily comprehensible.

In the first place, little was known about how these different and new people came across when one encountered them in everyday life, for example, in a Komsomol organization, or attempted to write about them beyond the terms of abstract celebration. V. Koroteev, an activist and frequent participant in the public debate of the late 1930s, encapsulated the prevalent perplexity about the young cohort in a small *mise-en-scène* in one of his 1940 pieces of correspondence in *Pravda*. Remembering his own meeting with a member of the new generation, Koroteev began his story by describing his shock upon encountering someone radically different from himself: 'I nearly gasped. This guy was born the year I joined the Komsomol.' He remembered becoming absorbed in contemplation of the young fellow. As Koroteev was 'watching him' he was thinking to himself, 'this is indeed the new generation of Komsomol members', the 'true face' with which the author of the article confessed not to be familiar.[5] Koroteev's framing of the unknown young fellow as a silent object of contemplation with whom he did not enter into conversation captured the mood of the 1930s, during which the older generation attempted, with only partial success, to understand their juniors.

In the 1930s, literature and the press produced a more focused investigation of the new generation alongside the abstract celebration. Journalists, Party and Komsomol workers, writers and literary critics attempted to fill in the gaps in their knowledge and to dissipate their own and others' anxiety about the new people. However, instead of answering questions and calming concerns, the concrete discussion of the new people only heightened social anxieties.

In a society divided by and aware of the issue of generation, the exploration of the new people inevitably took place in relation to the only other heavily celebrated generation – the revolutionary generation that came of age before 1917 and had the Revolution and the victory in the Civil War to its name. The new cohort was processed through expectations and ideals of its seniors, who in the 1930s occupied positions of authority in the Party-state and the press, and enjoyed greater access to public debate.

From the point of view of this revolutionary generation, the most immediate obvious cultural difference between themselves and the new people was culture itself or, to put it in the terms of the period, the particular relationship that the young people enjoyed with education and culture. In accordance with the terms of the 1930s discussion, Soviet journalists, writers, and officials defined 'education' not as basic literacy but as a special quality of interaction between an individual and culture – a process by which culture became an intrinsic part of one's life. From this perspective, the intimate connection between the new generation and culture was the true divide between generations.[6]

For the revolutionary generation, culture had several interrelated meanings and corresponded to several phases of experience. In the first place, it meant the challenge that they confronted late in their lives when they went through several years of intensive, nerve-breaking, and unsystematic specialized schooling in workers' colleges, evening schools, and factory workshops. This type of acculturation was simultaneously the fulfilment of a dream, a cultural shock, a traumatic experience, and a reminder of their unprivileged pre-revolutionary position. These sentiments entered the generic portrait of the generation in the press and literature. In his acclaimed 1936 novel *In the East* (*Na vostoke*), for example, Petr Pavlenko presented the revolutionary generation through a character named Shershavin, who became a 'schoolboy with a beard' at the age of 30 and whose early 20s had been devoted to fighting for the Soviet republic. A strong-willed Bolshevik tempered in revolutionary struggle, Shershavin also personified the pain and rage of the 'uncultured, illiterate, and ridiculed'. For him, as for many of his generation, culture – that is, reading, writing, and knowing – never became second nature but remained a challenge and an effort – something that could always let them down in a social situation or at the workplace.[7]

The generation of new people, on the other hand, not only did not share this traumatic attitude towards culture and knowledge but, as journalists and writers of the period pointed out, could not even conceive of culture as a painful and traumatic experience. They, by contrast, felt entirely at home with books and knowledge both general and professional. Reading, a fundamental part of an educated and cultured life, was presented as intrinsic to young people's personalities. Representations in the press did not invoke revolutionary battles but posed young men or young women as confident readers absorbed in a book in the privacy of their homes.[8]

In the mid- and late 1930s the young generation began appearing in Soviet novels. As old and young Soviet literati began to take notice of the post-revolutionary generation, they added youth to their general depiction of Stalinist society. In Petr Pavlenko's *In the East*, youth, represented by a young woman named Ol'ga, is just one of many protagonists that Pavlenko uses to draw a portrait of Stalinist Russia. Ol'ga is simultaneously an intrinsic part of the Stalinist social landscape and the cultural antithesis of the old generation. A young specialist and a former student, she embodies intellectual and professional confidence and sharply contrasts with the revolutionary but culturally insecure hero of the Civil War, Shershavin. Soviet writers who themselves belonged to the post-revolutionary cohort turned their coevals into the main characters of novels and explored their relationships with the revolutionary generation.[9]

Besides serving as subject matter for Soviet fiction, the young generation announced itself as a group of new readers with unprecedented critical skills and literary demands, readers that Soviet writers were not used to. Most strikingly, new readers announced themselves in letters to their favourite writers. One of the most esteemed writers of the old generation, Aleksei Tolstoi, correlated the coming of age of the first post-revolutionary generation with the appearance of a new genre of letter writing which he called the 'individual letter'. In this new type of letter, written in flawless language without grammatical mistakes, the young reader shared with the writer his individual and critical point of view.[10]

In the 1930s, the best-known public image of this educated, cultured, confident, and critical generation was created by the Party apparatus itself.

In 1935, when Soviet schools graduated the first cohort of students with ten years of systematic and uninterrupted schooling, the event was publicly celebrated at the Hall of Columns in the Moscow House of Soviets. It monopolized the front pages of Soviet newspapers and produced a condensed image of the generation that had culture and education as key markers of its identity.[11]

The Class of 1935 represented the elite of the generation of the new people. They had nothing but culture to their name. Purposefully prepared for institutes and universities, they were to get even more education and to join the workforce as highly qualified and expensive white-collar workers who would not go near manual labour at any point on their life trajectory. As the vanguard of the new generation, they possessed a feature that, in the 1930s, began to define the generation as a whole. This feature was especially well captured in the public celebration devoted to the Class of 1935. Indicative of the Stalinist discourse on the post-revolutionary generation as a whole, the press coverage contained a spectacular omission. In their addresses to and analysis of the young people, Party and Komsomol leaders, journalists, and writers continuously overlooked the category of 'class', this crucial category of identification for Bolshevik ideology and for the revolutionary generation.[12] Uniformly educated and deprived of working-class experience, these new Soviet people looked nothing like the previously imagined ideal of the new man as an educated worker.

Young people's diverse social roots seemed to have been obscured by their unique educational capital. In the press and literature, young people thus acquired 'culture' as their new mark of social distinction. The new signifier was a double-edged sword, however. On the one hand, it liberated them from their parents' class origins and expanded their identities beyond the existing class mentality. On the other hand, it excluded them from a category of identification intrinsic to the world view of several preceding generations and put them in a vulnerable position. As a central category of identification, 'class' structured all of Soviet life on the principle that there was a direct correlation between class, class consciousness, and dedication to the Soviet cause. The elimination of such an essential marker invited questioning of young people's identities regardless of all public celebrations of their historical novelty. What they gained in culture, they seemed to lose in distinct class identity.

Apart from not having a distinct class affiliation, young people, according to Soviet journalists and Komsomol leaders and activists, had not had first-hand experience of the class society of the Tsarist regime. Nor had they proven their identification with the working class during the Revolution or the Civil War. Simultaneously celebrating and lamenting the arrival of a new cohort, Soviet journalists noted the fact that young people had never suffered class exploitation. A disturbing conclusion was implied: young people did not have any worthy biography to speak of. Nor were their proper class consciousness and identification with the Stalinist state guaranteed.[13]

The question of who these young people in fact were continuously loomed large in Party and Komsomol discussions. Would the new generation be able to embrace and internalize the proletarian cause without authentic and first-hand experience of Tsarist class society? Could they develop the necessary class consciousness and class hatred under the new Soviet conditions? If culture was what they had and reading was their best skill, could they embrace the working-class world view through reading and learning about the past? Could learning and reading substitute for authentic pre-revolutionary class experience?

Responses from the grass roots seemed to deliver a resolute 'no'. Ever since the early 1930s, the older generation consistently failed to see in the post-revolutionary generation any familiar features either of themselves or of their ideals. At workplaces, in Party and Komsomol organizations and in universities, the young generation became objects of suspicion, mistrust, and even animosity. Writing to *Pravda*, older grassroots activists complained about young people's apparent internal inconsistency, aloofness from society, and unreliability. The educated, cultured, refined, confident, and critical new person was in the eyes of the revolutionary generation a chameleon-like character who behaved 'one way at home, another way at work, spoke one language at the meeting and another in private talk'. Special mention was made of the privileged position that private pursuits seemed to occupy in the life of the young generation at the expense of the collective. The gift of culture seemed to generate non-collectivist behaviour, since studying and reading required that much time be spent on one's own with a book and not with the collective.[14]

The qualities that the revolutionary generation saw in young people – inconsistency, aloofness, individualistic inclinations, and unreliability – clearly indicated that older comrades perceived the celebrated new people as an 'intelligentsia' type of personality. A term with many negative and derogatory meanings and associations, 'intelligentsia' had most recently been used in Stalinist official discourse as virtually interchangeable with the notion of 'class enemy'.

A slightly less condemnatory sense of the intelligentsia as not an independent class but a derivative of other classes that was intrinsically detached from life and unreliable at testing historical moments was also alive and well in the 1930s. One of the leading theorists and propagandists, Emel'ian Iaroslavskii, explicated these ideas in a 1939 booklet on the intelligentsia. Iaroslavskii's pamphlet undoubtedly represented an effort on the part of Party leaders and journalists to come to terms with the well-educated young generation. In the public discourse of the 1930s, the young generation was referred to as the new Soviet intelligentsia on and off.[15]

However, as the terms of Iaroslavkii's booklet might begin to suggest, the attempted alliance between young people and intelligentsia seemed only to contribute to popular anxieties. Despite the efforts, not always consistent, to create a positive notion of Soviet intelligentsia, suspicion of individuals who looked and acted like intelligentsia did not lessen over the decade and induced Stalin to highlight hostility towards 'the Soviet intelligentsia' during his speech at the 18th Party Congress in 1938. A valuable indication of serious social tensions, Stalin's speech could hardly negate popular animosity towards the intelligentsia. Nor could it erase it, given its deep roots and purposeful cultivation in Bolshevik and Stalinist culture.[16]

I want to conclude this overview of the Stalinist generational discourse by recapitulating my earlier suggestion that, despite the prevalent academic association of Stalinist official culture with coherence and clarity, the issue of young Soviet people was never resolved in the 1930s, either discursively or socially. Throughout the decade, both before and after Stalin's 1938 speech, the young generation was simultaneously celebrated, lamented, and deeply distrusted in the press. This state of official discourse inevitably created general confusion and exacerbated anxieties.

As long as the post-revolutionary generation whose maturation coincided with Stalinist industrialization was discussed from the class point of view, the contradictory nature of public discourse was inevitable. The Bolshevik class-centred discourse and the idealization of the working class as the most progressive embodiment of humanity did not easily fit the post-revolutionary generation that marked Russia's entry into modernity.

Confronting the new generation in Soviet literature: A case study

The futility of resolving the contradictory perceptions of the post-revolutionary generation and attempting to answer questions about its true identity from a class-centred point of view was especially striking in the realm of Soviet literature. In professional literary circles, the looming problem of young people's unreliable identity acquired a new dimension: it created a genre of writing that could give access to young people's inner world. The production novel – a genre of the initial years of industrial development in the late 1920s and early 1930s – was under direct attack by Soviet literary critics in the mid-1930s. Focusing on industrial processes and the massive scale of Stalinist transformations, the production novel portrayed a hero from the 'outside' as he strove for grandiose achievements. It was singularly unsuited to providing a detailed depiction of the inner making of the young generation. Elena Usievich, the most prominent and influential critic of the period, demanded that writers use the inner life of the new generation as the new organizing principle of their narrative.[17]

The most immediately acclaimed effort to fulfil the new needs of the time belonged to Vera Ketlinskaia, who published her novel *Courage* in 1938. Ketlinskaia herself was a member of the post-revolutionary generation: born too late to participate in the Revolution or to have conscious recollections of the period. The daughter of a tsarist officer who sided with the Revolution and was assassinated for his decision, Ketlinskaia acquired a good education at home and later at school and spent her childhood and teen years in pioneer and Komsomol organizations. She was an interesting exemplification of the hybridity of the new people – the daughter of a tsarist officer who lost her social origins early on and devoted all her life up to 1938 to proletarian youth organizations. In the 1930s, she began writing about youth-related novels and working for the main newspaper of the Communist Youth League, *Komsomol'skaia pravda*. The distrust that the young generation provoked in her older contemporaries and colleagues was very familiar to her.[18]

Courage was her first national best-seller, and it gained her admission into the Soviet Union of Writers as well as eliciting hundreds of letters from young readers. The first edition of her novel numbered 10,000 copies and quickly became a book for which readers were lining up and compiling waiting lists in libraries all over the country. As became clear from the letters that Ketlinskaia started to receive as early as 1938, her novel was phenomenally popular. Letter writers typically told of waiting approximately two weeks for the book, rushing madly to read it in a few nights, passing it unwillingly to the next in line, and then missing it and its characters.[19]

The inner world of the new generation was indisputably the organizing perspective of the book. The novel was devoted to 600 actual Komsomol members who in 1932 went to the Far East to build a city that, in accordance with the second Five-Year Plan (1933–7), was to become the centre of the Far Eastern economy and a military 'outpost of socialism'. Within four years, the Soviet map featured a new Far Eastern city, named Komsomol'sk in honour of its builders, that could boast a train station, hospital, primary school, radio station, cinema, and above all, a shipbuilding plant, along with 20,000 inhabitants. The story of how a place where there was nothing but taiga became the town of Komsomol'sk was told intimately by Ketlinskaia through the eyes of her characters.

Having secured this inner perspective by making her characters the primary vehicle for her literary exploration, Ketlinskaia made the question of the class identity of the post-revolutionary generation her key issue. She treats the 600 young people as a test sample to find out whether their generation could have a working-class personality even without proper proletarian experiences or proletarian past. Her understanding of what a working-class identity entails comes right out of the Bolshevik romantic-revolutionary canon: a deep and unselfconscious identification with the proletarian goal of changing the world, the psychological and physical preparedness to carry out this task under any circumstances, and, finally, self-sacrificing readiness to defend revolutionary ideals and to die for them if necessary. The Far East, with its unindustrialized backwardness and strategic military importance was a perfect place for the post-revolutionary generation to make its entrance, to change the environment in accordance with the proletarian master plan, and to prove the strength of their identification with this plan.

What makes Ketlinskaia's book a full-blooded participant in the larger Stalinist discourse on the new generation is the book's inability to shed anxiety about the nature of the youth's true self. The book starts with a troubled question about who the young people are and ends with the same question hanging in the air unanswered.

In line with her overall project, Ketlinskaia starts her novel with close-up portraits of her main protagonists: the former army diver Epifanov, the highly skilled mechanic Kolia Plat, and the inventor and future engineer Sema Al'tshuler. They share the familiar and publicly celebrated features of the new generation: self-confidence and a sense of personal uniqueness and ability. Epifanov cannot help but 'feel heroic' and 'unprecedented' and 'respect himself more than usual' on his way back from the army even before he joins the Far Eastern project. His future co-worker and roommate in the Far East, Kolia Plat, also takes much pride in his status as a mechanic of the eighth grade and in the 'respect' paid to him by his peers. Sema Al'tshuler, the most talented member of the group, finds enough material in his life to raise questions about the 'role of the personality' in history in relation to himself. None of the three men, to the best of their knowledge of themselves and each other, harbours any doubts about their bond with the proletarian epoch. They head for the Far East fearless and full of enthusiasm, ready to confront the timeless inertia of the region and turn it into another Stalinist project.[20]

These young people – self-admiring dreamers full of youthful energy – are set up by Ketlinskaia for admiration and inspiring envy. Who would not want to feel like them and to be in the company of people of that kind and quality? In her introductory portraits, Ketlinskaia does not articulate any direct questions and concerns regarding youth. And she really does not need to do so. If we take a step away from the novel for just a moment and see it against the larger backdrop of Stalinist official culture, we see that Ketlinskaia did not have to raise disturbing questions, because they already constituted the inevitable larger cultural context of her book. Anxieties about youth's true nature could be detected simultaneously outside the book, as a part of the Stalinist generational discourse, and inside the book, as the book's agenda; either way, they did not require explicit articulation.

Instead of tackling directly these anxieties, Ketlinskaia uses the two-week-long train ride that her characters take to the Far East to introduce more of their typical features. What the young people effortlessly carry with them to the Far East is their acute sense of professionalism and their habitual intimacy with books. They spend their days on the train reading books and articles about their destination. On the long journey, an adventure book about the Far East takes on the dimensions of a significant cultural event, revealing the presence of many zealous readers on the train: 'The book began to move from one reader to another. A waiting list was organized and reading time was specified – no more than four hours. "Read faster", they would tell the next reader, "get on the upper berth and race through to the final full stop."' The train even has its own poet, Grisha Isalov, a future journalist who announces his poetic aspirations by reading his verse to the attentive audience in his carriage. When taking a rest from their books, the young travelers gaze out of the window and exhibit their secondary school knowledge of physical geography as they trace the train route on their mental maps from the Urals to Lake Baikal, and onward to the Amur River.[21]

Having pictured books – that is, culture itself – as central to the life of the post-revolutionary generation, Ketlinskaia then deals with the young people's arrival at the Far East as a transition from a book-centred life to a life of tangible hardship, suffering, and danger. Working through widespread social anxieties concerning the post-revolutionary generation, Ketlinskaia strips her protagonists of their privileged 'specialist' status and of their 'culture' and 'education' as she sets them to work on the unskilled, manual tasks of unloading and rooting out trees, timber felling, and building. The young people are to test the depth of their identification with the proletarian cause not on the pages of their books but in everyday struggle. For several hundred pages, for days, evenings, and nights, the young men and women work in freezing marsh water up to their waists. Undernourished and overworked, they suffer from 'chicken eyes' and scurvy without medical support or hope of a food delivery. Having spent the first summer and autumn in damp tents beset by swarms of gnats, they face the onset of the Far Eastern winter without proper housing.

Not every enthusiastic volunteer manages to withstand the conditions and the demands of the construction project. As difficulties accumulate, many lose their enthusiasm, self-confidence, self-admiration, and ambition. They protest against the unbearable conditions, food shortages, and the lack of Party attention and, ultimately, desert the construction site. Once again, Ketlinskaia does not overtly condemn the protesters and deserters. Instead, she creates a social situation for her characters in which uncertainty about their own and others' true identity dominates their everyday life and causes much emotional turmoil and suffering. Everyone is being tested to reveal their true selves and facing the challenge of discovering the true selves of those around them. During the first phase of construction, each character personifies the very concerns and anxieties that were being expressed in discussions about the post-revolutionary generation in the central press.

Of the three protagonists with whom Ketlinskaia started the book, Kolia Platt turns out to be an unexpected and disconcerting deserter. Eager reader, specialist, and Komsomol member, he turns out not to 'imbibe' the proper personality deeply enough. Underneath his cultured and refined exterior, there hides a 'philistine essence' incapable of withstanding an encounter with the reality of life and struggle. He deserts, secretly abandoning his friends at the most difficult moment of construction. His roommate Epifanov, he of the 'heroic feeling', finds the fact of Kolia's desertion difficult, nearly impossible, to comprehend. The implicit question that Ketlinskaia invites here concerns not only Kolia's true self but also others' selves: if Kolia could not handle the pressure, who else might buckle? Epifanov himself withstands everything heroically and with distinction. However, thanks to Ketlinskaia's arrangement of the plot, his heroic deeds (as well as his true identity) remain unknown to his friends for a while. The third friend, Sema Al'tshuler, also succeeds in the face of the challenges of the Far East and proves his identification with the goals of the construction, despite his poor health. Out of the three friends, Sema has to withstand the most physical suffering. At the end of the novel, Epifanov and Sema are confirmed as heroes who can point to the built city as the material embodiment of their proletarian self.[22]

Ketlinskaia's highly praised and promoted book can hardly be accused of a happy socialist realist ending. The novel is a thriller whose suspense is produced by unpredictable sequences of questioning, searching, and either discovering or losing one's proletarian self. Replicating the conflictedness of public discussion on the meaning of the post-revolutionary generation, the author, herself a member of this generation, turned out to be unable to go beyond it. At the beginning of the novel, no one – neither the characters as they are presented by the author, nor the author, who gives out no clues – knows who out of these self-admiring and self-confident 600 will withstand the stern test of living, working, and fighting in the Far East. At the end, no one can explain why some members of this new and cultured generation go through the Far Eastern hardships unwaveringly and why others, in no way different from them, fail miserably. The only certain thing in this thriller about the post-revolutionary generation is the very absence of certainty concerning the post-revolutionary generation.

The post-revolutionary generation as readers of Ketlinskaia's *Courage*

What about the young people themselves who, in the late 1930s, were lining up and compiling waiting lists in local libraries to read Ketlinskaia's book? What was it in this highly ambiguous book about the new generation that made it such a success among this very generation?

As early as 1938, young readers began writing to Ketlinskaia to thank her for the book and tell her about the feelings and thoughts that it provoked in them. Preserved in Ketlinskaia's personal archive at the Russian State Archive of Literature and Art, these letters, which span the period from 1938 to 1948, bring individual perspectives and individual agency into my story. They take us back to the questions raised at the beginning of this article, questions that can now be considered in relation to the preceding discussion of Stalinist official discourse on the post-revolutionary generation and Ketlinskaia's book. Can the categories of belief and disbelief, internalization and rejection, sufficiently explain the types of relations that existed between members of the post-revolutionary generation and Stalinist culture if we do not assume the latter to be coherent and contradiction-free? Or, to rephrase the question, how does one believe or reject a culture that does not provide a neat set of ideals and narratives to believe in or to reject?

Letters that young people wrote to Ketlinskaia between 1938 and 1948 attend precisely to these questions. They present us with a Stalinist subject that is neither lost in Stalinist culture nor securely untouched by its ideals and demands. The most provoking feature of the letters is that the majority of Ketlinskaia's readers do not identify with either positive or negative characters of the book at the point when their particular identities become clarified. They make a different choice in their readings.

In the first place, they uncompromisingly insist that the book is 'true to life' and that they effortlessly recognize themselves in the book's heroes. Some, such as the 23-year-old female student I. Arapitova, who wrote in 1938, defined their experience of Ketlinskaia's characters as 'feeling close' to them and being able to 'understand' them. Others resembled a 23-year-old turner and Komsomol member, who in 1939 assured Ketlinskaia on behalf of his comrades and contemporaries that the 'psychology and feelings of [her] heroes' was the 'psychology and feelings of my friends'. What these readers happened to 'recognize' and 'feel close' to was, however, something emotionally destabilizing. It was, as one reader put it, the 'emotional turmoil' that the book's characters went through as they measured their ambitious confidence, culturedness, and self-admiration against the proletarian-scale challenges of the Far East. Although this turmoil was resolved for the individual heroes of the book at its end, it was far from over for the readers, at least at the time they wrote to Ketlinskaia. The intensely emotional and agitated tone of their letters is proof of this.[23]

Attempting to capture the emotional impact the book had on him, one reader, a 25-year-old special correspondent for a regional newspaper, refused to use the neutral verb 'read'. He asserted that he 'lived through' the book, which, in his case, meant he 'suffered' along with its characters.[24] Hyperbolic emotional confessions of this kind were no exception. A young married woman, Nina Nazarenko, described the emotional upheaval that the book created in her in even stronger terms. 'There were moments', she remembered in her letter, 'when I had to stop reading' the book because 'tears blocked the page'. A 16-year-old schoolgirl and Komsomol activist, Anna Fomicheva, unambiguously stated that *Courage* and its characters emotionally distressed her and destabilized her everyday life: 'Something incomprehensible is happening in my life ... Your book had very strong resonances for me,' she started her letter to Ketlinskaia. Fomicheva's stated reason for writing to Ketlinskaia was to ask for help and advice on how to deal with this psychological commotion that refused to fade away. Such responses were typical of the general reaction to the book. Readers consistently mentioned tears, spasms, laughter, and tears.[25]

As well as describing the powerful emotional impact of the book, readers also reflected on it. They did not, of course, supply a detailed and exhaustive analysis of the book, its characters, and the mechanisms of the emotional turmoil that they went through. What they did provide was a scattered and highly agitated discussion of the book in relation to their 1930s lives: not so much what the characters did in the book as what the book and its characters did to them in their everyday life. Thus, while describing their state of mind, they unintentionally revealed the content of their inner turmoil, which combined incredible personal ambition for greatness and uniqueness (that is, the striving to become somebody non-ordinary) with a painful sensation of non-existence, irrelevance, and inadequacy.

If we continue reading Fomicheva's letter, which started in such a dramatic manner, we find a rather detailed account of the impact that Ketlinskaia's book and Stalinist generational discourse had on her life and on the life of her generation. The 'strong resonances' of Ketlinskaia's book prevented Fomicheva from finding any 'meaning' in her daily activities in her school's Komsomol organization; they also stimulated in her a craving to be noticed and recognized as someone worthy of notice and recognition. Measuring herself against the lives of Ketlinskaia's heroes, she felt sharply the pointlessness and inadequacy of her own life. Sometimes the feeling was so acute that Fomicheva, as she admitted, appeared to herself to be invisible in her daily routine: 'The most important thing', she wrote, 'is that it seems to me that if I do not go to school tomorrow, no one, no one will notice that I am not there.' Her fear of 'not being noticed' was tantamount to her need to 'be noticed' personally and implied a conviction that she fully deserved attention. What she wanted from life was to be able to 'do something big' like Ketlinskaia's heroes.[26]

While not typical in the amount of detail she provided in her letter, Fomicheva was typical of Ketlinskaia's reader-correspondents for the way that she exhibited the range of issues that troubled readers of

Courage: an acute awareness of self-worth and an ambition for greatness were bound up with an acute sense of inadequacy and irrelevance. The stimulus for such emotional turmoil was the conflicted general perception of the young generation, a perception that the book made only more acute. Far from providing a resolution, *Courage* reactivated anxiety about the young generation among young people themselves. Young men and women who read and wrote about the book made a very convincing case that they had internalized the contemporary discourse on the 'new Soviet people'.

Here, however, we should avoid the temptation to produce another variation on the theme of the emotionally charged and self-policing Stalinist subject. For there is something that Stalinist official culture fails to do for this generation of young people. Having internalized the conflicted Stalinist discourse about them, young people did not and could not find a solution to their emotional turmoil and suffering. Official culture could not help them to work through their emotional turmoil or, at least, to achieve some kind of emotional equilibrium. I do not want to imply that internally conflicted individuals absolutely have to resolve their internal conflicts. But I do wish to suggest that, in the absence of a means of achieving such resolution, young people were left with the opportunity to exercise agency and find some resolution on their own. What is more, this cohort of young people was perfectly culturally equipped to construct, out of the available cultural material, self-narratives that official culture called for but did not provide.

Conclusion

The Bolshevik–Stalinist discussion of the 'new person' was framed by two pre-revolutionary preoccupations: class and generation. Bolshevik intellectuals expected this new being to arise from the working class and to form a generation of young people who neither knew nor were marked by the social divisions of pre-revolutionary Russia. This ideal of the new person dominated Soviet culture in the 1920s.

When the abstract generation of the new people began in the 1930s to take specific shape in Soviet schools and universities and to receive close-up attention in literature and the press, it turned out to have culture and education in abundance but also to lack identifiable class experiences. Party leaders, Komsomol activists, journalists, and writers found it difficult to accept this social rootlessness. The official public discourse was characterized by a profoundly contradictory attitude to young people, who were simultaneously celebrated for their cultural distinction and doubted for their seemingly uprooted, and hence suspicious, identity. Official Stalinist culture thus lacked a uniform and coherent image of the young generation. This tension in public representations of youth presented the 'first Soviet generation' with the opportunity and the imperative to reconcile the contradictions in their public image by participating actively in the construction of their identities.

The early Soviet experience suggests a way of talking about generation as an analytical category that avoids the binary opposition between 'false', 'invented' generations, and 'real' empirically verifiable cohorts. Of course, notions of the 'new Soviet people' depended on an ideologically controlled public discourse, and they were dominated by the image of the elite young people who gained an education and were about to launch themselves on white-collar careers: the 'young generation' was far from being statistically average or sociologically representative. Yet, at the same time, the Stalinist generation of young people was far from being an abstraction removed from the sociocultural transformation that Russia underwent in the 1930s and that young people embodied. Nor was it removed from the hopes, fears, and experiences of Soviet society: it existed in a close and fluctuating relationship with social forces, ideological and cultural articulations, and people's experiences and emotions.

Notes

1. For an extended discussion see my earlier article, 'The Tenacious Liberal Subject in Soviet Studies', *Kritika: Explorations in Russian and Eurasian History*, 1 (2000), 119–46.
2. See especially J. Hellbeck, *Revolution on My Mind. Writing a Diary under Stalin* (Cambridge, MA, 2006), and I. Halfin, *Terror in My Soul: Communist Autobiographies on Trial* (Cambridge, MA, 2003).
3. See Basile Kerblay's discussion of Soviet generations in historical perspective: Kerblay, *Modern Soviet Society* (New York, 1983), pp. 24–7. For a discussion of multigenerationality in the twentieth century, see the contributions by Pat Thane (Chapter 10) and Stephen Lovell (Chapter 11) in this volume.
4. 'Pokolenie velikogo budushchego', *Pravda*, 29 June 1935; see also in *Pravda*: 'Rovesniki Oktiabria', 4 June 1935, and 'Moral'nyi oblik Bol'shevika', 20 September 1937.
5. V. Koroteev, 'Nabolevshie voprosy Komsomol'skoi raboty', *Pravda*, 7 June 1940.
6. E. Krekshin, 'Molodye liudi nashego vremeni', *Znamia*, 1 (1939), 281.
7. Petr Pavlenko, *Na vostoke* (Moscow, 1937), pp. 212, 218–19. On the revolutionary generation and the cohort of *vydvizhentsy*, see Sheila Fitzpatrick, *Education and Social Mobility in the Soviet Union, 1921–1934* (Cambridge, 1979) and Moshe Lewin, 'Society, State, and Ideology during the First Five-Year Plan', in idem, *The Making of the Soviet System: Essays in the Social*

History of Interwar Russia (New York, 1994), pp. 209–40; see also Kerblay, *Modern Soviet Society*, especially pp. 155–8.

8. See N. Kren, 'Na proverochnykh ispytaniiakh po literature', *Pravda*, 2 June 1936; Aleksei Tolstoi, 'Vpered, k schast'iu!', *Literaturnaia gazeta*, 20 March 1937; Elena Usievich, 'Muzhestvo' (1938), in *Puti khudozhestvennoi pravdy* (Moscow, 1958); Krekshin, 'Molodye liudi nashego vremeni'. On the role of 'culture' in the self-identification of the post-revolutionary generation itself, see Iu.P. Sharapov, *Litsei v Sokol'nikakh: Ocherki istorii IFLI* (Moscow, 1995).

9. Symptomatic of the change was the appearance in Soviet literature of new characters: a young specialist, a student, a recent graduate, or a young educated worker. In novels from the late 1930s by such acclaimed Soviet novelists as V. Ketlinskaia, Iu. Krymov, and V. Gerasimova, the social distinctiveness of the new generation began to reside in their skills and knowledge, which were to mature and further reveal themselves as the new epoch gained momentum: see V. Ketlinskaia, *Muzhestvo* (1936–38); V. Gerasimova, *Khitrye glaza* (1937); Iu. Krymov, *Tanker Derbent* (1939).

10. Tolstoi, 'Vpered, k schast'iu!'. Note also Anna Karavaeva, 'Pis'ma k pisateliu', *Literaturnaia gazeta*, 10 April 1937, and A. Lozovskii, 'Kakoi tematicheskii plan nuzhen sovetskomu chitateliu', *Literaturnaia gazeta*, 15 September 1938.

11. 'Pervye vypuskniki desiatiletki', *Pravda*, 2 June 1935. See also 'Tsvetushchaia iunost' Rodiny', *Komsomol'skaia pravda*, 2 June 1935.

12. 'Pervye vypuskniki desiatiletki'.

13. See the following articles in *Pravda*: 'Vospityvat' dostoinuiu smenu', 15 February 1937; A. Kosarev, 'Uzlovye zadachi Komsomol'skoi raboty', 24 May 1937. And in *Komsomol'skaia pravda*: 'Tsvetushchaia iunost' Rodiny'; 'Nasha molodezh' ne znaet tragedii proshlogo', 5 August 1938; 'Pomoch' molodoi intelligentsii ovladet' bol'shevizmom', 1 March 1939.

14. S. Obraztsov, 'Kto vinovat?', *Pravda*, 11 August 1940. See also in *Komsomol'skaia pravda* two essays by E. Kononenko: 'Egoisty', 21 March 1938, and 'Chest' devushki', 28 August 1938; and Koroteev, 'Nabolevshie voprosy'.

15. E. Iaroslavskii, *O roli intelligentsii v SSSR* (Moscow, 1939). See also M.P. Baskin, 'Sovetskaia intelligentsiia', *Komsomol'skaia pravda*, 26 December 1936.

16. I.V. Stalin, 'Otchetnyi doklad na 18-om s"ezde partii o rabote TsK VKP(b)', *Pravda*, 11 March 1939, p. 6.

17. Usievich, 'Muzhestvo', p. 76. See also the following articles in *Literaturnaia gazeta*: S. Brailovskaia and M. Rybnikova, 'Net chteniia dlia shkoly', 15 April 1937; K. Simonov and M. Matusovskii, 'Predstaviteli na fone', 15 September 1938; A. Gurvich, 'Chuvstvo vremeni', 5 January 1940.

18. See Ketlinskaia's autobiographical novel *Vecher, okna, liudi* (Moscow, 1974).

19. Readers' letters to V. K. Ketlinskaia, in Rossiiskii gosudarstvennyi arkhiv literatury i iskusstva (RGALI), f. 2816, op. 1, d. 362, ll. 29, 46; d. 363, l. 6; d. 364, l. 15.

20. V. Ketlinskaia, *Muzhestvo* (Moscow, 1972), pp. 12, 29.

21. Ibid., pp. 47, 49, 50, 92, 96–7.

22. Ibid., pp. 152, 223, 234.

23. RGALI, f. 2816, op. 1, d. 362, l. 30; d. 363, l. 53; d. 362, l. 39.

24. RGALI, f. 2816, op. 1, d. 362, l. 39.

25. RGALI, f. 2816, op. 1, d. 363, l. 24; d. 364, ll. 1, 18.

26. RGALI, f. 2816, op. 1, d. 364, l. 1.

7
Age Groups, Political Conflict, and Sociological Thought in Interwar Spain

Sandra Souto Kustrín

Introduction

Spain's relative backwardness in establishing a democratic system and achieving socio-economic modernization meant that policies favourable to the development of defined and independent age-based groups were also later in arriving than in many other European countries. Although such groups have biological components, their growth is mainly a social and historical phenomenon, as the role they play depends upon the economic and social order and the political status of their society. As one indication of the consequences of this delay in Spain's development, the first law restricting child labour in Prussia was passed in 1839, but in Spain not until 1873.[1]

This meant that the political mobilization of the masses and the formation of youth organizations with their own identity separate from adult organizations was also a much slower process than elsewhere. However, following the end of World War I almost all European countries saw a surge in the number of youth organizations. These groups grew in number and aimed for greater autonomy, spurred on by the consequences of the war, economic crises, the abandonment of traditional social values, and the arrival of new ideologies such as fascism and communism that placed emphasis on the role of the young. At the same time, young people began to participate to a much greater degree in politics and to adopt more radical positions than those of adults. This phenomenon occurred in almost all European countries and in all ideological spheres; from Czechoslovakia to the youth section of the French Radical Party.[2] This has led some authors to speak of a 'generation of the Great Depression' in Europe.[3]

This same process was repeated in Spain, allowing the nation to take a full part in the process of mass political mobilization that was happening in the rest of Europe at that time. The interwar period, as in the rest of the continent, was a critical moment in Spanish history. Despite Spain's neutrality during World War I, the economic consequences were of particular importance for a country with such limited and unequal economic development. The country had exported to all the belligerent powers during the Great War, the end of which led to a loss of markets and the subsequent economic crisis. Socially and politically, the liberal regime of Monarchist Spain (1876–1931), headed by the Bourbons, showed itself to be incapable of integrating the increasingly important workers' organizations and would not or could not evolve towards a genuinely democratic system. In fact, the liberal regime underwent a period of deep crisis, which in turn led to the dictatorship of General Miguel Primo de Rivera (1923–30).

The complicity of the king, Alfonso XIII, with the dictator meant that, following the end of the dictatorship, the municipal elections became a plebiscite on the future of the political regime. The victory of Republican candidates in urban Spain revealed the extent of popular disaffection with the Monarchy and led to the coming of the Spanish Second Republic on 14 April 1931, which gained momentum as an attempt to modernize the country, not only economically and politically, but also socially and culturally. However, a variety of factors weakened the consolidation of the Republic: an unfavourable international situation made worse by the economic crisis of 1929 and the growing European political tension caused by the rise of the fascist movements, the resistance to change of traditional sectors of society, who still held economic power and control of the administration, all of this combined with the inability of the pro-Republican parties to agree a political agenda. The failed military uprising of 18 July 1936, in defence of traditional political interests, developed into a bitter civil war (1936–9), the eventual triumph of the rebel forces, and the almost 40 years of General Franco's dictatorship.

Although youth movements, especially those involving students, had their origins in the nineteenth century and the youth activism of the more economically and socially developed areas, such as Catalonia, in the latter part of that century,[4] it was only in the late 1920s and early 1930s that specifically youth-orientated organizations took shape. Until that time, they had lacked specific objectives and were merely tools of the political parties to which they were affiliated. However, the social and political mobilization of young people is a virtually unstudied topic in Spain. Young people, principally students, played an important role in the fall of the Primo de Rivera dictatorship. The coming of the Second Republic, with its aim to socially modernize and democratize the country, prompted the rise of new mass organizations and a general social and political mobilization concentrated in the youth movements. Finally, young people would play a vital role in the civil war itself, occupying important political and military office, especially in the Republican zone. The more hierarchical and regimented style of politics on the Francoist side made it more difficult for this to happen.

Given these circumstances it cannot be considered unusual that a generational school of thought, centred on the philosopher Jose Ortega y Gasset, arose in interwar Spain. This chapter will offer an analysis of the social and political mobilization of young people that occurred in Spain during that period, showing how this favoured the development of one of the first sociological theories on generations to exist in the social sciences. However, in my concluding reflections on the use of the concepts of generations in history, I will also point out the limitations of this theory.

Youth movements and political mobilization

The first signs of youth mobilization in Spain can be traced back to the consolidation of the liberal regime from the late 1860s onwards, and they were due primarily to the activities of university students. The first examples of youth movements that aimed to endure can be found at the beginning of the twentieth century. The Radical Republican Party was the first to design and develop a culture of mass political mobilization in an urban setting, mainly in Barcelona, the most developed and cosmopolitan city in Spain at that time. It placed great emphasis on youth activism, the occupation of urban space and the propagation of combat-based rhetoric. The 'young barbarians', as the party's youth organization became known, were at their strongest between 1906 and 1909. Their actions included low-level violence such as intimidating demonstrations, street brawls, physical attacks on newspaper offices, and assaults on opponents, especially during election campaigns or at times of great division between political parties.[5]

It was at this time, immediately before World War I, that Ortega first briefly approached the theme of generations. Although he did not manage to define them properly, he did distinguish within them 'individuals who enjoy social privileges' and the 'rabble'. He believed that generations could be 'historically condemned' if they did not undertake the tasks which had been assigned to them, and criticized the lack of political participation of the newer generations, that is, the young people of Spain.[6]

The economic growth caused by the Great War made possible an increase in the numbers of university students. The arrival in higher education of the children of the urban professional middle classes and small businessmen favoured the development of student organizations. However, it was during the dictatorship of General Primo de Rivera that students first noticeably became protagonists in political conflict. The debate on the freedom to teach without intervention by the Catholic Church caused a division between neutral students (that is, liberals) and Catholics. In 1927, the Federación Universitaria Escolar (Federation of University Students, FUE) was founded, which, in spite of describing itself as non-confessional and apolitical, took a liberal and socialist line and mobilized students against the dictatorship. The regime had already in 1924 set up the Juventudes de Unión Patriótica (Youth of the Patriotic Union, JUP) under the auspices of the dictator's party, the Unión Patriótica (Patriotic Union), itself an imitation of Italian fascism. However, the JUP was hardly a true youth organization, its student membership remained low, and its influence upon them was weak. The regime never granted the JUP autonomy and its failure to influence youth was clearly demonstrated by the student protests. These forced the dictatorship to consider ways of mobilizing the mass of young people. But it was already too late. In spite of its various declarations of good intentions, little was done to convert the JUP into an important organization within a national setting.[7]

The conflict in the Spanish universities, which broke out in 1928, was initially due to the suspension of the socialist professor, Luis Jimenez de Asúa. It intensified following the university reforms at the end of the same year, which gave Catholic colleges the right to issue university degrees. The repressive reaction of the dictatorship to the student protests caused them to spread from Madrid to other universities. The situation became serious enough to bring the closure of the universities for several weeks; faculty boards were shut, prominent professors were expelled, and the army occupied some colleges. The student protest became a political protest not only against the dictatorship, but also against the monarchy. The historians Javier Tusell and Genoveva García Queipo have stated that the student movement 'established an identification of the youngest generations with the patriarchs of the anti-dictatorship resistance'. Although the integration of the student movement into a wider political front caused it to lose its independence, it also radicalized intellectual protest and lent impetus to the anti-monarchist movement by opening it up to greater sections of Spanish society.[8]

As the historian Santos Juliá has stated, between 1925 and 1930 the intellectual sections of Spanish society were influenced by a group of young people born more or less at the turn of the century: Francisco Ayala, the poet Rafael Alberti, the Falangist politician Ramiro Ledesma, José Antonio Maravall, Pedro Laín, and Julián Marías. These men organized discussion circles in Madrid's cafes and were convinced that, following the fall of the dictatorship, 'pens should be at the service of ideas' although 'each one would choose his own way'.[9] Meanwhile, young workers' groups, the most important of which was the Socialist Youth Federation (FJS), the youth section of the Spanish Socialist Party (PSOE), were weak. After the internal crisis of the socialists between 1918 and 1920, the majority of the FJS had separated from the socialist movement to form the first communist party in Spanish history. Although the Spanish Communist Party (Partido Comunista de España, PCE) was minuscule during that period, the FJS was left as a shadow of its former self. The anarcho-syndicalist union, the CNT (National Confederation of Labour, Confederación Nacional del Trabajo), did not have an official youth section and its work suffered far greater repression.

In this period, distinguished Spanish intellectuals were calling upon the members of youth groups to be rebels, while the youth organizations themselves gave this conflict a generational character. In 1928, the prestigious doctor Gregorio Marañón wrote in *Renovación*, mouthpiece of socialist youth, that the 'fundamental duty' of the young was 'rebellion', while in 1929 Luis de Zulueta stated in the same publication that 'this is a time for the young', of whom he asked that they lead the way. It is not surprising that in 1929 the culturally important book series 'Biblioteca de la Revista de Occidente' published in Spanish Eduard Spranger's *Psychologie des Jugendalters*. The same year, Luis Jiménez de Asúa stated that 'the youth of Spain as a group are up in arms to reclaim [...] the helm of the national ship', although he also considered that adults with 'a juvenile impetus' should point out to young people their political goals, indicating the basis on which youth organizations would struggle against their adult counterparts across the political spectrum. Several days before the proclamation of the Second Republic, *Renovación* approached the problem in terms of generations: 'the young people of today have a historic mission to undertake: to lead the public along the true path, towards a revolution which goes further than the objectives of the bourgeois parties'.[10]

However, the youth organizations in general lacked truly youth-orientated objectives and a programme of demands of their own until the time of the Second Republic. This can be seen in the case of the FJS, which would include in its political agenda the right to vote from the age of 21, using as justification the role played by young people in the coming of the new regime (the Republican Constitution of December 1931 had established the right to vote at 23). The involvement of young people in anarchism pre-dated by many years the creation of an anarchist youth organization, which did not come about until 1932, with the foundation of the Iberian Federation of Libertarian Youth (Federación Ibérica de Juventudes Libertarias, FIJL). In spite of the continued presence of young people within the anarchist movement, there were no particular discourses directed specifically at them and orientated towards their objectives, problems, and characteristics until the Second Republic.[11]

As has already been stated, the coming of the Second Republic as a democratic regime favoured the rise in youth organizations, which played an important if not principal role in the social and political conflicts of the time and were in the forefront of new types of collective action. One of the most noticeable characteristics of Spanish political life during the 1930s was the development of specifically youth organizations connected to the main political parties. One example of the growth of these organizations is the case of the FJS, which went from 1500 registered members at its congress of 1929 to 12,000 at its fourth congress in 1932 and to more than 20,000 at its fifth (April 1934). Student groups of various shades of political opinion also appeared. In 1931, while the FUE was praised for its role in bringing about the Republican regime, the organization itself began to suffer from internal divisions. Within the FUE, republican, communist, and socialist students attempted to co-exist, which at times led to confrontation. The official recognition of the FUE by the regime meant that it was attacked by the right and entered into competition with organizations such as the Students' Association of the traditionalist monarchists or Carlists (Asociación de Estudiantes Tradicionalistas, AET), which had been created in the spring of 1930, and the SEU (Sindicato Español Universitario, Spanish University Union), created in 1933, which was affiliated to the Spanish Falange (Falange Española, FE), founded by José Antonio Primo de Rivera.[12]

In general, all of the political parties maintained difficult and conflictual relationships with their youth organizations, as they found themselves obliged to support young people's activism while at the same time trying to avoid granting them full participation in the real political decision-making process.[13] Practically all the youth organizations went through a process of radicalization which led them to adopt more extremist attitudes than their respective parties and to attempt to widen their independence from these organizations. This is what happened in the main Catholic political organization of the Republican years, the Spanish Confederation of Right-Wing Groups (Confederación Española de Derechas Autónomas, CEDA), whose youth organization, Juventudes de Acción Popular (JAP), adopted an antidemocratic position similar to that of the fascists and reproduced their imagery. The activities of the JAP centred on propaganda and demonstrations in places famed for their historic value which could evoke past national and imperial glories. The most important was a celebration on 22 April 1934 near the El Escorial Monastery, although throughout the following year more were to take place in other famous sites, such as Santiago de Compostela. The JAP also organized the mobilization of members and sympathizers to face the consequences of labour and political strikes. In February 1934, the JAP undertook the creation of a section for 'civil mobilization' to 'provide public services needed by the people' in the possible case of a national strike.[14]

Relations between the PSOE and the FJS were also a constant cause of conflict, made worse by the internal divisions of the Spanish socialist movement in this period and by the demands of the youth section not only for autonomy but also for the right to speak in their own name and put forward their own point of view in the socialist movement as a whole.[15] On the pages of *Renovación*, socialist youth rejected the idea that they were a 'subordinate body' of the PSOE: they were its 'shock troops' while the party stuck to a left socialist line, but if the PSOE 'went off' that line, they 'would not consider themselves to have any obligation to the party'. *Renovación* stated that every generation 'is assigned a role in history' and that the 'new Spanish generation', precisely because of its youth, 'has to be the vanguard of the revolution'. In this way, the Federation of Socialist Youth converted itself into the spearhead of the radicalization that the socialist movement underwent in this period, both in theory and in practice.[16]

The youth organizations of the left republican parties, Republican Youth Action (Juventud de Accion Republicana) and Independent Radical Socialist Youth (Juventud Radical Socialista Independiente), complained on 4 November 1933 about 'the anti-Republican and anti-patriotic policies' of the new conservative government then in power, and expressed their readiness to take to the streets 'united with the proletariat', because 'if the dilemma is between fascism and social revolution, we will shout with all our force and enthusiasm, "Long live social revolution!".' Some anarchist leaders, such as Manuel Buenacasa, also identified the most radical elements of the CNT ('faístas') with young people, while the more moderate (called 'syndicalists') were the older members. Scholarship has shown that this difference really existed, at least among the leaders.[17]

As in other parts of Europe, the use of violence was a salient feature of political mobilization during the Second Republic. Violence was seen as another instrument to achieve political and social objectives, and was utilized as much by working-class organizations as by sections of the traditionally dominant classes. It gained adherents in all parts of the political spectrum except the republican bourgeoisie. Young people, as protagonists in violent actions up to the beginning of the Civil War, played a major part in this process. This led the Republican government to forbid party membership for the under-16s and to demand that those under 23 obtain their parents' permission.[18] The public justification offered for this decree indicates the intensity reached by youth violence in this period. It contained a list of politically motivated violent incidents in Madrid involving young people from 1 January 1934 until the passing of the decree. Among those aged between 15 and 24, there were 13 dead and 31 wounded. The prominent role of students in violent direct action was also clear: eight of the wounded and five of the dead were students, and these figures could possibly be an underestimate, since many people among those listed lacked any indication of occupation. Incidents between members of the FUE and members of the SEU were frequent. Student groups also included those in secondary education, so secondary schools, in addition to FUE centres and Madrid University faculties, became battlegrounds in this period. Although Madrid, as the main Spanish university centre, was at the forefront of these incidents, violence also broke out in other Spanish universities such as Zaragoza and Seville.[19]

In February 1934, the Spanish Falange joined forces with the other Spanish fascist group, the Juntas de Ofensiva Nacional Sindicalista (JONS), run by Onesimo Redondo, giving rise to the Falange Española de las JONS. Yet, although Spanish fascism had since its beginning had a particularly strong youth orientation, its membership was no more than 2000 by the end of 1933 and one year later had hardly reached 5000. (It is quite possible that this figure would be three times higher if under-21s were included.) In May 1934, the traditionalist monarchists reorganized their youth sections, concentrating them in a Special Youth Delegation, which also included the AET. From this moment, the militant activism of these youth sections became undeniable, as did their direct participation in the acts of violence which would lead to the anti-Republican military uprising and the Civil War.[20]

The internal political crisis of mid-1933 coincided with an economic crisis and the rise of European fascist movements. The breakdown of the Republican–Socialist alliance and the subsequent triumph of the Right in the 1933 elections meant the end of the reforms of the first two years. The defeat of the Austrian Social Democratic Party – along with its German equivalent, which had served as a model for interwar European socialists – in their belated attempt to counteract the authoritarianism of Dollfuss in February 1934, was the final straw needed to convince many workers' groups that bourgeois democracy was incapable of stopping fascism. The common vision of a 'fascist danger', along with the struggle of members of the Spanish Falange and other right-wing groups against the young workers' organizations, led to calls for unity of action among the latter. However, numerous divisions remained. In addition to socialist and anarchist youth groupings, the Left was represented by the Communist Youth Union of Spain (Unión de Juventudes Comunistas de España, UJCE), the youth organization of the Comintern-affiliated Spanish Communist Party, and the smaller youth sections of the Trotskyist organization. In September 1934, the clearest understanding appeared to be between the FJS and the UJCE, but the only palpable events they had managed to organize together were the funerals of young activists killed by the rightist groups (the Socialist Juanita Rico and the Communist Joaquín de Grado), as well as some joint meetings against government resolutions or against right-wing rallies. This rapprochement was, moreover, achieved despite the official positions taken by the respective parties (which included rejection of the PSOE).[21]

Party militias were one of the most novel and widespread political phenomena of the period. They were to be found as much among monarchist and fascist groups as among Catalan and Basque nationalists, socialists, and communists (although they were rejected by both the JAP and the anarchists), and young people played an important role in them.[22] Just as political violence was not exclusively Spanish and took place in the context of the new-style militaristic mass politics that arose in interwar Europe, so the prominence of youth in Spanish politics had parallels elsewhere. Many historians have drawn attention to the continuous confrontations between young Nazis and Communists in Germany, where approximately 84 per cent of those arrested for political violence in Berlin between 1929 and 1932 were below 30, and more than a third of those were under 21. Of similar importance was the participation of the young in the Austrian Socialist Militia, the *Schutzbund* (the Republican Defence Corps), and in the Vienna insurrection of 1934.[23]

The most important militia milestone in Spain before the Civil War was the workers' uprising of 1934. The new government formed in October of that year included three ministers from the CEDA, a party that had never officially recognized the legitimacy of the Republic and had praised fascist regimes in its publications and speeches. This led to calls for a general strike, which developed into insurrection in some regions and a true social revolution in the northern mining area of Asturias. The role of the young in the insurrection was of great importance. Salazar Alonso, Home Office Minister until October 1934, noted the role of the Socialist Youth in the conflicts of the summer of 1934 and in the events of October. The socialist leader, Luis Araquistain, also wrote that 'the revolution was the work of proletarian youth. A majority of adult party leaders withdrew from the movement or were swept along in the wake of the youngsters'. The socialist militias that took part in the events of October 1934 could not have been formed without the participation of the young. *Renovación*, the newspaper of the Socialist Youth, became a source of information on the organization of the militias and the insurrection. The socialist militias of Madrid were also mainly composed of young people, and it was they who, in the absence of party coordination and direction, took part in the most important acts of violence and took the lead in Madrid. However, it was also mainly the young people who brought about the social reaction against the workers' mobilization. In Madrid, the authorities gave the youth sections of the right and centre-right parties control of supplies to hospitals, old people's homes and orphanages, and markets, and during the days of the strike these sections helped to run the trams, supply provisions, and make bread. The newspapers published during that time were sold by young people, who were sympathetic to their political stance. On 13 October 1934, the pro-monarchist paper *ABC* wrote that 'a large part of the young gentry, who are selflessly taking on the possible risk of losing their lives for the country, have come out on to the streets when the fear of the majority has left them deserted, and have done their civic duty with exemplary enthusiasm'.[24]

The joint participation in the mobilization of October 1934 of different workers' youth organizations and the great repression which followed it, which left many of their leaders in prison, also helped to bring them together as they fought for an amnesty for political prisoners. These factors speeded up the process of rapprochement between the UJCE and the FJS, who from November 1934 established a National Liaison Committee and regional and local liaison committees, while in January 1935 rupture occurred between the FJS and the Trotskyist youth organizations. Although the FJS and the UJCE met with representatives of the FIJL to organize a joint campaign for the freeing of political prisoners, and although the leadership of the FIJL defended their participation, its regional sections rejected it. In spite of the numerous ups and downs in relations between the FJS and the UJCE, the mainly clandestine propaganda activities were undertaken as a joint venture by the two organizations at both local and national levels. In spite of orders received from the leaders of the PSOE and their union, propaganda touched just as much on themes related to the post-October 1934 repression as it did more general questions such as the meetings of the JAP or the Italian occupation of Abyssinia. *Joven Guardia*, mouthpiece of the UJCE, drew attention to the many propaganda tasks that had been completed 'since the beginning ... on the basis of the united front with the Young Socialists'.[25]

Although the youth sections were important for mobilizing in favour of an amnesty during 1935, their role in the process of forming the Popular Front (the centre-left coalition which won the elections of February 1936), and in the choice of the different candidates put forward for those elections, was rather limited. Some leaders of the main youth organizations were included on the lists of candidates: for example, Trifón Medrano, Secretary of the UJCE, was a candidate for the Popular Front in Ciudad Real, Carlos Hernández Zancajo, President of the FJS, featured in the city district of Madrid, and Prudencio Sayagués, President of the Left Republican Youth (Juventud de Izquierda Republicana, JIR) took part in Huelva. Although it is difficult, if not impossible, to measure the youth vote, it must have been important for the victory of the Popular Front given that the Spanish population was characterized by its youth. For example, Hernández Zancajo was the socialist candidate in Madrid who received the most votes after the two heavyweights, Julián Besteiro and Luis Jiménez de Asúa, and received more votes than any other socialist left-wing candidate.[26]

The process of unification between the young socialists and young communists was completed with the signing by both organizations of an agreement that gave rise to the Unified Socialist Youth (JSU) in March 1936. The spring of 1936 also saw the creation of a Youth Front

(Frente de la Juventud), which linked the united youth organization with the different progressive Republican youth organizations: the JIR, the Republican Union Youth (Juventud de Unión Republicana, JUR), the Federal Left Youth (Juventud de Izquierda Federal, JIF), the Radical Socialist Youth, and the FUE. This umbrella organization would form the basis of the Anti-Fascist Youth Alliance (Alianza Juvenil Antifascista, AJA), which would be founded in the Republican zone during the Civil War. Meanwhile, on the Right, the electoral disaster suffered by CEDA caused the mass defection of the most radical members of the JAP (estimated at between 10,000 and 15,000) to the theoretically more combative Spanish Falange, leaving the Catholic conservative youth organization almost nonexistent immediately before the outbreak of the Civil War.[27]

Young people played a tremendously important role in the Republican war effort, and their mobilization was principally undertaken by the JSU and the FIJL. Although this youth participation has not been pointed out by many historians,[28] the contemporaries of these young people were more than conscious of it, starting with the very same youth organizations who asserted the role of young people in the failure of the military uprising of July 1936. They especially insisted on the importance of the young in the Republican Army and in the war leadership. On 22 October 1936, no fewer than ten leaders of the JSU were included in the Republican General Staff, and this youth organization stated at its conference in 1937 that, of its 300,000 members, 150,000 were members of the Republican Popular Army.[29] It was also the JSU who came up with the initiative of pre-military education for young people aged between 14 and 20 through the *Alerta!* organization, with the objective of preparing adolescents for the army. Later, the FIJL also joined this initiative when both organizations, together with the republican youth sections, formed the Anti-Fascist Youth Alliance (AJA) in August 1937.[30] The JSU also demanded new rights for young people, the majority of which were adopted by the AJA upon its foundation. These included the fight against illiteracy in rural areas, the equality of women, maternity leave funded by the state, and political and union rights for over-18s, including members of the armed forces.[31]

The clearly hierarchical and militaristic structures created by the Francoists at the very beginning of the uprising did not allow the young to take on such a central role in their organization. However, it has been claimed that numerous young people played a part in the Fifth Column and at the war's end many were given official positions 'if not of importance, at least of some influence'. This would explain why in 1940 a young intellectual such as Dionisio Ridruejo could demand power for his generation, which had not only fought the war but also 'provoked it, understanding its deepest reasons and embodying all of its revolutionary dimensions'. The Francoist state systematically dismantled the left youth organizations in a decree issued on 13 September 1936, which declared illegal all political organizations of the Popular Front. The unity of the right-wing parties and their associated organizations was forced upon them by the Decree of Unification of 19 April 1937, which led to the creation of Falange Española Tradicionalista y de las JONS and designated the Youth Organization as one of the 'national services' of the new one-party state. The SEU, the AET, and other student associations of the right were officially integrated into a unified SEU on 12 October 1937. Finally, the founding law of the Young People's Front (Frente de Juventudes) on 6 December 1940 was the final step towards bureaucratizing and establishing state control over Spanish youth.[32]

Historical reality and sociological thought

Although the term 'generation' dates back to the ancient Greeks and the Bible, theorizing about generation started in earnest at a time when Europe, including Spain, was in a state of economic and socio-political crisis, and youth was mobilized to an unprecedented degree. Contemporary observers of the interwar period frequently pointed out the activism of the 'younger generations'. As the French socialist leader Léon Blum stated, 'it was an age in which everyone assumed the right to speak in the name of youth, in which everyone tried to attract the young ... It seems that it is their approval, their participation, upon which success is based today: for a party, for an idea or for a social formation'.[33]

The two most important theories to come out of interwar Europe were those of the Spaniard José Ortega y Gasset and the Hungarian Karl Mannheim. Since that time, all explanations as to the growth of generations emphasize the important role played by adolescence and the early years of adulthood in the acquisition of a self-identity by members of different generations, which are defined as 'a group of people who being contemporaries and coevals present a certain relationship of co-existence, that is, they have common interests, analogical preoccupations or similar circumstances'. A generation agglutinates during its youth but generally has force in adult life.[34]

José Ortega y Gasset developed his theory in various studies, the most outstanding of which are *El tema de nuestro tiempo* (known in English as *The Modern Theme*), published in 1923 as an extension of the inaugural lecture of the 1921–2 year, and *En torno a Galileo. Esquema de la crisis* (translated as *Man and Crisis*), based upon a series of 12 lectures given in 1933 in the Central University of Madrid.[35] Although the theories of Ortega had their followers in the 1940s, especially Pedro Laín Entralgo and Julián Marías, they have never given rise to a sociological school of generations.

The main reasons for this can be found in the limitations of these theories and in the political and historical context in which they were developed. As Antonio Elorza has observed, the concept of generations allowed Ortega 'to express the intensity of the failure he identified in the years immediately before', as he felt himself to be a member of the type of generation whose principal feature was nothing other than 'to have failed in its historical duty', because it had not completed its social mission. For Elorza, Ortega was reflecting his feeling of helplessness in the face of the Spanish economic, social, and political crisis.[36] For his followers, the theory of generations opened up a form of reflection on their own life experience in the dark social and political setting of 1940s Spain, the hardest years of the Francoist dictatorship. As C. Feixa has analysed, for young Spaniards of the 1930s, the Civil War became the 'generational event' *par excellence.* However, the interviews undertaken by that same author show that the assessments those young people make with hindsight are contradictory. On the one hand, they emphasize that they became adults far too quickly, while, on the other, they have a positive image which emphasizes the value of emancipation from family and social control, of solidarity and direct participation.[37] One of the main problems caused by applying the concept of generation to any age group is that the members of a cohort never form a homogeneous whole. Rather, age groups reflect the economic, social, and political divisions that already exist in society.[38] Outstanding historical events affect all members of the age group experiencing their formative years, but in different ways.

However, Ortega and his most direct followers, Pedro Laín Entralgo and Julián Marías, saw generations not as collective subjects but as historical agents structured according to Ortega's favourite dichotomy: the 'minority' versus the 'masses'. 'Select individuals' were deemed to establish a clear relationship of domination over the 'rabble'.[39]

For Ortega, generations are the engine of history, and he believes that each one has a particular mission to perform, although at times that mission is not completed. Ortega's vision can be summed up in the words with which he defined a generation: 'a new type of integral social body, with its select minority and its masses, which has been thrown across the backdrop of existence on an already determined life path. The generation, a dynamic compromise between the mass and the individual, is the most important concept in history and, so to speak, the hinge upon which history makes its movements.'[40]

Even less coherent is the manner in which Ortega proposed to distinguish between generations: the prime indicator was the date when the person considered 'eponymous for a generation' was at the age of 30, although he did not specify how to identify such outstanding individuals. Once this key point of reference had been established, Ortega argued, other dates could be found to form 'the centre of the date zone which corresponds to each generation. Therefore, those people who celebrated their thirtieth birthday seven years before or seven years after that date belonged to that generation.' Nor does the idea of his follower, Julián Marías, to draw up lists of outstanding generational 'representatives' seem much of an improvement.[41]

Karl Mannheim thought of generations as possessing a distinct collective character. His more nuanced sociological approach was totally opposed to the elitist bias of Ortega and enabled him to develop the more refined analytical tool of 'generational units'.[42] Mannheim further contrasts with Ortega because he denied that the generational factor was decisive in history. He based his ideas on the 'accidental' character of generational movements and at the same time pointed out the existence of inter- and intragenerational conflicts.[43] However, John Hood-Williams, considers that 'the generational units are, as likely as not, non-generational since shared belief systems separate generations as is recognized and unite members of different age groups. With this criteria it is difficult to see what the "concrete bond" of the generation as actuality might consist of'. One of the principal problems of the concept of generations since its origins is that it has been given so many different meanings: kinship, cohort, life stage, historical period, and so on. For David Kertzer, the majority of studies on generational conflicts are really discussing relationships between people in different life stages. Annie Kriegel argues that 'a generation could only be the sum of all those who reach the same age or the same seniority at the same time; thus the concept of generation should be biased towards the mass, individualized only by age or by seniority', which in practice means that it is a 'fundamentally elitist' concept, and that the generation 'is only constituted when a system of collective references has retrospectively been set up and accepted as a system of collective identification' and its leaders chosen to represent their contemporaries.[44] However, all European countries, including Spain, are marked by the long shadow of missing war generations, which could be one of the reasons why this concept is so attractive.

In the words of Hans Jaeger, 'the ideological split among the young generation, which the First World War brought about, and the gross political contrasts within the same generation during the Weimar period' in Germany, and we could add in Spain, indicate conclusively that 'a massive uniform imprint during the formative years does not have to lead to the establishment of a generational community'. There may be a uniform context in the sense of a community of contemporaries facing common problems, but this does not amount to a generational unity whose members will put forward uniform solutions to these problems.[45]

All of this gives greater importance to forms of analysis that focus on psychological and social characteristics and distinguish, in each historical period and society, different age groups. That is, the term 'age cohort' is more useful epistemologically than that of generation, and age or generation is just one more type of social classification, given that social reality is almost always complex and difficult to understand. In spite of the fact that 'the world is different for persons of different age and generation, even if they share in common, sex, class and nationality and occupation', members of particular cohorts are still differentiated from each other by their geographical location, their position in the social hierarchy, their gender or race. The notion of a generational 'gap' was announced loudly by *Renovación*, the mouthpiece of the Federation of Socialist Youth, in March 1936: 'we are bothered by the old, especially because they feel the undeniable obligation to instruct and advise us, in the belief that all their advice has the obvious virtue of being correct, while just as obviously all the opinions of the young are wrong'.[46] Four months later, however, the young socialists would be fighting alongside these 'old people' and against other people, both young and not so young, in a vicious civil war.

This does not mean that the generation concept is devoid of value in historical inquiry. To specify generations is no more arbitrary than to specify social classes, ideologies, or political movements. When we suspect that age differences are historically important, we can mark out age groups from the chronological continuum to see whether observations about their collective behaviour and their relations with other groups are useful in explaining historical phenomena.[47]

Notes

This work has been made possible by my participation in the research project 'Grupos profesionales, corporativismo y políticas sectoriales del Estado durante la Dictadura de Primo de Rivera, 1923–1930' and to a contract from the Consejo Superior de Investigaciones Científicas (Higher Council for Scientific Research, CSIC), Spain. I would also like to say thank you to Jill Parsons for her help with the translation of this article from Spanish into English.

1. C. Wallace and S. Kovatcheva, *Youth in Society. The Construction and Deconstruction of Youth in East and Western Europe* (Basingstoke, 1998), pp. 11–13; M. Mitterauer, *A History of Youth* (Oxford, 1992), pp. 86–7; A. Soto Carmona, *El trabajo industrial en la España Contemporánea (1876–1936)* (Barcelona, 1989), p. 702.

2. See, for example, the studies of different European countries in B. Bianchi and M. Fincardi (eds), 'Giovani e ordine sociale', *Storia e problemi contemporanei*, 27 (2001), 7–202, Commission Internationale d´Histoire des Mouvements Sociaux et des Structures Sociales, *La jeunesse et ses mouvements. Influence sur l'évolution des sociétés aux XIXe et XXe siècles* (Paris, 1992), and D. Dowe (ed.), *Jugendprotest und Generationenkonflikt in Europa im 20. Jahrhundert. Deutschland, England, Frankreich und Italien im Vergleich* (Bonn, 1986). See also P. Dogliani, *Storia dei Giovani* (Milan, 2003). A synthesis of the evolution of youth movements in interwar Europe can be seen in S. Souto Kustrín, '"El mundo ha llegado a ser consciente de su juventud como nunca antes": Juventud y movilización política en la Europa de entreguerras', *Mélanges de la Casa de Velázquez*, 34 (2004), 179–215.

3. R.G. Braungart, 'Historical Generations and Youth Movements: A Theoretical Perspective', *Research in Social Movements, Conflict and Change*, 6 (1984), 95–142, here 130.

4. G. Samper i Triedu, *La Joventut fa Catalunya. 1900–1985. Aproximació a la història de les associacions de Joves* (Barcelona, 1987), pp. 30–6.

5. J.B. Cullá i Clara, *El republicanisme lerrouxista a Catalunya (1901–1923)* (Barcelona, 1986), pp. 139–55, and idem, 'Ni tan jóvenes, ni tan bárbaros. Las juventudes en el republicanismo lerrouxista barcelonés', *Ayer*, 59/3 (2005), 51–67.

6. 'Vieja y nueva política', lecture given on 23 March 1914, in J. Ortega y Gasset, *Obras Completas*, vol. 1 (Madrid, 1966), pp. 265–307, especially pp. 270–3.

7. A. Quiroga, 'Perros de paja: las Juventudes de la Unión Patriótica', *Ayer*, 59/3 (2005), 69–96. The organization which should properly be called the Federal Union of Hispanic Students (Unión Federal de Estudiantes Hispanos, UFEH) was based on student unions within each faculty, which were coordinated in each university district by the FUEs, which in turn were coordinated nationally in the UFEH: see R. Casterás Archidona, *Diccionario de organizaciones políticas juveniles durante la Segunda República* (La Laguna, 1974), p. 50. However, the name FUE was more commonly used.

8. E. González Calleja, 'Rebelión en las aulas: un siglo de movilizaciones estudiantiles en España (1865–1968)', *Ayer*, 59/3 (2005), 21–49; S. Ben-Ami, 'La Rebellion universitaire en Espagne, 1927–1931', *Revue d'Histoire Moderne et Contemporaine*, 26 (1979), 365–90; S. Ben-Ami, 'Los estudiantes contra el Rey.

Papel de la F.U.E. en la caída de la dictadura y la proclamación de la República', Historia, 16/6 (1976), 37–47; J. Tusell and G. García Queipo de Llano, *Los intelectuales y la República* (Madrid, 1990), p. 59.

9. S. Juliá, 'Ser intelectual y ser joven, en Madrid, hacia 1930', *Historia Contemporánea*, 27 (2003), 749–75, quote on 775.

10. Renovación, 15 March 1928, 2, and 15 March 1929, 8; *Juventud. Conferencia de Luis Jiménez de Asúa y réplica de José López Rey* (Madrid, 1929), pp. 28, 17. *Renovación,* 20 February 1931, 1; E. Spranger, *Psicología de la edad juvenil* (Madrid, 1929).

11. S. Souto Kustrín, 'Entre el Parlamento y la calle: políticas gubernamentales y organizaciones juveniles en la Segunda República', *Ayer*, 59/3 (2005), 97–122; S. Tavera, 'Escola de Rebellia. La joventut i l'anarcosindicalisme', in E. Ucelay da Cal, *La joventut a Catalunya al segle XX. Materials per a una historia* (Barcelona, 1987), vol. 1, pp. 138–51.

12. Federación de Juventudes Socialistas, *Memoria del IV Congreso* (Madrid, 1932), p. 6, and *Memoria del V Congreso* (Madrid, 1934), p. 13; M.A. Ruiz Carnicer, 'Estudiantes, cultura y violencia política en las universidades españoles (1925–1975)', in J. Muñoz, J. L. Ledesma, and J. Rodrigo (eds), *Culturas y políticas de la violencia. España en el siglo XX* (Madrid, 2005).

13. I analyse only the main Spanish youth organizations, leaving aside the question of young people's political participation in Basque and Catalan nationalisms, although in both cases the number of young people and their political role would be important. The youth organization of the Basque Nationalist Party (Partido Nacionalista Vasco, PNV) would always be more dependent upon the party than the youth section of the Catalan Republican Left (Esquerra Republicana de Catalunya, ERC). See E. Ucelay da Cal, 'Violencia simbólica y temática militarista en el nacionalismo radical catalán', in *Ayer*, 13 (1994), 237–64, here 239; J. L. de la Granja, *El nacionalismo vasco: un siglo de historia* (Madrid, 1995), 157.

14. About the JAP, see J. R. Montero, *La CEDA. El catolicismo social y político en la Segunda República* (Madrid, 1977), vol. 1, pp. 582–656; E. González Calleja and F. del Rey Reguillo, *La defensa armada contra la revolución. Una historia de las 'guardias cívicas' en la España del siglo XX* (Madrid, 1995), p. 237; and J. M. Báez, 'El ruido y las nueces: la Juventud de Acción Popular y la movilización "cívica" católica durante la Segunda República', *Ayer*, 59/3 (2005), 123–45.

15. The political differences within the PSOE – the party that was the main support of the Republican government between 1931 and 1933 – and its union, the General Workers' Union (Unión General de Trabajadores, UGT), were apparent from the early days of the Second Republic but became more pronounced after the electoral defeat of the centre-left in November 1933. The Spanish socialist movement was divided into three factions. Firstly, a right wing that was hostile to the idea of revolutionary insurrection. Secondly, a centrist faction that supported a new left republican–socialist alliance, which they saw as the best means of ensuring the implementation, in a more thoroughgoing fashion, of the legislative reforms attempted between 1931 and 1933. Finally, a left-wing group who talked of social revolution and the dictatorship of the proletariat. See, for example, M. Bizcarrondo, 'Democracia y revolución en la estrategia socialista de la

Segunda República', *Estudios de Historia Social*, Madrid, 16–17 (1981), 227–461, passim.

16. *Renovación*, 11 November 1933, 1 and 3. See also 9 December 1933, 2, and 18 April 1934, 1. I have analysed the role of socialist youth in this radicalization in S. Souto Kustrín, 'Taking the Streets: Workers' Youth Organizations and Conflicts in the Spanish Second Republic', *European History Quarterly, 34 (2004), 131–56*, and *Y ¿Madrid? ¿Qué hace Madrid? Movimiento revolucionario y acción colectiva (1933–1936)* (Madrid, 2004), passim.

17. Archivo Histórico Nacional, Audiencia Territorial de Madrid, Criminal (Spanish National Archive, Madrid Province Courts of Justice, criminal section [hereafter, AHN, ATM, Cr.]), box 205/1, court number 18, summary 349/33; S. Tavera, 'Escola de Rebellia', 142–3.

18. The decree can be seen in *El Sol*, 29 August 1934, 4. In the 1930s, 15- to 24-year-olds formed the largest Spanish age group: see J. López Santamaría, 'Les joventuts llibertaries durant la guerra civil', in E. Ucelay da Cal, *La joventut a Catalunya*, pp. 152–67, here p. 153.

19. In a congress held in Seville in March 1934, the FUE declared itself antifascist: see M. F. Mancebo, 'Una élite estudiantil: los primeros congresos de la Unión de Estudiantes Hispanos (UFEH)', *in Les élites espagnoles à l'époque contemporaine* (Pau, 1982), pp. 362–93. Incidents were also common between worker youth groups and members of rightist youth organizations or the police: examples included the clashes in Madrid on 10 June 1934, which resulted in several dead and wounded, and led the Home Office to forbid groups with political insignia and to set up checkpoints in Madrid, especially on bank holidays: see *El Socialista* (mouthpiece of the PSOE) and *El Sol*, 12 June 1934, 2.

20. S.G. Payne *Falange: Historia del fascismo español* (Madrid, 1985), pp. 89ff. See also the memoirs of the Carlist J. del Burgo, *Conspiración y Guerra Civil* (Madrid and Barcelona, 1970).

21. I have analysed in detail the debate between the different youth organizations in Souto Kustrín, *Y ¿Madrid? ¿Qué hace Madrid?*, pp. 86–101; some of the joint actions are discussed on pp. 125–68.

22. See the various articles in J. Aróstegui (ed.), 'La militarización de la política durante la Segunda República', *Historia Contemporánea*, 11 (1994).

23. E. Rosenhaft, *Beating the Fascists? The German Communists and Political Violence 1929–1933* (Cambridge, 1983), p. 193; C. Jeffery, *Social Democracy in the Austrian Provinces, 1918–1934: Beyond Red Vienna* (London and Cranbury, 1995), pp. 208–9.

24. AA. VV., *Octubre 1934. Cincuenta años para la reflexión* (Madrid, 1985); R. Salazar Alonso, *Bajo el signo de la revolución* (Madrid, 1935), p. 227; L. Araquistain, 'La revolución española de Octubre', in AA. VV., *La revolución española de Octubre* (Santiago, 1935), pp. 19–20; Souto Kustrín, *Y ¿Madrid? ¿Qué hace Madrid?*, pp. 169–287.

25. Proceedings of the meeting on 1 November between the FJS and the UJCE, Fundación Pablo Iglesias (Archives of the Pablo Iglesias Foundation), Mixed Archives, CV-18; *Boletin Interior de la JCE-ICE*, 25 April 1935, 11–13. AHN, ATM (Cr.), box 1/1, court no. 20, summary 174/35; box 230/1, court no. 6, summary 274/35. *Octubre*, underground newspaper of the FJS, 3 (1935), 2; *Joven Guardia*, 6 (1935), 7, and 7 (1935), 3; Archivo Histórico del

Partido Comunista de España (Spanish Communist Party Historical Archive), film XIII (165) and film IX (125). *Joven Guardia*, 2 (1935), 7. The repression also affected the FUE, whose centres were closed and official status removed.

26. *Mundo Obrero*, 15 February 1936, 4. The joint propaganda undertaken by the leaderships of the FJS and the UJCE is listed in a joint comunicado signed by both organizations published in *Mundo Obrero*, 4 February 1936, 4. *Boletín Oficial de la Provincia de Madrid*, 18 February 1936, supplement to issue 42, 17. The JIR was formed in 1934 by the merger of the Republican Youth Action (Juventud de Accion Republicana) and the Independent Radical Socialist Youth (Juventud Radical Socialista Independiente).

27. R. Viñas, *La formación de las Juventudes Socialistas Unificadas (1934–1936)* (Madrid, 1978), passim; *Mundo Obrero* (newspaper of the PCE), 26 February 1936, 4, and 21 April 1936, 4; *Juventud. Diario de la Juventud en Armas* (mouthpiece of the JSU), Madrid, 28 October 1936, 4; S.G. Payne, *Falange*, p. 120.

28. Among the exceptions are the British historian Helen Graham (*The Spanish Republic at War* (Cambridge, 2002), p. 176), who considers the JSU to be one of the principal sources of the PCE's strategy of permanent mass mobilization during the Civil War.

29. See *Juventud*, mouthpiece of the JSU, 28 October 1936, 4; *Tierra y Libertad*, anarchist newspaper, August 1936, reproduced in E. Ucelay da Cal, *La joventut a Catalunya al segle XX*, vol. 2, p. 175; *Octubre*, newspaper of the JSU, 5 September 1936, 1; *Juventud*, 22 October 1936, 1. Archivo General de la Guerra Civil (Spanish Civil War Archive, Political and Social Section, Extremadura Region (PS Extremadura)), box 3, file 7, Minutes of the Conferencia Nacional de la Juventud (National Youth Conference), undertaken by the JSU, p. 1; F. Muñoz Arconada, *La juventud en la defensa de Madrid* (Madrid, 1937), p. 19.

30. *Ahora*, newspaper of the JSU, 8 January 1937, 4–5; Juventudes Libertarias. Comité Regional de Centro, *Rutas juveniles* (Madrid, 1937), passim; *Ahora*, 2 September 1937, 3–4.

31. JSU, *Las diez reivindicaciones de la juventud* (Valencia, n.d.); *Ahora*, 25 June 1937, 3 and 6, and 27 June 1937, 4–5. This newspaper insisted on 18 July 1937, 4, that 'Spanish young people, with a great sense of their sacrifice, must be considered. Their civil and political rights must be recognized'. The Republican Association Law of 8 April 1932 stated that the union committee members must be aged over 21: see A. Martín Valverde et al., *La legislación social en la Historia de España. De la revolución liberal a 1936* (Madrid, 1987), p. 739.

32. V. Alba, *Historia social de la Juventud* (Barcelona, 1979), p. 190. The importance of the role of the young in the Madrid Fifth Column is evident, even if the author does not emphasize it, in J. Cervera, *Madrid en guerra. La ciudad clandestina, 1936–1939* (Madrid, 1998). D. Ridruejo, *Arriba*, newspaper of the unified Falange, 5 May 1940, quoted in I. Saz, *España contra España. Los nacionalismos franquistas* (Madrid, 2003), p. 300. The Francoist organization of youth from above is analysed in J. Sáez Marín, *El Frente de Juventudes. Política de juventud en la España de la postguerra (1937–1960)* (Madrid, 1988).

33. In the nineteenth century, several researchers adopted the concept of generations to define literary or artistic phenomena: see P. Laín Entralgo, *Las generaciones en la historia* (Madrid, 1945), pp. 207ff. On the situation in the 1930s, see W. T. Winslow, *Youth. A World Problem. A Study in World Perspective of Youth Conditions, Movements and Programs*, (Washington, 1937); S. Neumann, 'The Conflict of Generations in Contemporary Europe: From Versailles to Munich', *Vital Speeches of the Day*, 5/20 (1 August 1939), 623–8. The quotation is from L. Blum, *La Jeunesse et le socialisme. Conférence prononcée le 30 Juin 1934* (Paris, 1936), p. 3.

34. An overview of the different theories of generations and their problems can be found in H. Jaeger, 'Generations in History: Reflections on a Controversial Concept', *History and Theory*, 24/3 (1985), 273–92. The definition of generations is taken from J. Zarco and A. Orueta, 'La idea de generación: una revisión crítica', *Sistema*, 144 (1998), 107–14, here 109; the role of the early adult years is discussed in the same article, 112. Note also P. Laín Entralgo, *Las generaciones*, p. 309, and J. Marías y M. Rintala, 'Generaciones', in *Enciclopedia Internacional de las Ciencias sociales*, vol. 5 (Madrid, 1975), pp. 88–94, here p. 92.

35. Editions used for this work: *El tema de nuestro tiempo* (Madrid, 1988) and *En torno a Galileo. Esquema de la crisis* (Madrid, 1965).

36. A. Elorza, *La razón y la sombra. Una lectura política de Ortega y Gasset* (Barcelona, 1984), pp. 137–8.

37. C. Feixa, *La ciutat llunyana. Una història oral de la joventut de Lleida (1931–1945)* (Lleida, 1993), pp. 6, 11–12.

38. See, for example, P. Bourdieu, 'La « jeunesse » n'est qu'un mot', in P. Bourdieu, *Questions de Sociologie* (Paris, 1980), pp. 143–54, and Wallace and Kovatcheva, *Youth in Society*, pp. 19–20, 34, who also point out other social differences, such as gender and race.

39. Ortega y Gasset, *El tema de nuestro tiempo*, p. 57, and P. Laín Entralgo, *Las generaciones*, pp. 295, 305.

40. Ortega y Gasset, *El tema de nuestro tiempo*, 57. P. Laín Entralgo, *Las generaciones*, p. 329, disagreed with his master and denied that generations are fundamental units for historical change.

41. J. Ortega y Gasset, *En torno a Galileo. Esquema de la crisis*, pp. 70–1. J. Marías, *El método histórico de las generaciones* (1949), in idem, *Obras*, vol. 6 (Madrid, 1970), pp. 13–172, here pp. 141ff.

42. On the theories of Mannheim, see K. Mannheim 'El problema de las generaciones' (1928), *Revista Española de Investigaciones Sociológicas*, 62 (1993), 193–242 (first Spanish edition), passim; and I. Sánchez de la Yncera, 'La Sociología ante el problema generacional. Anotaciones al trabajo de Karl Mannheim', *Revista Española de Investigaciones Sociológicas*, 62 (1993), 147–92.

43. Laín, although following Ortega's elitist view, identified within the leading minority what he called 'generational sub-groups', which he defined as groups that differ in their preferred themes and styles although they share common ground: see Laín Entralgo, *Las generaciones*, pp. 297–8, 305–6.

44. J. Hood-Williams, 'The Problem of the Problems of Generations', *Youth and Policy. The Journal of Critical Analysis*, 10 (1984), 41–3 and 56, the quotation on 42; D. I. Kertzer, 'Generation as a Sociological Problem', *Annual Review of*

Sociology, 9 (1983), 125–49, 134; A. Kriegel, 'Generational Difference: The History of an Idea', *Daedalus*, 107/4 (1978), 23–38, 29. A defence of Mannheim's theories against Ortega's can be found in J. Pilcher, 'Mannheim's Sociology of Generations: An Undervalued Legacy', *British Journal of Sociology*, 45 (1994), 481–95.
45. Jaeger, 'Generations in History', pp. 285, 289.
46. M. Rintala, 'A Generation in Politics: A Definition', *The Review of Politics*, 25 (1963), 509–22, 509; *Renovación*, 3 March 1936, 2.
47. A.B. Spitzer, 'The Historical Problems of Generations', 1358; H. Jaeger, 'Generations in History', 284.

8
The War Child: A German Trauma?

Nicholas Stargardt

When Germans gathered to commemorate the sixtieth anniversary of the end of World War II in May 2005, the talk everywhere turned to the suffering of German civilians. Perhaps understandably given their age, it was the generation of war children which took centre stage, as journalists, psychotherapists and historians tried to interpret what it meant for those aged between 65 and 75 to have mass bombing and mass flight among their earliest and deepest memories.

In all wars, children are victims. World War II differed in the unprecedented extent to which this was true. At least one million Jewish children perished in the 'final solution', and we still do not know how many of the 216,000 victims of medical killing were children. Children were shot by German soldiers and militia men in droves in occupied Poland and the Soviet Union. Starvation and disease killed the elderly and the very young throughout occupied Europe, but especially in the east. And children were incinerated with their mothers in the firestorms of Hamburg, Dresden, Hildesheim, Darmstadt and a host of German cities, or froze to death in the mass flight of German civilians along the snow-bound roads from Silesia and East Prussia in 1945. And still greater numbers of children suffered in the war, losing their homes and belongings, their parents or older siblings.

But being a victim of war carries many different possible meanings, and those who want to extend this status to German civilians in general, and to the generation of 'war children' in particular, are treading on morally and politically cluttered ground. In the 1950s, the West German government published a multivolume compilation of German eyewitness accounts of flight and expulsion from eastern Europe. Much of this had a deliberately self-exculpatory purpose: in these accounts, the 'golden age' of normality ended, not with the German invasions of 1938, 1939 and 1941, but only with the approach of the Red Army in 1944 and 1945. And this matched a West German diplomatic stance which anticipated using German suffering to counter the claims of its east European neighbours in eventual peace negotiations. That this did not happen probably has more to do with the fact that no peace treaties were negotiated than with the moral and political stance of West German politicians in the post-war decade: certainly, in the event of the treaty Adenauer did sign, in Moscow in October 1955, much was made in the West German press about the suffering of the last 10,000 German prisoners of war in the Soviet Union, who were now released.[1]

The child's perspective appealed to West German writers like Heinrich Böll in the early 1950s as they looked for symbols of hope and regeneration in the post-war world. But as the literary critic and survivor of the Warsaw ghetto Marcel Reich-Ranicki remarked in an acid review of Böll's early work, the limited horizon of the child could also provide an excuse for avoiding all the broader issues of the Nazi war of annihilation waged in the East.[2]

The current revival of public discussion of German suffering in the war has a different vocabulary and carefully eschews the relativization of the Holocaust and the *ressentiment* which underscored so many contributions during the 1950s. Responses to the best-selling account of the bombing of German civilians made this distinction very evident. When Jörg Friedrich published *Der Brand* (*The Fire*) in 2002, the emotional immediacy of his evocation of civilians' plight moved German audiences deeply. But when he began referring to the bomber fleets as '*Einsatzgruppen*', as if they were the mobile killing units of the SS, or to asphyxiating air-raid cellars as 'gas chambers', then he also went too far. After so much public discussion of German responsibility for the murder of the Jews, most commentators found these terms unacceptable and strongly rejected any attempt to equate German and Jewish suffering.[3]

The one group of Germans strikingly absent from these new chronicles is the overwhelming majority of the Third Reich's war dead – soldiers. Some 400,000 German civilians were killed by Allied bombing; an unknown number, perhaps over one million, died in the mass flights and post-war expulsions from eastern Europe. But 4.8 million German soldiers died in the war. Whereas Andreas Hillgruber was all too happy to invoke the memory of their sacrifice in the *Historikerstreit* of 1986 to hold out against a Holocaust-centred interpretation of the Nazi period, and whereas conservatives condemned the exhibition on Wehrmacht 'atrocities' in the 1990s for slandering military honour, now these voices have fallen silent. With them died the hard talk of moral equivalence of Nazism and Stalinism, or of killing Jews and resisting the Red Army.[4]

What we find now is something different, a soft talk of equivalence through a general emphasis on innocence, victimhood and trauma. This is the talk not of the destruction of nations but of the suffering of persons. And this has set the tone for the handful of works which have now appeared based on interviews with war children. For the first time, interviewers have wanted them to tell their stories. Amid talk of 'breaking the silence', the new emphasis has been on the worst moments of their wars, on bombing, flight and hunger. Seeking to give voice to the suffering of the innocent is not unfamiliar: for the same means have been used to present the memories of Holocaust survivors, in the process 'empowering' the victims by according them high moral standing and political recognition.[5]

But recognition as a victim can also have a curiously disempowering effect, as historical subjects trying to make difficult calculations in terrible predicaments are turned into the passive objects of history. With the best of empathetic intentions, our culture turns to notions like victimhood and trauma with an ease which creates enormous obstacles to understanding the past. Such terms are neither apolitical nor neutral. They give suffering a particular emotional colouring, highlighting innocence and recovery, and redemptive sides of pain, while casting destructive ones such as hatred, rage and envy into deep shadow.

National and personal redemption in the wake of defeat is not a new idea. The German Right of the 1920s was unanimous in staking militant claims about the power of the blood sacrifice made by the defeated on the battle fields of World War I, and the 1950s articulated a more pacific vision of national rebirth through reconstruction. But now the redemptive message is quite a different one, a search for cure through public talk. Steeped in liberal and human rights centred values, the current discussion draws on a tradition which was developed in the 1960s and 1970s for speaking about German guilt. This is a tradition of testifying in public, treating public debate as itself a kind of social therapy, as if by variously talking out the Nazi past, the Holocaust, collaboration in the former East Germany with the *Stasi*, or – most recently – the suffering of the war will itself cleanse and cure society of their effects. It is in many ways a Protestant tradition, given secular guise by the terms of a social psychoanalysis first marshalled by the Mitscherlichs in their classic *The Inability to Mourn*. Whether individual therapy is ever so straightforward or so in step with public discussion is of course doubtful.[6]

The chief difference between the earlier debates about German guilt and the current one about German suffering is stance. As former Hitler Youths reread their teenage diaries in the late 1980s and asked themselves hard questions about their own moral responsibility for Nazism, they were deliberately confronting their former selves as if they were not merely older, but morally separate beings.[7] By contrast, little self-interrogation is demanded of witnesses once their childhood suffering is endowed with the unquestionable status of 'survivor testimonies'. And this easily shades into an uncritical kind of narcissistic self-absorption. Just as Reich-Ranicki found that Böll's early work used the limited horizon of the child to avoid the wider perspective of the Nazi war of annihilation waged in the East, so the new works on German war children help to restore an exclusive and homogeneous national narrative of the war, as if there were not millions of forced foreign labourers in their midst.

It is a paradox that, although children's experiences are homogenized in people's memories of the war, they were in fact profoundly marked by the forms of discrimination and social tension that existed in Nazi Germany. For children provided a crucial measure of the Nazis' success in realizing their utopian visions. They saw the pure-bred, well-educated and upright German child as the racial future of the nation, and they were only too aware that this was the first generation they could nurture and shape from infancy. In pursuing their utopian vision, the Nazis drew children into their field of action to an unprecedented degree, in order to separate German and Jewish, Polish and Czech, Sinti and disabled children along racial lines, dividing them into those who were destined to rule and those who were to serve; ultimately into those who were to live and those who were to die. Children's experiences deserve to be understood across the racial and national divides, not because of their emotional similarities but because their extreme social contrasts help us to see the Nazi order as a dissonant whole.[8]

Here I want to delve into some of the ways children and teenagers experienced things at the time, rather than how these were reconceived of in successive reworkings of 'generational experience' afterwards. First of all, I shall consider the ways in which the experiences of different children under the Nazis became sharply distinct from one another, depending, above all, on their national and ethnic belonging, but also on their age group and the peculiarities of the wartime events in the region in which they lived. Then I shall consider what common emotional elements emerge from children's diverse experiences of violent conquest and occupation.

* * *

In 1939, children had no idea what a major war would be like and most younger ones did not even know what the word meant. For Wanda Przybylska 'the war' was bound up with roses. The nine-year-old could not grasp why this strange word made her mother weep, surrounded by the white roses whose scent hung heavily over her parents' garden on 1 September 1939. In those first days, children in Germany and Poland simply listened to the war on radio. The schools remained closed, and children hung around the gates as they watched reservists flocking in to register for military service.[9]

Within three weeks, most Polish children had learned the meaning of fear, defeat and occupation. When the Germans occupied Wanda's village of Piotrków Kujawski in western Poland, they arrested her father, the local school teacher. Wanda and her family were forced to flee to Warsaw. Later on, in 1942, when she was travelling along the branch line to the Varsovian summer swimming resort at Świder, she witnessed the massacres and deportations of the Jews at wayside stations. The next day, overwhelmed by what she had seen, she struggled for words to describe the 'crowds sitting without moving in the heat', 'all the corpses', 'the mothers hugging their babies'. As she sat on the veranda of the country house at Anin, she could not look at the stars. 'Everything is dead inside me,' the 12-year-old wrote. With every round of machine gun fire she could hear in the distance, she imagined a body falling. All the forests, the fields of wheat and the birds' song which had seemed to express her own inner vitality now felt totally lost to the barbarity and power of the enemy. For nights afterwards, the girl lay awake at night weeping, unable to explain to herself why it was happening: 'Because they are of such and such a nationality? Because they are Jews? Because they don't resemble them?'[10]

By the time Wanda recalled the day the war began and the heavy scent of the roses, nearly five years had passed. The nine-year-old had just turned 14 and the rose garden in Piotrków Kujawski had been lost long ago. A few weeks later, Wanda was killed by a stray bullet during the Warsaw Uprising of 1944.

While Wanda was learning the meaning of war through invasion, the arrest of her father and flight to Warsaw, German children continued to follow the war on the radio, marking the advance of the Wehrmacht with coloured pins on maps hung in their classrooms or in their living rooms at home. Many kept war diaries too. In Essen, 14-year-old Marion Lubien copied down bits of the military bulletins into hers. On 3 September, she noted the capture of Tschenstochau (Czestochowa), on 6 September, 'the industrial area of Upper Silesia virtually unharmed in German hands', and on the 9 September, her bulletin read, 'Lodz occupied. The Führer in Lodz.' But this 14-year-old girl kept to the clipped and stilted language of the Wehrmacht bulletins to the home front. The war itself was still remote. Not until the first bombs fell near her house in October 1940 would Marion's chronicle of the war leap into the first person.[11]

Even in the big cities of northern and western Germany many children first experienced the bombing later still, in 1942–3: it was then that war became real, establishing new routines of being woken nightly by the wail of air-raid sirens, stumbling half-asleep downstairs to their cellars, and learning the meaning of fear from the shaking adults around them.[12] As a boy at the Burg-Gymnasium in Essen wrote ten years later:

> I was born just at the outbreak of war so that I cannot remember the first [war] years. But from my fifth year on, much is irradicably etched in my memory. I sat through long nights of bombing in the cellar or bunker between shaking adults.[13]

Or as a boy at the vocational school put it: 'Then it started in the bunker where people crouched in every corner and angle. With every bomb that fell the "Our Fathers" sounded louder.'[14] Having to endure months of twice or thrice nightly alarms under the entire flight path of the bomber fleets took its toll on sleep and nerves. By the time that Liselotte G. had endured six weeks of continuous bombing in Berlin, the 16-year-old's constant moral demands on herself were narrowing in focus: she must not, she repeated to herself like a refrain, break down. By 3 January 1944, she found that her religious faith too was inadequate: 'Yes, I tell you,' she wrote in her diary, 'I am religious [...], but my heart is too weak, human fear of the end is so unimaginably great that in the immediacy of death nothing actually survives from the strength and belief in God's will other than a quaking human heart.'[15]

Children did not experience war and violence just in one way. Events divided older and younger children more sharply than before. As a 16-year-old *Flakhelfer*, Klaus S. manned a flak battery in Hamburg's Stadtpark throughout the week of Operation *Gomorrha*, 25 July–3

August 1943. In the letters he wrote to his mother late at night by the light of the firestorm, he maintained a far more level, matter of fact tone than the Police President achieved in his official report. Klaus never mentioned a single corpse, never described the hurricane-force winds, never admitted to his own fear or his comrades' – except to say that he could not get through an attack without smoking, but even this was an acceptable military practice. When Klaus wanted his mother to know what they had gone through, he preferred to quote the senior lieutenant in his flak battery who had told him that the bombing of Hamburg was worse than anything he had experienced on the Polish or French campaigns.[16]

What it cost these well-brought up boys like Klaus to summon up such cool poise is impossible to calculate, but they did so in the self-image of having finally grown up and entered the world of men. For them, the new airforce and naval uniforms were not only the realization of a dream long-cherished through their years in the *Jungvolk* and Hitler Youth. The uniforms were also sacralized once these boys had withstood the ordeal of serving under fire. As Hitler Youths became members of the *Volkssturm* in the final months of the war, they would be drawn into a totality of violence. Sent to fight Soviet tanks with rifles and bazookas, some, like Martin Bergau, were also called out to participate in the massacre of concentration camp prisoners. Theirs was a willingness to sacrifice themselves – and others – which often continued until the end of the war.[17]

Younger children in the German cities saw the bombing through quite different eyes. They often watched the bombing of their cities with awe and wonderment, thrilled by the vividness of the colours and wild beauty of the sights. Living in Hamburg before the July 1943 raids, Harald H. could see the oil tanks burning after a raid on the port of Harburg. For the 13-year-old boy, tired out from being woken twice by air-raid sirens in the same night, the colours were completely captivating and magical:

> I gazed fascinated at the play of colours, into the yellow and red of the flames, which mingled and divided again against the background of the dark night sky. Neither before nor afterwards did I see such a clean, radiant yellow, such a blazing red, such a vibrant orange into which both colours merged.[18]

Nor did the first appearance of Allied planes overhead necessarily evoke terror in children. One five-year-old girl watching from her home outside

Berlin as the planes flew in to bomb the city in 1943 remembered that 'the sight of the threatening and growling aeroplanes was such that I thought I was dreaming and in a magical world'.[19] She wrote this in a school essay 12 years later, when she had very good reasons to replace her wonderment with fear. Again and again children compared such sights to being at the theatre, to watching a show greater than any they had ever seen. Whereas children often found great beauty in these instruments of destruction, even in the fires themselves, only very rarely do adults comment on this side of the air war.[20] Although in popular slang they too spoke of the coloured flares which slowly fell as 'Christmas trees', and even though soldiers often wrote about the the destruction they wrought on others in aesthetic terms, adult civilians probably felt inhibited about talking about the destruction of their neighbours' homes in such language. It was not just that younger children lacked this particular sense of shame; they may also have found it hard to understand their own – and others' – proximity to death.

The bombing gave rise to new children's games. Collecting *Flak* splinters was particularly prized by boys, who traded them in their school yards just as their older brothers had once swapped cigarette cards. But some other games no longer made any sense at all: one six-year-old girl found no fun anymore in one of her favourite games, jumping off the roof of the chicken hutch screaming 'Stuka!' as loudly as she could. She stopped playing the game after Essen was bombed in March 1943. The make-believe had become all too real.[21]

As they watched their houses burn and collapse in front of them, older children and adults had words for expressing their disbelief and their pain. Younger children often did not. After the destruction of their homes, women might count the plates and glasses which had miraculously survived, as if they stood for all that they had lost. Small children consoled themselves with the shoes, books and dolls which were rescued from the rubble.[22] But loss also divided small children from adults. For children who had been captivated by the spectacle of the 'Christmas trees' and fires, the real destruction of the bombing often came unexpectedly. Three-year-old Uwe Timm could only summon up fragmentary images of the destruction of his Hamburg home in July 1943 – the two porcelain figures his elder sister carried outside; the line of burning torches down each side of the street; the small fires which seemed to hang in the air. When Uwe Timm's older brother, Karl-Heinz, read his father's account, the young SS man wrote back from the eastern front immediately: 'That is not a war, but just a murder of women and children – and it is not humane.'[23]

This was not an isolated viewpoint. Many adult civilians reacted with outrage too, finding their explanation for the barbarity of the bombing in Goebbels' tireless propaganda about the Jews as the arch-enemy in the war, the hidden power controlling the Allied war machine. Some sought an outlet by writing to Goebbels demanding that Jews should be executed in reprisal for the deaths of German civilians. Others bemoaned the fact that Germany's 'radical solution of the Jewish question' had prompted such Jewish retaliation against German civilians.[24] To make sense of the ferocity of what people universally called the 'terror bombing' required a conspiracy by an enemy who was filled with an implacable hatred of Germans and Germany. Even in the Austrian countryside, older children might intone, 'War guilt is the Jew's' at the start of class each day.[25] But, in the bombed cities themselves, younger children did not have access to such words to express their anger and fear; often they lacked even a concept for death, until it bore in upon them. The dividing line here did not separate children from adults so much as younger children from prematurely socialized, older ones.

* * *

What children did do was to construct their own chronologies of the war through key events; the moment when *their* war became real. When exactly their secure world collapsed became a defining moment, dividing the war from a previous 'golden age'. For Jewish children in Germany, Austria and the Czech lands, that moment almost certainly came before the war, often with their emigration, especially if that involved family separations. For Poles, this often happened in 1939–40 , with the mass shootings, deportations and – for Polish Jews – ghettoization. For German children in the cities of the Rhineland and Ruhr, it came with the onset of heavy bombing in 1942. For children in the eastern German provinces, that moment was usually the mass flights of 1945. For many other German and Austrian children, their intact and safe world did not end until occupation and the collapse of the Third Reich: for them, the events shaping their inner sense of time were more likely to be the capitulation of 8 May 1945 and the hunger years which followed than the Nazi period itself.[26]

As children's memories of Nazi Germany divided between those who remembered it as a time of normality and those who recalled it with fear and horror, the exact events they recollected mattered. For key dates and events marked the boundary between a war followed with coloured pins on maps and one experienced in their own bodies. Hunger, fear and death may be universal human experiences, but neither adults nor children saw them this way at the time, and the immediate post-war years saw a continued nationalization of memories about the war. There would be no European consensus about the meanings of 1939, 1940, 1941 or 1945, or about what counted as victory, defeat or liberation. In West Germany in the 1950s, public attention dwelt on the mass flight and expulsions of ethnic Germans from east of the Oder and Neisse, the mass rape of German women by Red Army soldiers and the plight of prisoners of war in the Soviet Union, while in Poland the German occupation was depicted as a national martyrdom leading to resurrection.[27]

We have come a long way in the last 50 years from the exclusive nationalisms of the 1950s, even though the danger still exists of reawakening those debates about who the real victims of the war were as soon as discussions focus exclusively upon the suffering and victimhood of a particular national community. But there is another danger too, not of exclusivity but of homogenizing and blending all experiences together. This came to the fore when the *Neue Wache* memorial was reconsecrated in reunited Berlin in 1993: the claim on its plaque to represent the 'Central Memorial of the Federal Republic of Germany to the Victims of War and Tyranny' immediately provoked a storm of debate about relativizing the Holocaust.[28] Intellectually, the same danger is present when historians, journalists and psychologists start invoking 'trauma' as a universal term to explain the suffering of war children on all sides.

There clearly were children whose responses to their plight cut them off from others, and can only be explained as 'traumatized'. I would think here of the small German girl who could only think of rescuing her shoes from the rubble of her house, or the five-year-old Polish girl who had to be taught to speak again after her liberation from a concentration camp.[29] But how useful is it to think of a whole society of individuals unable to communicate with one another? This is the implication of recent works on German war children which take their cue from giving speech back to the 'survivors', as they 'break their silence'.[30]

At the time, most children were neither silent nor unable to engage with their environment or relate to others: if we want to find children's own wishes and responses to events it is to their activities that we should look. During and immediately after the war, across Europe adults were rattled by the confidence and activity of children. From looking after younger siblings while their effectively single mothers went out to work, children took on ever greater responsibilities. They became beggars and smugglers to feed their families. At some point – as their parents broke down in the starving Jewish ghettos, or as they fled before the Red Army in the snows of 1945, or while they hid in their cellars during bombing raids – many children shouldered premature responsibilities, often for the whole family.[31]

In 1945, the Polish State Institute of Mental Hygiene studied the war's moral and psychological harm through a large-scale questionnaire. Many children claimed to have learned the patriotic virtues from their parents, teachers and the Resistance. But just as many children admitted that they had learned to lie, steal and deceive, hate, treat authority with contempt, feel indifferent to all ideals and had even lost faith in the sanctity of human life. Set against the evidence of teenage drinking, sex, absenteeism from work, theft and black marketeering which welfare workers, juvenile courts and psychologists were reporting across the European continent, such surveys confirmed their belief that the war had destroyed children's innocence.[32] It had also taught these children how to survive. It was, perhaps most of all, the experience of occupation which taught children the meaning of fear. And they learned it first from the sudden powerlessness of the adults around them who till that point had appeared so omnipotent.

During wartime and post-war occupations, and in the Jewish ghettos, children had asserted themselves on the streets and market. They had had fewer norms to unlearn than adults and often more drive and energy to adapt. But the same development also undermined their trust in the adult world and increased their sense of having to take responsibility for themselves. By 1946, German children were plying the black market too. Hunger drove children to become smugglers across the German–Belgian border, and it taught them not to trust strangers: however dysfunctional and unhappy their own families became, in conditions of social collapse they were generally the only institution on which children could rely.[33] In this premature and 'wild' activity of children lay their capacity for treating the most extreme conditions as *normal*.

In these moments when the war became 'real', the integrity of their family worlds broke apart and children felt that they needed to patch them up again. These specific moments shaped children's overall chronology of the war, establishing when the 'safe' or 'intact' world of childhood was destroyed. For Yehuda Bacon, bringing food to his father in Theresienstadt had marked his assumption of premature responsibility.[34]

For Ingrid B., it was taking care of her sister when her mother collapsed during the expulsion from Czechoslovakia.[35] For Wolfgang Hempel, it was setting out to find his father's grave and bring his papers home in the winter of 1945–6.[36] Events like these united intimately personal and wider social crises, making the preceding period seem like a 'golden age'. In the kaleidoscopic character of events, as one crisis succeeded another, the locus of the 'golden age' was also unstable. So, Yehuda Bacon recalled how he used to dream of his home in Mährisch Ostrau while he was in the Jewish ghetto of Theresienstadt. After his deportation to Auschwitz-Birkenau, that became too remote and he dreamed instead of the Czech boys' home he had left behind in Theresienstadt.[37]

Power and powerlessness also altered children's games. With the rise of the black market came new games like 'coal thief and engine driver', which were played in Poland in 1940 and in Germany in 1946.[38] Children's games have a limited and historically repetitive repertoire, but role play also changed in significant ways in these extreme moments of crisis, so offering a way of understanding what powerlessness and threat meant to different groups of children at the time.

Throughout World War II, children played war games. In Southern Westphalia in October 1939, Detlef was able to convey some of the excitement of his battles to his enlisted father, as the ten-year-old described how his side had retaken their position under 'murderous fire'. His side had used sticks as hand grenades, but the enemy had thrown stones. Then Detlef had led the charge, his 'sabre' raised, putting the enemy temporarily to flight. As battle resumed, Detlef's side attacked once more and withstood a fierce counter-attack: 'None of us cried out and we won,' he wrote triumphantly to his father.[39]

There was nothing very new about this. Only the roles which the children competed for altered over time. Children in 1757 in Aachen or in Cologne in 1810 wanted to be the 'king' or the 'robber captain'. By the interwar period, German and Austrian children were playing *Räuber und Gendarme*, cops and robbers.[40]

Play is as natural to children as talk is to adults. As the behaviour of children who *cannot* play reminds us, at its most essential play is an expression of fantasy. Play is creative in itself, and even destructive games satisfy some urge to appropriate space and objects and subjugate them to the will and whim of children.[41] For elaborate games to continue they also have to be secure from outside interruption, which is one of the reasons that kids who belonged to a gang liked hanging out together in their own territory, under the canal bridges in the Berlin neighbourhood of Kreuzberg, or on the staircases and backyards of the Warsaw ghetto. Being outside adult control of course meant that it was the children who would determine how long the game lasted and how violent it became. Anything which is historically specific about children's games in central Europe during World War II is only evident against the backdrop of these more general characteristics of children's playing.[42]

But defeat, occupation and imprisonment had an immediate impact upon children's games too. In Bromberg – or Bydgoszcz – four- and six-year-olds soon began re-enacting the mass executions the Germans carried out on the town square in the first weeks of the occupation, acclaiming most those who cried, 'Poland has not yet perished!' In Warsaw boys played at liberating prisoners, but they were also observed pretending to carry out Gestapo interrogations, slapping each other's faces in this 'wild' game. As reality invaded the make-believe, children were torn between models of heroic resistance and the allure of their conquerors.[43]

When eight-year-old Christoph had begged his older brother Werner to send him a French 'Képi' from France in 1940, he was adding a dash of contemporary colour and a frisson of the German victory to an age-old game.[44] But, for the conquered, bringing the old games up to date often meant playing with real humiliations and threats. In the Jewish ghetto in Vilna, children also began to play with a daily reality. There was only one main gate in and out of the ghetto, and each evening the Jewish police searched the Jewish workers as they returned from the workshops on the Lithuanian side of town for smuggled food, and although they risked being beaten for it, children often lingered near the gate in the hope of getting something. They also played at what they saw. As children enacted 'Going through the gate', Tzvia Kuretzka recalled:

> Two main characters were selected; Levas, the hated head of the Jewish gate guards, and Franz Murer, one of the most murderous Gestapo men. The rest of the children played the Jewish workers who tried to smuggle some food into the starving ghetto and the guards who attempted to find the contraband. While the Jewish gate guards search everyone 'Murer' comes, which propels the Jewish police to intensify its brutality and, at the same time, precipitates a tumult and panic among the 'workers'. They try desperately to toss away the small food packages, but 'Murer' finds some with the incriminating evidence and the 'workers' are put aside and later are whipped by the police.[45]

The two biggest boys got to play Franz Murer and Meir Levas, leaving it to the smaller ones to take the role of the adult Jewish workers, who, in reality, would often have included their own older brothers, sisters, aunts, uncles and parents. Like the adults they were playing, they were powerless to protect themselves from the blows rained upon them, in this case by the bigger, stronger children. As in the war games of Christoph and Detlef, power still resided in the uniform. But the choice of role models was a stark one, as fear and detestation mingled with envy and longing. Where Detlef and Christoph wanted to be just like their fathers and elder brothers in France, for these children being like their elders promised only fear and suffering.

For ten months from September 1943 till July 1944, several thousand Jews from the Theresienstadt ghetto were kept in a special section of Auschwitz-Birkenau known as the 'family camp', just in case the SS were to open the camp to inspection by the International Red Cross. To the great envy of inmates in other sections of Birkenau, this so-called family camp had special blocks for children, and the inmates were allowed to keep their hair and the clothes they had come in. The children played organized games and sang, even performing a full-length musical loosely based on Walt Disney's *Snow White*. One of the Czech kindergarten teachers in the family camp also noticed the games the younger children played when they thought no one was watching. They played 'Camp elder and Block elder', 'roll call' and 'hats off'. They played the sick who were beaten for fainting during roll call, and they played the doctor who took their food away and refused to help them if they had nothing to give him in return.[46]

Games in concentration camps did not protect children from the reality around them by preserving an ideal world of make-believe. On the contrary, children reshaped their games to incorporate that reality. In so doing they drew the most extreme conclusion from the key lessons that defeat and occupation taught all children. The first thing that defeated children witnessed was the sudden impotence of the adults they had grown up thinking were all-powerful. Power and success, the strivings of ambition and envy, were suddenly incorporated in their enemies. In some cases, children could imagine themselves as partisan fighters or members of one of the underground armies of the Resistance. But complete defeat and capitulation left few positive role models. During the war years, conquered children did not just fear and hate their enemies. They had also profoundly envied them, often preferring to imagine themselves in the position of their enemies rather than their parents, their elder brothers and their sisters.

As the Third Reich crumbled in the rubble of Berlin during the last days of April and the first days of May 1945, German children began to express the dilemmas of their new predicament in their games. Before they had even emerged from their Berlin cellars, children started playing at being Russian soldiers. Waving make-believe pistols, they relieved each other of imaginary watches, crying, '*Uhri, uhri*' to mimic the Red Army looters. As they assimilated the real and terrifying power of their enemies and masters into their games, these Berlin children were also enacting their own impotence and envy.[47]

Yet, the very fact of children's *play* leaves a degree of openness and ambiguity about the meaning of their games: what does it mean for children to consciously enact such scenarios? When, in May 1940, Emmanuel Ringelblum overheard an eight-year-old Jewish boy in the Warsaw ghetto screaming, 'I want to steal, I want to rob, I want to eat, I want to be a German,' he was hearing the voice of pure desperation and rage.[48] But to *play* at robbing, stealing and being German was somehow different from this starving child's scream. Children knew it was a game, that one scenario that they could truly control, however powerless they might be in other respects. And then there were things they did not play at altogether – German children might enact Russian plunder, but not rape. Indeed, this pattern persisted later on: as German and Austrian children wrote about the end of the war over the next 50 years in school essays or unpublished memoirs, they might mention the ubiquity of rape but veered away from the subject again as soon as it touched on their own mothers.[49]

The 'family camp' in Birkenau was a rectangular barbed wire enclosure situated within sight of three crematoria. Their chimneys belched out three- and four-metre high flames when in constant use. Whereas the adults attempted to ignore their proximity to the gas chambers, the children drew them directly into the fabric of their daily lives. The older ones played games with death, daring each other to run up to the electric fence and touch it with their fingertips, knowing the high voltage current was usually – but not always – switched off during the daytime. One day one of their teachers came upon the younger children playing 'Gas chamber' outside their block. They had dug a hole and were throwing in one stone after the other. These were to be the people who were going into the crematorium and the children mimicked their cries. In one way, their game broke down here. Whereas in their normal games of 'Roll call', the little children may have had to submit to beatings for 'fainting', here no one jumped into the hole which was the gas chamber. They had to use stones instead.[50] Even the smaller children, who were routinely dragooned into playing roles where they were punished or beaten, could not be those people: we may surmise that to do so would, like playing at rape, have been too psychologically self-destructive. In any event, these unspoken limits to children's games suggest that, however much they may have envied their enemies, their primary drive was to adapt in order to survive.

The war was not just something that had happened to children. As they strove to survive in it and to parent their parents, it also tore apart their inner emotional world. Through their games, children simultaneously protected themselves from and adapted to a reality in which they recognized their enemies as the image of victorious strength and their parents as impotent failures. Children's games, as much as their other precocious activities, demonstrated that they were not just the mute and traumatized witnesses to this war. By the war's end, almost all European children had experienced military defeat and occupation. Although the level of violence and the policies of the German and Allied occupations could not have been more different, everywhere children became acquainted with hunger, cold and the powerlessness of adults, as well as the fluidity of once secure social structures. By finding new roles for themselves and adapting with a speed and practicality which shocked many adults, they demonstrated just how profound were the social transformations wrought by Nazism and war: children found these things *normal*.

* * *

It is difficult enough to fix what such experiences meant at the time. What to make of them afterwards has often been a matter of symbolic politics in public and private reticence. But whatever the current claims may be, it is clear that however emotionally formative key wartime experiences may have been, their meaning was neither obvious nor fixed. As a cohort, the children who lived through World War II under Nazi rule did not all share the same experiences and did not all respond to those they did share with others in like manner. Even in this most destructive of wars, the entire cohort of war children was made into a generation not by their common experiences but by the different ways in which they and the generations above and, later, below them talked about these events.

At the very heart of the notion of the 'formative experience' lies a paradox. For, the more violent and overwhelming events became, the more destructive they were to children's sense of self, leaving them less able to reconcile their own contradictory desires and understandings of reality. Finding in such experiences a stable set of meanings was bound to be not only as politically tendentious as such acts of public commemoration always are, but also peculiarly partial and fragile in psychological and emotional terms. This was a cohort whose formative experiences could be made to fit all the frames of generational belonging created in post-war Europe, each version similar to its predecessor only in its incompleteness and pre-emptive bid to offer moral closure.

Notes

1. R. Moeller, *War Stories: The Search for a Usable Past in the Federal Republic of Germany* (Berkeley, 2001), Chaps 3 and 4; L. Niethammer, 'Privat – Wirtschaft. Erinnerungsfragmente einer anderen Umerziehung', in idem (ed.), *'Hinterher merkt man, daß es richtig war, daß es schiefgegangen ist.'* *Nachkriegserfahrungen im Ruhrgebiet* (Bonn, 1983), pp. 29–34; M. Beer, 'Im Spannungsfeld von Politik und Zeitgeschichte: Das Grossforschungsprojekt "Dokumentation der Deutschen aus Ost-Mitteleuropa"', *Vierteljahrshefte für Zeitgeschichte*, 49 (1998), 345–89; F. Biess, 'Survivors of Totalitarianism: Returning POWs and the Reconstruction of Masculine Citizenship in West Germany, 1945–1955', in H. Schissler (ed.), *The Miracle Years: A Cultural History of West Germany, 1949–1968* (Princeton, NJ, 2001), pp. 57–82; H. Knoch, *Die Tat als Bild: Fotgografien des Holocaust in der deutschen Erinnerungskultur* (Hamburg, 2001), pp. 314–23. On East Germany, see G. Margalit, 'Der Luftangriff auf Dresden: Seine Bedeutung für die Erinnerungerspolitik der DDR und für die Herauskristallisierung einer historischen Kriegserinnerung im Westen', in S. Düwell and M. Schmidt (eds), *Narrative der Shoah: Repräsentationen der Vergangenheit in Historiographie, Kunst und Politik* (Paderborn, 2002), pp. 189–208 .
2. H. Böll, *Haus ohne Hüter* (Cologne, 1954), and the critique by Marcel Reich-Ranicki, *Deutsche Literatur in West und Ost: Prosa seit 1945* (Munich, 1963), p. 133; on this see also D. Reed, *The Novel and the Nazi Past* (New York and Frankfurt, 1985), p. 55; D. Pinfold, *The Child's View of the Third Reich in German Literature: The Eye among the Blind* (Oxford, 2001), pp. 27 and 149–50.
3. See the recent debate about Jörg Friedrich, *Der Brand: Deutschland im Bombenkrieg 1940–1945* (Munich, 2002), in L. Kettenacker (ed.), *Ein Volk von Opfern: Die neue Debatte um den Bombenkrieg 1940–45* (Berlin, 2003), some of whose themes are reprised in the exclusively German focus of Oliver Hirschbiegel's film *Der Untergang*.
4. Numbers of German military dead, R. Overmans, *Deutsche militärische Verluste im Zweiten Weltkrieg* (Munich, 1999), pp. 238–46 and 316–18; A. Hillgruber, *Zweierlei Untergang: die Zerschlagung des Deutschen Reiches und das Ende des europaischen Judentums* (Berlin, 1986); on the *Wehrmacht* exhibition, see O. Bartov, A. Grossman and M. Nolan (eds), *Crimes of War: Guilt and Denial in the Twentieth Century*, New York, 2002.
5. H. Lorenz, *Kriegskinder: Das Schicksal einer Generation Kinder* (Munich, 2003); S. Bode, *Die vergessene Generation: Die Kriegskinder brechen ihr Schweigen*

(Stuttgart, 2004); H. Schulz, H. Radebold and J. Reulecke, *Söhne ohne Väter: Erfahrungen der Kriegsgeneration* (Berlin, 2004); on Holocaust testimony, T. Kushner, *The Holocaust and the Liberal Imagination: A Social and Cultural History* (Oxford, 1994); and P. Novick, *The Holocaust and Collective Memory: The American Experience* (London, 1999).

6. On the cult of the fallen soldier, see George Mosse, *Fallen Soldiers: Reshaping the Memory of the World Wars* (New York and Oxford, 1990); A. and M. Mitscherlich, *Die Unfähigkeit zu trauern: Grundlagen kollektiven Verhaltens* (Munich, 1967).

7. See N. Stargardt, *Witnesses of War: Children's Lives under the Nazis* (London, 2005), introduction; G. Rosenthal (ed.), *Die Hitlerjugend-Generation: Biographische Thematisierung als Vergangenheitsbewältigung* (Essen, 1986); D. von Westernhagen, *Die Kinder der Täter* (Munich, 1987); P. Sichrovsky, *Schuldig geboren: Kinder aus Nazifamilien* (Cologne, 1987); and esp., D. Bar-On, *Legacy of Silence: Encounters with Children of the Third Reich* (Cambridge, MA, 1989).

8. See Stargardt, *Witnesses of War*.

9. W. Przybylska, *Journal de Wanda*, ed. and trans. Z. Bobowicz (Paris, 1981), pp. 86–7: 30 June 1944; on children at the start of the war, Stargardt, *Witnesses of War*, pp. 21–4.

10. Przybylska, *Journal de Wanda*, pp. 28–9, 40–1: 1, 17 and 21 August 1942.

11. D. Wierling, '"Leise versinkt unser Kinderland" – Marion Lubien (pseud.) schreibt sich durch den Krieg', in U. Borsdorf and M. Jamin (eds), *Überleben im Krieg: Kriegserfahrungen in einer Industrieregion 1939–1945* (Hamburg, 1989), p. 70.

12. On the bombing war, see especially O. Groehler, *Bombenkrieg gegen Deutschland* (Berlin, 1990).

13. Wilhelm Roessler-Archiv, Institut für Geschichte und Biographie der Fernuniversität Hagen: Burg-Gymnasium Essen (hereafter, RA), UII/516, anon., 16 yrs, 14 February 1956, 1.

14. RA, Berufschule M2/6, 1, praying in bunker, 16 yrs, 21 January 1956.

15. Liselotte G., in I. Hammer and S. zur Nieden (eds), *Sehr selten habe ich geweint: Briefe und Tagebücher aus dem Zweiten Weltkrieg von Menschen aus Berlin* (Zurich, 1992), p. 291.

16. Kempowski-Archiv, Nartum, 4709/2, Klaus S., letters to mother, 28, 30 and 31 July, 1 and 10 August 1943; Police President of Hamburg in J. Noakes (ed.), *Nazism: A Documentary Reader*, vol. 4, *The German Home Front in World War II* (Exeter, 1998), pp. 554–7.

17. In general, see Stargardt, *Witnesses of War*, Chaps 8 and 10. Sixteen-year-olds were called up to the *Flak* for the first time by a decree issued on 26 January 1943: K.H. Jahnke and M. Buddrus, *Deutsche Jugend 1933–1945: Eine Dokumentation* (Hamburg, 1989), pp. 359–61; see also the oral history project of Rolf Schörken, *Luftwaffenhelfer und Drittes Reich: Die Entstehung eines politischen Bewusstseins* (Stuttgart, 1984), pp. 101–61; Kempowski-Archiv, Nartum 2554, Werner K., '20 Monate Luftwaffenhelfer: Tagebücher 5. Januar 1944–20 August 1945'. On participating in the *Volkssturm*, K.H. Jahnke, *Hitlers letztes Aufgebot: Deutsche Jugend im sechsten Kriegsjahr 1944* (Essen, 1993); and for a confessional account of his own role in a massacre, see M. Bergau, *Der Junge von der Bernsteinküste: Erlebte Zeitgeschichte 1938–1948* (Heidelberg, 1994), pp. 244–75.

18. Harald H., MS, 3 (author's collection): I am grateful to the late W.G. Sebald for sending this to me.
19. RA, Goetheschule Essen, OII, anon., b. 1938, 1.
20. A rare exception is Ursula von Kardorff, *Berliner Aufzeichnungen: Aus den Jahren 1942 bis 1945* (Munich, 1962), p. 159: 21 June 1944, on the swirling clouds of dust and flames after an air raid on Berlin.
21. *Flak* splinters in Harald H., MS, 1 (author's collection); 'Stuka' game in RA, UI/ no no., anon. 19 yrs, 16 January 1956, 2–3.
22. Rescuing the tale of Queen Luise, RA, Goetheschule Essen, UI/1, 23 January 1956, 3; finding a shoe, see RA, Luisenschule Essen, UI/5, 5; RA, Goetheschule Essen UI/3, 6: cannot imagine that all the toys have been destroyed along with the family home.
23. U. Timm, *Am Beispiel meines Bruders* (Cologne, 2003), pp. 27 and 34–7: letter from father, 6 August, and from Karl-Heinz, 11 August 1943.
24. See Stargardt, *Witnesses of War*, pp. 252–3, and M. Steinert, *Hitlers Krieg und die Deutschen: Stimmung und Haltung der deutschen Bevölkerung im Zweiten Weltkrieg* (Düsseldorf, 1970), pp. 260–1; V. Klemperer, *The Language of the Third Reich: LTI – Lingua Tertii Imperii: A Philologist's Notebook* (London, 2000), pp. 172–81.
25. Dokumentation lebensgeschichtlicher Aufzeichnungen, Institut für Wirtschafts- und Sozialgeschichte, University of Vienna, Edgar P., b. 15 September 1935, 'Die Russenzeit – ein Zeitzeugnis', MS, 1995, 9–10.
26. See Stargardt, *Witnesses of War*, especially chaps 1, 4, 8, 9 and 11.
27. In general for the 'Resistance myth' in Western Europe, see P. Lagrou, *The Legacy of Nazi Occupation in Western Europe: Patriotic Memory and National Recovery* (Cambridge, 1999), and his 'The Nationalization of Victimhood: Selective Violence and National Grief in Western Europe, 1940–1960', in R. Bessel and D. Schumann (eds), *Life after Death: Approaches to a Cultural and Social History of Europe during the 1940s and 1950s* (Cambridge, 2003), pp. 243–57. On Poland, see E. Dmitrów, *Niemcy i okupacja hitlerowska w oczach Polaków: poglady i opinie z lat 1945–1948* (Warsaw, 1987); M. Steinlauf, *Bondage to the Dead: Poland and the Memory of the Holocaust* (Syracuse, NY, 1997); on Israel, Boaz Cohen, 'Holocaust Heroics: Ghetto Fighters and Partisans in Israeli Society and Historiography', *Journal of Political and Military Sociology*, 31/2 (2003), 197–213; for Germany in the 1950s, see Note 1 above.
28. On the memorial discussion, see P. Reichel, *Politik mit der Erinnerung: Gedächtnisorte im Streit um die nationalsozialistische Vergangenheit* (Munich and Vienna, 1995); and more generally, see E. François and H. Schulze (eds), *Deutsche Erinnerungsorte*, vols 1–3 (Munich, 2002); J. Young, *The Texture of Memory: Holocaust Memorials and Meaning* (New Haven, 1993).
29. For these examples, RA, Luisenschule Essen, UI/5; K. Sosnowski, *The Tragedy of Children under Nazi Rule* (Pozna, 1962), p. 167.
30. See Note 5 above.
31. See Stargardt, *Witnesses of War*; on wartime Poland, see T. Szarota, *Warschau unter dem Hakenkreuz: Leben und Alltag im besetzten Warschau 1.10.1939 bis 31.7.1944* (Paderborn, 1985), pp. 101–130; G.S. Paulsson, *Secret City: The Hidden Jews of Warsaw, 1940–1945* (New Haven, 2002), pp. 26 and 61–6.
32. T. Brosse, *War-Handicapped Children: Report on the European Situation* (Paris, 1950), pp. 19–20 and 77–100; Sosnowski, *The Tragedy of Children under Nazi*

Rule, pp. 165–7; H. Radomska-Strzemecka, 'Okupacja w oczach młodzieży', in J. Wnuk and H. Radomska-Strzemecka, *Dzieci polskie oskarżają (1939–1945)* (Warsaw, 1961), pp. 195–379.

33. On post-war Germany, S. Meyer and E. Schulze, *Wie wir das alles geschafft haben: Alleinstehende Frauen berichten über ihr Leben nach 1945* (Munich, 1985), pp. 100–8; A.L. Lloyd, 'Germany's Child Smugglers', *Picture Post*, 4 October 1947, cited in D. Macardle, *Children of Europe: A Study of the Children of Liberated Countries: Their War-time Experiences, Their Reactions, and Their Needs, with a Note on Germany* (London, 1949), pp. 287–8.

34. Dokumentation des österreichischen Widerstandes, Vienna, 13243, Bacon, interview with Ben-David Gershon, Jerusalem, 17 November 1964, 57.

35. Kempowski-Archiv, 3915, Johannes W., 'Die Familie B. 1945/46 in Briefen und Dokumenten', MS, Frau B. to Dr Otto B., Kneese, 10 December 1945; Ingrid B. to father, Kneese, 10 December 1945. For other accounts of the expulsions through children's eyes, see A. Wagnerová, *1945 waren sie Kinder: Flucht und Vertreibung im Leben einer Generation* (Cologne, 1990).

36. Wolfgang Hempel, in H. Schulz, H. Radebold and J. Reulecke, *Söhne ohne Väter: Erfahrungen der Kriegsgeneration* (Berlin, 2004), pp. 31–2 and 88–9.

37. Yehuda Bacon, video interview in Terezín Foundation, *Terezín Diary*; and Dokumentation des österreichischen Widerstandes, Vienna, 13243, interview with Ben-David Gershon, Jerusalem, 17 November 1964, 61.

38. M. Maschmann, *Account Rendered: A Dossier on my Former Self* (London, 1965), p. 121; Kempowski-Archiv, 4622, Peter Laudan, 'Gefährdete Spiele', b. 1935, 34.

39. H. Lange and B. Burkard (eds), *'Abends wenn wir essen fehlt uns immer einer': Kinder schreiben an die Väter 1939–1945* (Hamburg, 2000), 97–8: Detlef, 17 October 1939.

40. N. Stargardt, 'Kinder zwischen Arbeit und Spiel', *Sozialwissenschaftliche Informationen*, 2 (1999), 123–30; E. Rosenhaft, *Beating the Fascists? The German Communists and Political Violence, 1929–1933* (Cambridge, 1983); H. Lessing and M. Liebel, *Wilde Cliquen* (Bernsheim, 1981). The upper classes were the first to withdraw their children from such wild freedom of the streets at the turn of the eighteenth century, in a sense setting the precedents for the wholesale withdrawal of the middle classes from the streets into private recreational spaces in the last third of the nineteenth century: J. Schlumbohm, *Kinderstuben: Wie Kinder zu Bauern, Bürgern, Aristokraten wurden 1700–1850* (Munich, 1983), p. 222.

41. See the classics by D.W. Winnicott, *Playing and Reality* (London, 1971) and his *The Piggle: An Account of the Psychoanalytic Treatment of a Little Girl* (London, 1978).

42. Kempowski-Archiv, 3024, Otto P., b. 1926, 'Himmel und Hölle: Eine Kreuzberger Kindheit', MS, 59–60; J. David, *A Square of Sky: The Recollections of a Childhood* (London, 1964), pp. 111–14.

43. For these games, see I. Flatsztejn-Gruda, *Byłam wtedy dzieckiem* (Lublin, 2004), pp. 37–8; Polish Ministry of Information, *The German New Order in Poland* (London, 1942), p. 27; Szarota, *Warschau unter dem Hakenkreuz*, p. 100, citing Stanisław Srokowski's diary for 20–21 June 1940.

44. Kempowski-Archiv, 3936, Marianne Walter (née Marx), b. 1922, MS letters from her younger brother, Christoph, and sister, Regina, b. 1932 and 1933,

to Werner, their elder brother by 13 years, c. 1940–44 , second, undated letter.

45. Tzvia Kuretzka cited in G. Eisen, *Children and Play in the Holocaust: Games among the Shadows* (Amherst, 1988), p. 77. For the context of this game, see Y. Rudashevski, *The Diary of the Vilna Ghetto: June 1941–April 1943* (Tel Aviv, 1973), p. 113: 28 December 1942; pp. 115–16: 1 January 1943; see also p. 99: 26 November; pp. 126–7: 27 January 1943; Y. Arad, *Ghetto in Flames: The Struggle and Destruction of the Jews in Vilna in the Holocaust* (New York, 1982), pp. 304–5.

46. Otto Dov Kulka, evidence given on 30 July 1964 at the Auschwitz trial, and Hanna Hoffmann–Fischel report for Yad Vashem, both reprinted in I. Deutschkron (ed.), *... Denn ihrer war die Hölle: Kinder in Gettos und Lagern* (Cologne, 1985), pp. 80 and 54; and Dokumentation des österreichischen Widerstandes, Vienna, 13243, Bacon, interview with Ben-David Gershon, Jerusalem, 17 November 1964, 47–8.

47. Anneliese H.'s diary, 1 May 1945, in E. Kuby, *The Russians and Berlin, 1945* (London, 1968), p. 226.

48. J. Sloan (ed.), *Notes from the Warsaw Ghetto: The Journal of Emmanuel Ringelblum* (New York, 1958), p. 39: 9 May 1940.

49. See Stargardt, *Witnesses of War*, pp. 321–3; A. Petö, 'Memory and the narrative of rape in Budapest and Vienna in 1945', in Bessel and Schumann, *Life after Death*, pp. 133–4 and 138; I. Bandhauer Schöffmann and E. Hornung, 'Vom "Dritten Reich" zur Zweiten Republik', in D.F. Good, M. Grandner and M.J. Maynes (eds), *Frauen in Österreich: Beiträge zu ihrer Situation im 19. und 20. Jahrhundert* (Vienna, 1994), pp. 232–3; also M. Baumgartner, 'Zwischen Mythos und Realität: Die Nachkriegsvergewaltigungen im sowjetisch-besetzten Mostviertel,' *Zeitschrift für Landeskunde von Niederösterreich*, 2 (1993), 80.

50. Hoffmann–Fischel report for Yad Vashem, reprinted in Deutschkron, *... Denn ihrer war die Hölle*, 54.

9
'Good Night, Little Ones': Childhood in the 'Last Soviet Generation'

Catriona Kelly

Family stories, generation stories

In Russia, as in Germany or France, though not Britain, perceptions that history is shaped by the different character of generations, in the sense of the varying experience and political tastes of those born in different decades, have carried great weight in cultural commentary. Generational evolution is held to shape literary history, as in the ubiquitous belief that the major novels of Turgenev (*Rudin*, *A Nest of Gentlefolk*, and *Fathers and Sons*) deal respectively with 'men of the 1840s', 'men of the 1850s', and 'men of the 1860s', or that writers and thinkers – from the 'Pushkin pleiad' and the 'Slavophile and Westernizer' controversy of the 1830s to the Symbolists and post-Symbolists born in the 1880s and 1890s – cluster in generational constellations.[1] Often, such representations emphasize more or less heroic failure, as in Mikhail Lermontov's 'Thought' (1838), which opens: 'It saddens me to look at our generation,' or an equally famous 1914 poem by Aleksandr Blok lamenting the fate of those born in 'the hollow years'. 'Generationalizing', to borrow Bernd Weisbrod's term, has been a characteristic strategy of social historians and social scientists too, with recent studies identifying 'the post-war baby-boomers' (i.e. those born in the post-war demographic surge of 1946–8) and 'the last Soviet generation' (those born in the 1960s) as specific groups in political, social, and economic terms.[2]

The assumption that a particular set of values is shared by all, or most, of the members of a given age cohort is a problematic expression of lived reality. As with the question so often invoked in historical discussion of whether experience is 'typical' or otherwise, we confront a set of values that express historical narrative's continuing, and in some cases unselfconscious, espousal of the perceptions and expressive devices of classical realism, and especially its unselfconscious implementation of social categories. Compartmentalizing changing historical experience according to 'generation' is convenient, but in signal respects misleading. It produces a hierarchy of social and cultural change that is event-driven, and which may obscure major shifts in experience that are difficult to link with a specific span of years. Thus, in my own area of recent interest, the history of childhood, there is extensive documentation of the effects of war on childhood, but much less of those brought by, say, widening access to antibiotics and to vaccination. At the same time, this latter process was highly significant in terms of lived experience. By 1960, children in the majority of European countries and in North America were extremely unlikely to lose a sibling or a friend to infectious disease; by extension, death in childhood (particularly violent death) came to seem 'unnatural', and hence peculiarly traumatic.

The masking of historical change through 'generationalizing' is pervasive in Russia too. Some 'generational' experience – the 'Blockade childhood' of wartime Leningrad, say – is famous and mythically recognizable, and thus seen as distinctive. Yet it is arguable that the suffering endured by the under-15s during World War II was actually part of a dismal continuum stretching back through collectivization and the Russian Civil War to the Revolution, or indeed the catastrophically accelerated urbanization begun in 1861, all of which brought rates of infant mortality and child death that were aberrant in international terms, as well as poverty, deprivation, and disease on a massive scale. Politically significant events and reforms to everyday life do not necessarily overlap in a straightforward way. So far as European Russia was concerned, the generational experience that is truly distinctive would begin in the late 1950s, when increased earning capacity in real terms, declining family size, better availability of consumer goods (despite shortages), and the Soviet equivalent of 'slum clearance' programmes (moving families from tenements [the notorious *kommunalki* or 'communal flats'] to private apartments), accompanied by large-scale house- and apartment-building in the countryside, transformed relations within the family, survival rates among young children, and the child's experience of domestic space. Equally, for a member of the 'small peoples' of the North, it was not World War II, but the large-scale development of boarding school education and the Russification associated with this in the post-war years, that marked a real cultural watershed.[3] Yet these social changes affected children at different rates depending on social status, place of residence, and local conditions. 'Baby boomers' born in 1946–50 whose parents were in the privileged groups able to buy co-operative apartments in the mid-1950s experienced them long before the children of factory workers, who were likely to be moved out of their communal or 'barrack' accommodation two or even three decades later.

A further problem, not unique to Soviet society, but especially rampant there, lies in the fact that family generations and age cohorts may not neatly overlap. The idea that they must do so is a product of recent Western demographic history, and particularly the rise to dominance of small nuclear families where child production is narrowly spaced. Even here, the age at which parents choose to have children may create ambiguities: the generational experience of a child born in the late 1950s whose parents were born in the late 1930s (and hence too young to have detailed memories of World War II) differed to a significant extent from that of children the same age born when their parents were in their 40s, or, conversely, of children born a decade later to parents born in the late 1930s. In Russia, an important additional factor in 'generational blur' is the relatively larger importance of grandparents as childcarers. In the post-war years, many war orphans were raised by grandparents; in the late Soviet period, grandparents continued to be important primary carers because of the very high rates of participation in the labour market by women, added to the continuing deficiencies of state childcare provision. Once children reached school age, grandparents might provide cover for a few hours in the late afternoon, between the time school ended (about two) and the time when most adults were able to get back from work (more like five), as well as for long stretches of the school holidays at the dacha.

Another factor in Russian 'generational blur' during the second half of the twentieth century was the prevalence, where there was more than one child in the family, of very broad spacing – gaps from 6 to 11 and even 12 years were not uncommon. This phenomenon, which I have named elsewhere as 'serial only children',[4] can mean that two individuals in a family who were 'children' in the sense that they were the descendants of the same parents might have totally different experiences, not just because their parents had aged in the interval (though in a high-stress society this factor was of considerable importance), but also because external circumstances might have altered significantly. An individual born in 1968 who left school in 1985 had life experiences that were in important ways different from those of a sibling born in 1978 who left school in 1995. Though the proportion of 'serial only children' is impossible to compute accurately, because published census records do not include information on family spacing, informal accounting suggests that such children represent a high proportion of families with more than one child.[5] The likelihood of 'generational overlap' in the late twentieth century was therefore considerable.

The amorphousness of the late Soviet period, not just with reference to the history of childhood, but in general terms, as reflected in the problems of imposing 'generational' mechanisms upon it, is one reason, one may suppose, for the relative neglect of the period by historians, compared with the first four decades of Soviet power. Thus, as Bernd Weisbrod rightly suggests, 'generationalizing' is accompanied by misleading emphases and ellipses; 'silent' generations (or perhaps more accurately, those that are unable to make themselves heard) succumb to generations that noisily clamour for attention, propelling their experience to the centre of national and/or group myths. And it goes without saying that 'generationalizing' primarily represents adult male experience, rather than the assumed continuities of child-raising and childhood itself.

At the same time, pointing to the obvious fact that constructs do not capture the totality of experience, and indeed may distort this, is only a first step. Adopting a 'myth' versus 'reality' approach involves another form of simplification, because it elides the issue of how historical subjects may themselves internalize myths. Among categories favoured by historians, 'generationality' is interesting precisely because what one might describe as the 'analytical laity' are prepared to espouse it. Few from the post-Romantic era would spontaneously recognize the term 'typical' as appropriate to themselves (it would seem equivalent to adopting the label, 'boring and ordinary').[6] On the other hand, the distinctiveness of generational experience is widely recognized, and particularly in cultures where mythic 'generationalizing' is pervasive. Thus, in Russia, asking the question, 'Which year are you from?' (i.e., 'when were you born?') is a standard way of 'placing' people in terms of cultural experience; people will refer in ordinary conversation to the characteristics of this or that *pokolenie* (generation).[7] Terms such as *shestidesiatnik* – 'nineteen-sixtyite' – are widely used and immediately evoke a concrete picture (in this case, a slightly ramshackle and hairy denizen of literary bohemia, a veteran of much fieldwork with the vodka bottle). Identification of this kind was encouraged, in the Soviet period, by the socialization of children, who were taught from early years where they should locate themselves on the generational map.

During the early years of Soviet history, this was mostly achieved by encouraging children themselves to think in generational terms. For example, those born in 1917 and 1918 were celebrated, in the 1920s and early 1930s, as the 'coevals of October' – those who would contribute to the making of a new society. As these 'coevals' reached adulthood, however, and the Soviet leadership itself moved into late middle age, the tone of propaganda began to change. Now, the task of children was held to be *continuing* the great work that had been done by their elders, and it was adult experience that dictated aspirations for the future.

This second phase of Soviet history accorded much better with the accepted norms of family life than had the first phase, when children were encouraged to see themselves as the vanguard of the revolution, and to take issue with parents who held 'backward' views. The legend of Pavlik Morozov – who had supposedly denounced his father to the authorities for subverting the cause of collectivization – was only the most (in)famous of a variety of young heroes as generational rebels. Heroes of this kind were promoted by specific interest groups in Soviet society, largely made up of young members of the Komsomol organization (though with a powerful patron in the writer Maxim Gorky, who himself had, according to his memoirs, experienced an abusive childhood that had turned him into a critic of the status quo). The Party youth organizations carried out fervent campaigns to encourage children to distance themselves from family life, as expressed with particular directness in an anonymous typescript dating from the mid-1920s, and now held in the central archive of the Komsomol in Moscow. (The translation reproduces the irregularities of punctuation, grammar, and style that were characteristic of the time.):

The modern family is complete[ly] alien to the Komsomol member in its way of life, customs etc., because it doesnt allow him to struggle and move forward, and so the new family of the Komsomol member should be the Komsomol cell. He should share his joys and griefs. the cell and the Komsomol members generally should be the family constantly surrounding him, only then will [the traditional family] not be in a position to influence him. of course its even better if the Komsomol member leaves his family altogether supposing it [his family] is petty-bourgeois, making his own hostels and communes – but thats not too easy right now and so the principle that the cell is the Komsomol members family is of first importance.[8]

Living up to these standards created significant tensions, particularly in Russian villages, where obedience to elders was the norm (though, as ethnographical records from the late nineteenth century point out, norms might be suspended if the household patriarch happened to be drunk or incapable).[9] Both memoirs and contemporary newspaper reports suggest that attacks on activist children were quite common.[10] The reversal to 'parent control' in the late 1930s no doubt did seem like a return to normality for many. The intergenerational conflict that might in other circumstances have emerged during such a period of restored conservatism was blunted by the material deprivation endured by Soviet society and by the common perception of the family as a refuge from social malaise, rather than a place that should be fled from. A highly visible population of street children (*besprizornye*) (cleared from view beginning in 1935, but re-emerging with a vengeance during World War II) reminded children and young people that the costs of rebellion were high. Open conflict with one's parents seems to have been a quite exceptional social phenomenon in the Stalin years.[11]

The first four decades of Soviet power thus saw a shift from widespread emphasis, in propaganda and ideology, on children and young people's capacity for radical action to a shift on their capacity for emulation. In turn, this emphasis on continuity flattened the individual character of different generations. Considerably more dynamic in terms of generational mythology was the era after 1956. Khrushchev's secret speech denouncing Stalin, and the period of de-Stalinization in symbolic terms that followed it, was accompanied by a deliberate return to the mythology of the 1920s, including the emphasis on youth activism. The 1960s saw a number of notable events to mark this, including the setting-up from the late 1950s of 'voluntary popular militias' (*dobrovol'nye narodnye druzhiny*) composed of Komsomol activists, and an upsurge of propaganda promoting child and teenage heroes. The fall of Khrushchev, on the other hand, marked the start of an era that was more conservative in this respect, as in many others. The post-Stalin era accordingly witnessed an important clash between the mythology of change and innovation and the mythology of continuity – between a generational history based on the deeds and attitudes of parents, and a generational history based on the deeds and attitudes of children. If the *shestidesiatniki* were one hegemonic group to emerge from the post-Stalin era (their lustre in terms of street credibility only increased by their rather precarious standing in terms of the Soviet cultural establishment), another was the much larger community of those who had 'defended the Motherland' between 1941 and 1945, a community that extended to some members of the politburo.[12]

The prominence and political and emotional load of 'generation' as an assumed link between biological age and social experience is such that to ask whether the term 'generation' has any empirical validity might appear from most respects a *question mal posée*. Nevertheless, I believe it is a question worth asking, if only because it is worthwhile to look beyond the history of the 'noisiest' age cohorts (who include not only *shestidesiatniki* and war veterans, but also a voluble band of self-apologists who reached maturity in the Stalin years).[13]

Narrating generational experience

Getting at the nature of 'experience' is, as always, a tricky activity. The evidence on which most of the discussion here is based is oral history – 37 interviews with informants born between 1957 and 1977, and brought up in a variety of different urban centres, ranging in size from small towns to large cities and the 'two capitals' of Moscow and Leningrad. Clearly, informants do not simply 'tell it like it was' in interviews: they are engaged in a process of performance, where the audience comprises not just the interviewer, but the social group that he or she is held to represent, 'educated people', 'social outsiders', and often also 'the younger generation' (since a standard situation is one where some member of a 'noisy generation' shares his or her memories with a person who has not been witness to those events). In Russia, the 'seniority cult' that obtained from the late 1930s onwards makes it common for elderly interviewees to take a strongly didactic approach to the interlocutor. A typical example is this excerpt from an interview of mine with an informant born in 1918, who is describing here the frugal circumstances in which he was brought up:

> We had to be very careful with everything. Water too. You couldn't save water in the vegetable patch, nothing will grow otherwise. But at home we watched every drop. We weren't allowed to overfill cups when we were using the kettle. You had to use as little water as possible when you were washing. You see? We treasured that water. That was what life was like [...] And I'll tell you another interesting thing: I still do save water. Whenever I turn on the tap, I try to let out just a little trickle ...[14]

Clearly, this informant is not just describing matter-of-factly the economics of the household in which he was brought up, but also relating them to an assumed context of extravagance and wilful waste, where people are prepared to pour gallons of water down the sink. As another informant put it more directly in an informal conversation: 'I can't bear to see food wasted because I was hungry all my childhood. But my children …!'[15] Conversely, informants brought up in the post-Stalin years employ a rather different set of tropes. Here, the contrast between 'then' and 'now' functions in order to suggest the idyllic character of the past, the supremely happy nature of childhood experience back then in the 1960s, 1970s, or 1980s. Take the following extract from an interview with a woman born in Penza in 1970:

> **Inf.:** Well, I think we had the best childhood you could possibly have, and the best we had was what we had in childhood. And now I'd like my children to have a childhood like that, a cloud-free, happy childhood.
> **Int.:** So you think that all the social muddle and confusion reflects …
> **Inf.:** I don't *think*. I *know*.
>
> [Oxf/Lev T-04 PF8A, p. 25][16]

But it is clear that, at the very least, interviews with different age cohorts reveal different methods of *describing* experience, alternative rhetorical stereotypes. Conversely, they reveal a striking communality in terms of narrating experience among the post-1954 group,[17] and one that is distinctive in terms of Soviet history. While Soviet propaganda spent a great deal of time dwelling on the state's munificent provision of a 'happy childhood' to all the nation's little ones, this fantasy – if one takes our informants on trust – came closest to being enacted in reality in the last decades of Soviet power. The experience of this particular generation (or these particular generations – the issue of how long a generation lasts being not much easier to answer than the classic question of the length of a piece of string) was exceptional in Soviet terms precisely because it was 'normal' – *normal'noe* – a term that in Russian, as in many other European languages, though not English, has the additional meaning of 'fine', 'good', 'just as it should be'.

Before moving to the discussion of this motif in more detail, however, some annotatory or framing material to supply information that the informants take for granted needs to be supplied. To begin with: why might this particular era be seen as a coherent entity? One possible answer is that this impression is illusory. The social upheavals since the late 1980s have left late Soviet experience as a kind of 'frozen memory', as static as the recollections of émigrés for whom the term was originally coined. Soviet culture no longer exists, and from the vantage point of the present, now seems a world in which, to quote the title of Alexei Yurchak's recent study, 'Everything Was Forever, Until It Was No More'. Yet in fact this was a usually settled period of Russian history, so far as the experience of the under-14s was concerned.[18] The oldest members of our group, those born in the late 1950s, began attending school in 1961 or later, when de-Stalinization had already peaked. It is most unlikely that any of them would have come across textbooks or posters celebrating the disgraced leader, but on the other hand, they would have been little exposed to serious discussions of the Stalin years either; it was customary to skate over the period with formulations such as 'the temporary suspension of normal democratic relations'.[19] At the level of high politics, this was the so-called period of stagnation, which brought an abrupt end to the questioning of the Soviet past begun under Khrushchev. Certainly, Stalin was not restored to the pantheon, but the cult of Lenin remained in full force, and children were enthusiastically exposed to this.

As had been the case from the mid-1930s, the vast majority of schoolchildren were members of the Pioneer (children's Communist) movement, whose influence on younger children had, indeed, been increased by the strengthening, from 1955, of the Octobrist organization for six- to ten-year-olds. The responsibilities of 'class supervisors', or form teachers, included, as had been the case since the 1940s, political and moral education, which was imparted in sessions of political discussion, and the assignation of material such as the lives of Pioneer heroes for homework reading. Children were cajoled or coerced into subscribing to newspapers and journals such as *Pioneer, Pioneer Pravda,* and *Leninist Sparks* (the Leningrad Pioneer newspaper), and had to prepare summaries of articles therein; 'political information' could not be avoided except by truancy. The vast majority of our informants recall receiving political education in some form, and everyone we spoke to was a member of the Pioneers. It was not until the end of the 1980s that this situation began to change, with teachers in subjects such as history abandoning the textbooks from which instruction had formerly been given, and Pioneer work becoming less and less important until, in 1991, it was abandoned altogether as the organization folded. By this time, all our informants had reached the age of fourteen anyway, so that all of them experienced a 'normal Soviet childhood' as intended by educational planners throughout their early years.

Our project concentrated on recording life histories from informants who had grown up in working-class families, since these individuals are under-represented in written memoirs. These interviews are not a door into the lives of the elite, but into those of the mainstream inhabitants of towns and cities, people mainly without special privileges and special experiences. Yet all came from settled families; in some cases their parents had divorced, and in one or two, a parent had died, or a father never been in evidence at all, but there are no accounts of catastrophic dysfunction or atomization. The official mechanisms of 'refusing one's baby' (*otkaz ot rebenka*) and 'deprivation of parental rights' (*lishenie roditel'skikh prav*) meant that children from marginal families (the children of poor single mothers or chronic alcoholics, for example) had a high chance of ending up in institutions – for the fortunate, mainstream orphanages and boarding schools, for the less fortunate, corrective and penal institutions such as strict regime boarding schools or 'youth colonies' (labour camps).[20] Our informants, then, are the 'success stories' of Soviet urban life, in a modest way. However, that is also true (indeed, all the more true) of our informants from earlier generations, so the difference in narrated experience in this group is still significant.

Toy tanks and white dresses

So what does this narrated experience tell us? On the evidence presented here, home life between the early 1960s and the late 1980s was in many ways homogeneous. To begin with, children were spared many of the political and social upheavals of other times. No one in this era remembers having a parent or relation arrested, a fairly common event in the recollected lives of our interviewees during the 1930s. No one mentions a murder, as they might have done when recalling childhood in the 1990s or 2000s. Certainly, some specific features of the command economy remained. Household moves, where they occurred, were more likely to be a result of *force majeure* than of personal choice: because one or both parents had changed employment, or been relocated in the course of their employment, or because the family had been allocated new accommodation. According to Soviet literature and journalism, the post-Stalin era was the great age of the 'exchange', of informal room or apartment swaps (sometimes accompanied by a cash incentive), whereby relatives might pool several rooms in order to shift from accommodation in a communal flat to a private apartment shared by two or three generations of the same family, or, conversely, move from a large family apartment into two smaller ones.[21] This celebrated manifestation of the exercise of limited consumer leverage within the Soviet housing market is not widely reflected in our interviews, which generally record relocations of more orthodox varieties – moves from communal flats into newly allocated state flats, or occasionally, the purchase of a co-operative apartment.[22] The mobility in the accommodation market that emerged during the Yeltsin years, with some families buying apartments, others 'privatizing' their own, and the emergence of a much larger private rental sector, still lay far in the future. It was common for families who had half-way acceptable accommodation to remain in this for decades. This in turn increased the chances that at least one grandparent would be present in the family household, since young married couples were likely to occupy space in one or other partner's birth family for at least a decade before they found separate housing (assuming they took this step at any stage).

Characteristically Soviet also, in terms of international comparators (and comparators from within Russian history), was the relative absence of markers of socio-economic distinctiveness. Late Soviet society, though multicultural and regionally diverse, had strongly entrenched social norms that were both enshrined in, and shaped, public discourse. Experience that did not fit with the customary models of social behaviour essentially did not 'exist' from the point of view of official discourse, such as journalism and literature. To judge by the recollections offered to us, these norms were internalized to a high degree. It is common for informants to observe that the circumstances in which they lived were 'like everyone else's'.[23] The concrete detail provided suggests that these perceptions had some objective foundation. None of our informants who lived in a one-family flat recalls having more than three rooms; the furniture remembered was usually strictly functional (beds, wardrobes, tables, secretaires, bookshelves, with decoration limited to pot plants, photographs, posters, in rare cases a few paintings, and perhaps a chandelier, rather than, say, marble sculptures or inlaid cabinets – any items in this last category that happened to be around would almost certainly be inherited from an earlier generation of the family).[24]

Yet underneath the surface, there were considerable changes afoot. Parents were now encouraged to create a 'children's corner', and it was, judging by informants' reports, indeed much commoner for children to have some kind of private space, even if this only amounted to a bed.[25] The era also saw further development of an autonomous children's culture in other respects as well. Numbers of books for children expanded; as well as the established classics of the 1930s and 1940s, the publishing houses 'Children's Literature' and 'Little One' (Malysh) issued reprints of books that had been quietly shelved since the early 1930s, such as

Panteleev and Belykh's orphanage classic *The Republic of Shkid*. A new feature was an upsurge in the number of translations, above all of Eastern European, but also of Western European titles, and not just classics, as in the 1930s and 1940s, but also twentieth-century best-sellers. Among the most popular titles of the period were Lindgren's *Pippi Longstocking*, Milne's *Winnie the Pooh*, and Gianni Rodari's *Cipollino*. Material of this kind did not languish in some kind of semi-permitted half-life, but was integrated into official culture – one school even named the *zvezdochki*, subgroups of Young Octobrists analogous to 'sixes' in the British Cub Scout movement, after characters from A. A. Milne.[26]

The late 1950s and 1960s onward also saw the emergence of a fully fledged autonomous cinematic tradition for children, celebrated, from 1974 onwards, in the specialist magazine *Eralash*, which carried narrative photo spreads about new titles. The material included both narrative films with human actors and more particularly cartoons, *mul'tfil'my*, an occasional genre of the Russian cinema back to the 1900s, but reaching unprecedented dominance at this period.[27] These cultural changes were symptomatic of something else as well – the increased importance of leisure activities in the Pioneer movement. Already in the 1930s, there had been a rising emphasis on the work of 'hobby circles', and on the provision of facilities for these through the network of 'Pioneer Palaces' in large cities, and 'Pioneer Houses' in smaller urban centres, and individual districts of conurbations. But the 1960s and 1970s saw growing numbers of children's clubs open up, both within the Pioneer movement and also outside it – housing co-operatives and city 'microdistricts' began providing centres where children could play sports or learn how to dismantle a radio, staffed by volunteers among local residents. All the informants recall taking part in some aspects of this vibrant culture for children – watching films, visiting hobby circles, using playground facilities, going to the theatre, and reading (though by no means all were enthusiastic readers, and among those who were, journals such as *Young Technician* were often as popular as fiction).

There was more on offer for children, then, than there had been in the late 1940s, when after rationing was abolished in 1947 working-class young Leningraders spent afternoons wandering into shops and simply staring at the goods that were for sale.[28] A still more striking change was the quantities of child-relevant goods available for purchase by parents or by children themselves. The official campaign to improve consumer provision initiated at the Twenty-Second Congress of the Communist Party in 1961 was followed by widespread press coverage of the need to provide special furniture, clothes, and toys for children. Certainly, official advice on baby management at this period was very simple. Unlike their pre-revolutionary predecessors, Soviet childcare gurus did not tell readers that they were supposed to have special changing mats, baby baths, layettes, and so on. But they did give advice on diet. 'Vegetables, berries and fruits contain minerals and vitamins that are absolutely vital,' advised *House Management*, a compendium of domestic life published in 1965.[29]

The expanding sense that it was necessary to provide generously for children did not stop at food. So far as older children were concerned, consumer goods were also mentioned. For instance, *House Management* told parents that toddlers should have toys such as balls, skipping ropes, sledges, and hoops.[30] At this period, newspaper coverage also began to stress consumer goods, from the point of view of quality as well as of acquisition in its own right. Parents were told that goods for children – furniture, clothes, shoes, etc. – should be attractive as well as hygienic and practical.[31] Sometimes Western items (in one case, Italian-made plastic laminated nursery furniture) were held up as models for Soviet design; on other occasions, 'cutting edge' Soviet items were featured.[32] The coverage included things that might have been described as luxuries – most egregiously, perhaps, a special children's umbrella with a handle shaped like a flower, designed by a team of psychologists, sociologists, artists, and engineers.[33] At other times, a touch of more realism was displayed – as in the case of designs for girls' dresses that could be adjusted to fit as the girl grew taller.[34] But whichever way, there was unprecedented attention to the fact that children needed large numbers of special things – from lace jabots to fancy hairdos.[35] As well as ensuring that the child's environment was pleasant from this point of view, Soviet normative literature had started to emphasize the importance of making children the centre of attention in other ways – for example, by organizing elaborate children's parties for birthdays, or spending time on decorating the home for New Year.[36]

The potential social tensions likely to be caused by encouraging children to expect material things were occasionally recognized in the Soviet press, particularly when the desirable items were of 'foreign' origin. A disapproving article of 1984, for example, scathingly portrayed a youth craze for a new style of trousers called 'bananas'.[37] And a new problem had appeared in advice literature – what to do with the quantities of things that the 'normal' child was now assumed to have.[38] Official magazines sometimes poked fun at the idea of the child consumer – with *Nedelia* running a cartoon of a baby in its pram scanning a fashion magazine.[39] But the balance was nonetheless towards encouraging consumption. Parents who indulged their children excessively might be ridiculed, in the latest manifestation of the tradition of warning against 'spoiling', but parents who did not pay due attention to their children's needs in terms of acquiring material things were the subject of harsher criticism.[40]

Thus, items that would, in earlier decades of Soviet power, have been seen as luxuries, or indeed not mentioned at all, began to be presented as simple necessities – despite the fact that their real existence was often rather elusive. Like the designer clothes in British fashion magazines that are described as 'made to order' (for which read, samples that are not available to the general public), the prime goods in Soviet magazines were not within the reach of ordinary mortals. Accommodating expanded expectations of what a child needed was far from easy. While the post-Stalin era did not – until the beginning of the 1990s, at any rate – see a repetition of the severe food shortages of the post-war era, providing children with the recommended amounts of nourishing foods, particularly milk, fresh vegetables, and fruit, demanded much time spent queuing, and often also large amounts of luck, or more likely, as the system of *blat* (personal pull) took hold, connections with shop staff or with well-placed friends. Food purchases could also be made at the semi-private collective farm markets, but here prices were high. In the context of Soviet life, fruits in particular could be classed as 'luxuries'. As Sigrid Rausing records in her study of post-Soviet Estonia, even in the 1990s imported fruit was considered an embarrassingly generous gift, in response to which 'I was sometimes overwhelmed with boxes of Estonian sweets or chocolate, or even crocheted table mats or decorations, objects that, to a Western way of reckoning, were far more valuable than a few oranges or kiwi fruit.'[41] In the 1970s and 1980s (as I can testify from direct personal observation), oranges and lemons were only available in collective farm markets, where they cost a rouble each (up to one per cent of an average monthly wage – say 10 dollars by today's standards). Expensive in cities, they were not available at all in the Russian countryside, where the imperative to provide fruit and vegetables could only have been satisfied by recourse to home-bottled produce. Children's clothes were also scarce, as were toys, games, and various types of sporting equipment; purchasing such items on the black market was prohibitive. And there was no official state allocation here, as there was with baby clothes.

Yet adults did what they could. If oral history is anything to go by, an ethos of 'everything for the children' was extremely widespread.

A woman whose children were born in the early 1980s recalled how her husband filled her younger daughter's pram with rattles:

> Where did he find them? It was very hard to buy them. And there was a whole pile of snow-white nappies. I'll remember it all my life. We always tried to buy books and educational games, paints and pencils and plasticine, we had all that in unlimited quantities. And I tried to make the most beautiful clothes I could. My daughter always wore white tights and light dresses. We tried to take them everywhere [...] to the park, the circus, the cinema. We bought everything that was necessary for childhood, we tried to do everything. I don't think there were any gaps. But we did ingrain spiritual and moral education into the children.[42]

One notes here the integration into 'everything that was necessary for childhood' of material objects that were from a practical point of view 'luxuries' – white and pale clothes were almost impossible to keep looking fresh in cities that were dusty or muddy depending on the season, and where water supplies were erratic and often tainted by rust or other stain-inducing substances. Where children were concerned, it would seem, no 'luxury' was classed as such.

Significantly, the early memories of informants from the 1960s and 1970s generations often hinge on material things. For example, a lorry driver's daughter from Leningrad born in 1969 warmly remembered trips with her father to 'Children's World', one of the chain of state-run toyshops whose flagship store was on Lubianka Square, next door to the headquarters of the Soviet secret police:

> **Inf.:** Well, the most vivid memory I have is of Dad taking me to 'Children's World'. He was very generous, and he always ... you know ... I'd arrive at the shop, and he'd buy everything I pointed at, I'd just say, 'I want that.' Although I wasn't spoilt, I was brought up knowing the value of money. But if I really wanted something, they'd try to go along with it.
> **Int.:** So what did you usually get there? What did you point at?
> **Inf.:** I don't know... somehow I remember this doll I got given, a big, big one, that walked all by itself and said 'Ma-ma.'[43]

Other kinds of first memory include time in the country, which for this generation often meant a dacha, rather than a trip to some village where their grandparents or other relations were permanently domiciled.[44]

The idea was that spending time out of doors was essential to a child's health; yet investment in the property required quite a considerable financial outlay, especially if it were only accessible, or most conveniently accessible, by car, which tended to be the case with the less prestigious (more affordable) settlements that were starting to be built during the 1960s and 1970s.[45]

Of course, one could argue that 'first memories' are made up of such experiences because they were relatively rare. And certainly informants are eager to emphasize (here, as always with oral history, having an eye to the present) that circumstances were constricted. Thus a man born in Leningrad in 1972, the son of a single-mother factory worker, remembered how he and the neighbours' boy, to his annoyance, had to make do with identical toys:

> When they were selling some nice children's toys, my mother would get a call, or my mother would ring them, and they'd buy the same things together … two sets of the same toys at once, for the two boys at the same time. Right. And so for some reason or other my mother would always make a mark on my toys with nail-varnish, so they didn't get mixed up. [...] They gave us two identical tanks that steered in the same way. Right. And we'd play with them … we were only nine or so, we had no idea the remote would do both tanks at once [...] And my mother read the instructions and said, when you're playing with that tank, see, there's a switch here, and you have to switch it off. It switched off the radio receiver. But the neighbour didn't switch off his tank, and he left it in the kitchen. So when I started playing with my tank, his tank fell off the shelf and got broken. They glued it together, but I felt happy inside: finally, my tank looked different from his.[46]

In comparable vein, a woman brought up in Taganrog in the 1970s and 1980s remembered that birthday presents had to last all year:

> Well, probably because there wasn't much money to go round, I don't really remember presents that. … If I got one big doll, then that was it for the rest of my life.
> **Int.:** So you didn't really have many toys.
> **Inf.:** No, really not many, although at that time … Some people did have them, those toys, but to be honest we really weren't too indulged.[47]

Another line of recollection is 'making do' without items that might be considered normal – one notes, for example, the emphasis in an interview with a woman from a working-class family in Perm (she was born in 1958) on growing up without a proper cot: 'We had a zinc tub hanging above the bath. And I would get told constantly: That's the tub, when you came back from the maternity home, we didn't have a cot, of course, you slept in that tub. That is, the tub was my cot.'[48] Thus an everyday object becomes a trigger of family mythology, a marker of times in the past when 'we didn't have a cot, of course'.

Despite this persistent tendency to self-assertion through recollected self-denial, though, informants brought up in the 1960s, 1970s, and 1980s do remember significantly more concrete items than most informants brought up in previous decades of Soviet history. Even children from working-class homes were likely to have purpose-made clothes, rather than outfits cut down from adult clothes, which might include say a sheepskin coat, a tracksuit, and zipped boots for winter days, as in the case of a boy born in 1972.[49]

The contrast with earlier decades is brought out particularly vividly by descriptions of two different first days at school, in 1948 and in 1977:

[1948] I was late going to school for the first time, I had nothing to put on my feet, I had to go barefoot, and since it was already September it was really cold. And so I arrived at the school, my grandmother had used a sack, she'd unpicked a sack and used onion skins to dye it, and she'd sewn me a dress. I put the dress on, and then I didn't know what to do with my exercise book, so my grand-dad made me this bag, and he put potatoes into the corners, and two straps on the back, for the bag. So I got to school wearing all that, and I'll always remember – I can still remember the teacher, her eyes, her hairstyle, the dress she was wearing, I was overwhelmed by how beautiful that woman was, my first teacher![50]

[1977] **Inf.:** Yes, I do remember my first day at school. I remember very well how my neighbour arrived – the son of a friend of my mother's, and he gave me a bottle of perfume, 'Tea Rose'. And that very day, 1 September 1978, a rose had come out that my mother was growing on the windowsill. And I put a bit of that 'Tea Rose' on the real rose, to make it smell, I can remember how I took that perfume to school on 1 September.
Int.: And the rose didn't wither?
Inf.: Yes, actually it did a bit, from that 'Tea Rose'.
Int.: From the perfume ...
Inf.: From the perfume. I'd sprinkled it with 'Tea Rose'.[51]

On the one hand we have a recollection where even essentials elude the child – shoes, a proper dress; on the other, the gift of scent, an ineffably useless item, which, in a nice gesture of childish literalism, the child uses to improve on nature. There could hardly be a clearer illustration of changing circumstances. As always with autobiographical recollection, one needs to allow for self-mythologization, but the self-mythologization in each case is of a very different order.

The consumer item that probably had most resonance for Soviet children of the post-Stalin years, though, was the television. Recollections of exposure to TV in the Stalin era are rare, and coloured by a sense of privilege. Children might be allowed, very occasionally, to watch a set owned by a neighbour in a communal flat, as briefly tolerated guests; they did not calmly sit down and enjoy a couple of hours on a regular basis.[52] Not surprisingly, the arrival or presence of a television is a regular high point in memories. The set itself was a precious item – its brand name and specifications likely remembered for years afterwards.[53] And watching was a strictly regulated activity – in part because of the official schedules:

> My parents had a bed. And a TV. They got the TV when I was seven [i.e. in 1967], I'd started going to school. Now that was something special! Because you could watch the TV, and not have to go out to the cinema. They only let me go on holidays, at least, they only gave me money then. That's what made the TV something special. But it didn't work like now, morning to evening. These days, you can turn it on at six in the morning, even at five, so far as I know. And before the programmes started … I don't think there were any in the mornings. They started in the afternoon, I think. And they didn't just let us watch it any old how, you know, turn on and watch.[54]

The cohort I describe here might well be named as 'the first Soviet TV generation', or even more exactly, the 'Good Night, Little Ones' generation. 'Good Night, Little Ones' was a kind of Soviet equivalent of 'Watch With Mother', first transmitted in 1964. An animation and fantasy special under the title 'Good Night, Little Ones', with a saccharine theme tune, 'Now the Tired Toys are Sleeping/And the Bears', it was broadcasted nightly on weekdays just before the main evening news programme, *Time* (Vremia), on Channel One.[55] The scheduling was intended to have, and in fact often did have, a normative effect on family life: the standard evening routine was supposed to consist of the entire family watching this programme, followed by bed for the little ones, while the parents and older children watched the news. The timetabling did not always work as neatly as this – children might be allowed to stay up longer than the schedulers anticipated, or, if they were sharing one room with their parents, might feign sleep while actually watching films 'for adult audiences' later on. But 'Good Night, Little Ones' is widely remembered as a feature of childhood existence; its popularity can be gauged from the fact that it is one of the few Soviet TV programmes (alongside the news) to have survived the transition era.

Television represented a case where encouragement to consume was readily combinable with the established commitment to social solidarity and the dissemination of Soviet patriotism. Though there were apparently cases where some Leningrad residents with dachas in Karelia could receive Finnish TV on their sets, most Soviet citizens (in contrast to the situation with the radio) were limited to what they could officially receive. The only ways of expressing complete dissonance were not to own a set, or never to turn it on, rather than to exercise choice in what one watched. Other types of consumer goods, however, including the 'innocent' items that might be purchased by children, could sow disharmony, particularly among children who were too young to have learned that materialism was wrong. Interestingly, envy comes up considerably more as a motif in interviews recalling upbringing in the 1960s and 1970s than at earlier periods. The case of the boy who was delighted when his neighbour's tank got smashed because his then became different has already been cited. Another slightly different expression of covetousness was remembered by a Moscow woman born in 1971, who decided, aged about two, on an act of personal redistribution when frustrated by her friend's possession of a nicer object:

> My friend had a watering can in the shape of the Frog Princess, it was lovely, but I just had an ordinary one and I so wanted a watering can like hers. And so I asked my mother. But my mother said, 'No, you've already got a perfectly good one.' She wouldn't buy me one. And so then I did something crafty – I pinched my friend's watering can.[56]

In this particular case, the situation was resolved as neatly as in a morality tale – the informant was found out, thoroughly shamed, and remembered the lesson for the rest of her life. But discrepancies in access to personal possessions were not always so easily resolved. And, while some informants recall the last decades of Soviet power nostalgically, as a time of social harmony and equality, others remember that stratification was starting to make itself felt. Children who had relatives living abroad, or black market connections, were likely to appear with foreign clothes, shoes, or chewing gum (a much-prized possession in this era); others were not. Equally, children might well get inducted at an early stage into the system of favour- and influence-trading known as *blat*. A baby whose mother was making frantic telephone calls in order to swap her precious foreign romper suit for the next size up would still be oblivious; a child sent to a different school from friends at nursery school because the parents had pulled strings to get him or her a place outside the catchment area would sooner or later come to independent conclusions about what was going on.

Whichever way, children born after the mid-1950s had experiences that were distinctive, in terms of Russian history more broadly, both in terms of presences (German dolls to play with, bicycles, birthday parties as high days and holidays) and in terms of absences (queuing and hunger were not part of the usual experience, nor, usually, was hard physical work from an early age). In some ways, these children were privileged by comparison with children from ordinary families in the West at the same period: it is rare for recollections to include the fact that the informant, as a child, badly wanted some object that his or her parents could not afford to buy.[57]

Certainly, the homogeneity of children's lives in the late Soviet period should not be overstated. As at other periods of Russian history, childhood experience was strongly nuanced by social status and by location. A child growing up in a small provincial town or a village was deprived in some respects (access to cultural goods), though he or she would also have more open space to play in and quite possibly also more space to live in. Boys and girls from working-class families were more likely to be beaten, though on the other hand they were usually spared the psychological browbeating and emotional blackmail that passed for child management in some intelligentsia families ('you're not my daughter any more'). Other factors with impact on children's lives included whether there were strong ties to the countryside – if so, a family that was not well off in terms of the supply system and access to holiday facilities, such as the 'houses of rest' run by the trade-union movement, might be able to arrange for parcels of food to be sent, and for the children to get a break in the summer (perhaps one that included a little light work on the vegetable garden, or helping herd chickens, and so on). Yet at the same time, there are many ways in which childhood experience in the late twentieth century was coherent, and profoundly different from childhood experience in earlier decades of Soviet history. Like all parents and children, those of the 1960s,

1970s, and 1980s contrasted their experience with that of their ancestors or descendants, which in part was a power gambit; but the concrete detail provided in their stories suggests there was some foundation for their claims that their experience was unique. Looking back on the late Soviet era, one can see definite evidence of real historical specificity in the experience of childhood at that era. Whether one chooses to name this specificity as 'generational' is a matter of terminology and taste.

Notes

The research for this article was carried out with the support of the Leverhulme Trust, grant no. F/08736/A, 'Childhood in Russia: A Social and Cultural History'. In particular, I draw extensively here on an oral history project sponsored by the grant, using semi-structured interviews with focus groups in Moscow, Perm', St Petersburg, Taganrog, and villages in Leningrad and Novgorod provinces. Interviews from this project are coded in the following way: Oxf-Lev SPb-03 PF3A, p. 1: project identifier (Oxf/Lev), place identifier (SPb, M, T, V – for 'villages'), year code (03, 04 etc.), tape number (PF1A etc.), page number in typed transcript (p. 13). The interviewers were Aleksandra Piir (SPb), Iuliia Rybina and Ekaterina Shumilova (M), Svetlana Sirotinina (Perm'), and Liudmila Terekhova (Taganrog). Interviews carried out by Catriona Kelly are coded 'CKQ', followed by a place identifier (SPb, M, E, Oxf – which last refers to interviews carried out in the UK, not just in Oxford). For more information about the project, including information about the informants, see the project website, www.mod-langs.ox.ac.uk/russian/childhood/. I also draw on interviews coded 'RAO': these were carried out as part of a training programme at the Russian Academy of Education, and were kindly made available to me by Vitalii Bezrogov.

1. A recent example of this approach is Lesley Chamberlain's popular history of Russian philosophy, *Motherland* (London, 2004), where each chapter deals with a specific generation, beginning with 'Men of the 1820s'.
2. D. Raleigh, *Russia's Sputnik Generation: Soviet Baby Boomers Talk about Their Lives* (Bloomington, IN, 2007); A. Yurchak, *Everything Was Forever, Until It Was No More: The Last Soviet Generation* (Princeton, NJ, 2006).
3. E. Liarskaia, *Severnye internaty i transformatsiia traditsionnoi kul'tury (na primere nentsev Yamala): avtoreferat dissertatsii na soiskanie uchenoi stepeni kandidata istoricheskikh nauk* (St Petersburg, 2003).
4. See Catriona Kelly, *Children's World: Growing Up in Russia, 1890–1991* (New Haven, CT, 2007), Chap. 10.
5. Of 69 informants consulted by Ekaterina Belousova for her survey of birthing experiences in the late Soviet and post-Soviet eras, more than two-thirds (48) had only one child. Of the other 21 informants, 14 had two children spaced between 5 and 11 years apart; only 5 had children spaced under 5 years apart (the other two cases were a family with twins, and a family of 9 children, both of which were for different reasons exceptions). Figures compiled by me from the list of informants in E. Belousova, 'Prima

materia: sotsializatsiia zhenshchiny v rodil'nom dome', *Trudy fakul'teta etnologii*, vol. 1 (St Petersburg, 2001), pp. 89–93. 'Serial only children' were frequent in our interviews as well. Interestingly, this phenomenon seems, going by my personal impressions, to be on the wane in post-Soviet Russia, with rather more families where the children are close-spaced, as in Britain or the USA.

6. True, informants who grew up in the Soviet era will often categorize material culture in analogous ways. It is common, when people are asked to describe what the family home looked like, what furniture there was, and so on, for phrases such as *tak, kak u vsekh* ('like everybody's, like everybody had') to be used. However, such phrases are not used when people describe their relationships with close family members or friends.

7. For an example, see Oxf/Lev SPb-03 PF36A, p. 15, where the informant (a man born in 1940) remarks, in answer to a question about whether grandmothers babysat the children in his family, 'That generation wasn't around' (*eto vot pokolenie ne bylo*).

8. 'Komsomol'skii byt' (unsigned and undated text of a lecture, c. 1924), Tsentr khraneniia dokumentov molodezhnykh organizatsii (TsKhDMO), Moscow, f. 1, op. 23, d. 245, l. 81. The complete text of this document is to appear in Vitalii Bezrogov and Catriona Kelly (eds), *Vzroslye o detiakh i deti o sebe: Istoriia russkogo detstva 1890–1991 v dokumentakh* (publication forthcoming).

9. For variations in the role of the *bol'shak*, see B.M. Firsov and I.G. Kiseleva (eds), *Byt velikorusskikh krest'yan-zemlepashtsev. Opisanie materialov Etnograficheskogo biuro kniazia V.N. Tenisheva (na primere Vladimirskoi gubernii)* (St Petersburg, 1993), pp. 192–9.

10. Memoirs include Mikhail Alekseev, *Kariukha. Drachuny* (Moscow, 1988); newspaper reports include the case of the much-mythologized Pavlik Morozov, on which see Catriona Kelly, *Comrade Pavlik: The Rise and Fall of a Soviet Boy Hero* (London, 2005).

11. Such conflict is recalled by only very occasional informants in interviews: for example, CKQ-Ox-03 PF5–6 (this particular case is a woman b. 1931, who was the daughter of a leading commander [later general] in the Red Army, and who grew up on the most elite residential street in Leningrad, Kamennoostrovsky prospekt, directly opposite the apartment occupied, until his murder in December 1934, by the Leningrad Party leader, Sergei Kirov). This is not to say that young people were involved in no social conflict in the Stalin years: as Juliane Fürst's work indicates, Soviet teenagers came into confrontation with the authorities fairly often, in the post-war years particularly.

12. On war mythology, see N. Tumarkin, *The Living & the Dead : The Rise and Fall of the Cult of World War II in Russia* (New York, 1994); C. Merridale, *Night of Stone: Death and Memory in Russia* (London, 2000).

13. See e.g. N. Korzhavin, *V soblaznakh krovavoi epokhi*, 2 vols (Moscow, 2005).

14. CKQ-M-04 PF5B, p. 20.

15. Pers. inf. (from conversation with male, b. late 1940s, St Peterburg 2003).

16. Money worries were in fact endemic in the Soviet system too – see the early 1960s questionnaire answers – but this is often not recorded in this and other recent interviews, where informants tend to contrast their own childhoods with the greater level of economic conflict in those of their own children.

17. The observations here and below are based on 36 semi-structured interviews with informants in this group, 22 female and 14 male, most of whom grew up in the families of manual workers.

18. The time limits of childhood are a subject of extensive discussion. Both here and in *Children's World*, I am concerned primarily with children from the onset of mobility and speech (two or three) and the onset of puberty – notionally taken to be 14. This age threshold was significant in terms of Soviet children's public experience less because of biological changes (the subject generally of embarrassed silence) than because the early teens marked the start of a time when more was expected from children in a social and moral sense. Fourteen or fifteen was the lower-age threshold of the Komsomol, a much more serious organization than the Pioneers; it was the upper-age limit for children in orphanages; and it marked the time when the majority of children were expected either to leave education and go into employment (as was the case until the 1960s), or to transfer from academic into vocational education (the introduction of compulsory full secondary schooling for all was accompanied by the retention of a multi-track pattern of institutional provision, with some pupils at vocational schools, colleges, and technicums, and others at academic ten-year schools).

19. I remember this phrase, *vremennoe prekrashchenie normal'nykh demokratich-eskikh otnoshenii*, being used in Soviet history (*stranovedenie*) classes when I was a student at a Soviet university in 1980–81.

20. These institutional stories were also recorded in our project: e.g. Oxf/Lev P-5 PF14 (male, b. 1976, specialist school for the educationally backward); Oxf/Lev SPb-04 PF47, p. 48 (female, b. 1967, orphanage); Oxf/Lev T-04 P5 (female, b. 1972, orphanage); and at second hand in interviews with child-care professionals, e.g. Oxf/Lev P-05 PF1, p. 2 (guard in youth colony from 1984); Oxf/Lev SPb-04 PF45, p. 46 (female, supervisor in boarding school from 1970); Oxf/Lev SPb-04 PF62, p. 63 (male, supervisor in closed-regime boarding school from 1974). All of these interviews indicate that material conditions, while still difficult by Western standards (in boarding schools, children were allocated only one pair of tights per year, and girls were not issued with bras) were significantly better than in previous generations.

21. The classic literary depiction of this social institution is Iurii Trifonov's *The Exchange* (1969), which was turned into one of the most popular plays on the stage of Iurii Liubimov's Taganka theatre and also entered the English-language repertory in a translation by Michael Frayn.

22. On a move from a room in state accommodation to an apartment, see e.g. Oxf/Lev SPb-03 PF14A, p. 4; on co-operatives see e.g. Oxf/Lev P-05 PF5A, p. 2; a rare reference to an exchange is Oxf/Lev P-05 PF15A, p. 2. The scarcity of experiences in this last category might in turn raise questions about the actual extent to which the exchange system operated. Obviously, participating in this required a degree of privilege – access to accommodation that someone else might want.

23. See, e.g., M-03 PF 10A, p. 4: 'Well, [the things we had] were like everyone's, in any working-class family.'

24. As in the case of the couple interviewed in CKQ-M-04 PF5, CKQ-M-04 PF6, p. 7, whose interior decoration included inherited portraits, a bust of Dante, etc.

25. Though there are cases of siblings sharing beds even in this generation, e.g. Oxf/Lev SPb-03 PF14A, p. 2 (lorry driver's daughter, b. 1969).
26. Oxf/Lev SPb-03 PF29A, p. 40.
27. A. Golembievskaia, 'Kto liubit mul'tfil'my?' *Nedelia* [henceforth *N*], 27 (1968), 10–11. Cf. the item on *Zamarashka, N*, 5 (1962), 19; on *Belaia shkurka, N*, 13 (1969), 19–20. For general introductions to animation, see David MacFadyen, *Yellow Crocodiles and Blue Oranges: Russian Animated Film since World War II* (Montreal, 2005); Birgit Beumers, *Pop Culture Russia!* (Santa Barbara, CA, 2005), pp. 99–104.
28. Oxf/Lev SPb-03 PF8B, p. 27 (man from manual-worker background, b. 1933).
29. *Domovodstvo* (Moscow, 1964), pp. 19–55.
30. *Domovodstvo*, p. 45.
31. E.g. (on clothes), *N*, 48 (1962), 21; *N*, 10 (1963), 23; *N*, 6 (1965), 20–1; *N*, 33 (1966), 20; *N*, 50 (1968), 19; *N*, 2 (1971), 15; *N*, 31 (1971), 14; *N*, 34 (1976), 14–15; *N*, 32 (1979), 24; *N*, 42 (1980), 16; *N*, 1 (1982), 12; *N*, 21 (1982), 18–19; *N*, 32 (1983), 14–15, and so on.
32. *N*, 26 (1973), 22–3; cf. *N*, 5 (1977), 16 (Italian furniture); *N*, 29 (1980), 5 (Soviet made cutting-edge children's bicycles).
33. *N*, 29 (1980), 9.
34. *N*, 32 (1983), 14–15.
35. *N*, 44 (1979), 18–19 (lace jabot for a baby); *N*, 13 (1977), 19–20, *N*, 38 (1978), 14 (hairdos).
36. On parties, see *N*, 52 (1971), 19, ibid. 30 (1970), 13; on trees and other New Year decorations, ibid. 51 (1970), 16–17.
37. *N*, 3 (1984), 19.
38. See e.g. *N*, 4 (1972), 10, which shows an attractively presented 'children's corner' in the living room, with shelving space for toys and games.
39. *N*, 6 (1979), 6.
40. On criticism of parents for not doing enough for children, see e.g. the satirical story 'Detskii mir', *N*, 21 (1971), 20, where some parents spend the family money on clothes for themselves rather than a birthday present for their son.
41. S. Rausing, *History, Memory, and Identity in Post-Soviet Estonia* (Oxford, 2004), p. 73.
42. Oxf/Lev P-05 PF8B, p. 20 (woman b. 1959, factory settlement, Perm' province, mother clerk, father crane driver).
43. Oxf/Lev SPb-04 PF 14A, p. 1.
44. See, e.g., CKQ-Ox-03 PF12A, p. 1 (woman b. 1958, Leningrad, father architect, mother designer).
45. See S. Lovell, *Summerfolk: A History of the Dacha, 1710–2000* (Ithaca, NY, 2003).
46. Oxf/Lev SPb-03 PF 28A, p. 3.
47. Oxf/Lev T-04 PF 19B, p. 19 (woman b. 1968, Taganrog, father lorry driver, mother cashier).
48. Oxf/Lev P-05 PF21A, p. 2.
49. Oxf/Lev SPb-03 PF 28A, p. 6.
50. Oxf/Lev T-04 PF21, p. 12 (woman b. 1941, factory settlement, Briansk province, raised by grandmother, a factory worker).
51. Oxf/Lev T-04 PF 7A, p. 12 (woman b. 1970, Penza, mother housepainter, father turbine operator).

52. See e.g. CKQ-Ox-03 PF1A, p. 3 (woman b. 1936, daughter of senior officials in the Ministry of Trade).
53. As e.g. in Oxf/Lev M-04 PF24A, p. 2: (man b. 1968, factory settlement, Moscow province, father building worker, mother teacher). In this case, the set was a 1970s TEMP brand with a large screen, in black and white.
54. Oxf/Lev P-05 PF12A, p. 2 (woman b. 1960, small town, Perm' province, mother cook, father lathe operator).
55. Limited information about the history of 'Spokoinoi nochi, malyshi!', still running at the time of writing, can be found on the programme's website, http://www.rutv.ru/prog?rubric_ud=606&brand_id=360 (accessed 22 August 2005).
56. RAO M-05 PF13A, p. 2 (female informant, b. 1971, satellite town, Moscow [*prigorod*], father and mother workers).
57. Conversely, recollections among members of this generation of being unable to buy particular consumer goods for one's children are fairly common, e.g., CKQ-Ox-03 PF4A, p. 12 (woman b. 1957, Odessa province): 'There were too many tempting things around, and it was all very tough, especially for parents.'

10
Generations and Intergenerational Relationships, Public and Private, in Twentieth-Century Britain

Pat Thane

Introduction

The concept of 'generation' has had little resonance in the national politics of modern Britain. This is probably because for at least two centuries the country has not undergone the sharp historical breaks – hostile occupation, defeat in war, revolution – which other European countries have experienced and which have created in these societies a sense of real separation between different age cohorts. It is true that the country, which at the beginning of the twentieth century headed a vast international Empire, was a major world power and a leading player in the international economy, by the 1960s, at the latest, was none of these things. But this profound change in Britain's international roles was experienced by British people gradually, unevenly and rarely as cataclysm. There are no clear differences between imperial and post-imperial generations, though perhaps some of the most profound intergenerational differences are within the post-imperial immigrant groups who have come to Britain from former colonies in Asia, Africa and the Caribbean.

The notion of a 'lost generation' had a certain, negative, resonance in Britain after the 'Great' war of 1914–18, when it was felt that the high casualties, and especially the exceptionally high levels of loss of upper class young men, had destroyed many of the 'brightest and best', thus depriving the country of a cohort of potential leaders.[1] The closest Britain has come to generational terminology in recent British politics has been in references to 'Thatcher's children', an ambiguous tribute to the political leader who tried harder than any in the twentieth century to challenge established British institutions and cultural certainties, with some successes. It implies a generation which grew to maturity during

Mrs Thatcher's premiership, from 1979 to 1990, whose values – those promoted by the Thatcher governments – are said to be more individualistic, competitive and materialistic than those of older generations.

Ideas about generations have entered British political life more frequently in relation to concerns about the impact of demographic change upon the economy, society and politics. And both the idea of generational difference and the experience of intergenerational relations have mattered greatly in the everyday lives of most people.

'Age groups'

How, then, has 'generation' been conceptualized in Britain within these very different, public and private, discourses? Firstly, let us explore 'public' definitions of age groups. Since the later nineteenth century generational age groups have come to be more strictly defined by age in official discourse, as age of entry to and exit from the adult workforce came to be regulated by state legislation. Capacity and eligibility to work have long been the prime marker of generational boundaries. The introduction of compulsory education from 1880 defined childhood dependence as lasting until the age of 12–13, a threshold that rose gradually to 16 by the 1970s. For increasing numbers of people it is now 18 or 21, since 40 per cent of 18-year-olds enter university for at least three years (the proportion was only 7 per cent even in 1970). The introduction of state old-age pensions in 1908, paid at age 70, began the process whereby at a certain age people were defined as 'old' and expected to retire from the workforce. This official pensionable age fell to 65 in 1925, and for women to 60 in 1940, though gradually raising the pension and retirement age to 68 is currently under discussion.[2] As we will see, it was only after World War II, in the 1950s, that retirement from paid work at the state pension age became normal for most people.[3]

Similar changes in the ages of leaving and entering the workforce occurred throughout Europe from the mid-nineteenth to the mid-twentieth centuries. To take the example of pensions, between 1889 (when Bismarck introduced the first scheme of social insurance for old age in Germany, payable at age 70) and 1946 (when Switzerland introduced its first compulsory old-age insurance scheme), most European countries introduced state pensions payable at ages ranging from 60 to 70.[4]

Throughout history the age at which young people acquired adult responsibilities – above all the responsibility to support themselves by work – had been highly diverse, varying particularly with income level and social class. In popular, and sometimes in official, discourse individuals were defined as 'old' at highly variable ages. There have always been substantial numbers of people who have been perceived and described as 'old' in any European community.[5] Contrary to a popular belief that it is only very recently that substantial numbers of people have lived past middle age, those who had survived the hazardous years of childhood have for centuries had a respectable chance of living at least to their sixties, especially if they were female. Women still tend to outlive men in all European societies.[6] Even in the early eighteenth century about 10 per cent of the English population are estimated to have been aged 60 or above, as were 8.6 per cent of the population of Austria in 1779;[7] within eighteenth-century France the numbers averaged 8–10 per cent across the regions.[8] In most countries there were some communities of high outward migration by younger people where the proportion of older people was much higher. In addition, the proportion of any population who 'looked old' would have been higher than the statistics suggest, due to the visible ravages inflicted on the poor by hard lives and on the rich by excessive consumption of luxury foodstuffs. Sugar consumption among the seventeenth-century European elite caused widespread tooth decay.

The ages at which people 'looked old' and were regarded in their communities as old were highly variable and determined above all by appearance and physical fitness.[9] Thus in eighteenth- and nineteenth-century England people could be first awarded poor relief by reason of incapacity to support themselves due to 'old age' at ages ranging from their fifties to their eighties.[10] In the debates preceding the introduction of state pensions in Britain in 1908, representatives of the labour movement argued unsuccessfully against a fixed pensionable age on the grounds that, in their experience, people varied in the ages at which they became incapable of supporting themselves by regular work, even in heavy manual occupations such as coal mining.[11] Similar debates went on elsewhere in Europe.

Nevertheless, in public discourse throughout Europe, official and unofficial, in the twentieth century the lower boundary of old age came to be defined by eligibility for the state pension. In Britain 'old-age pensioner' became the popular term for older people, and at this age people were expected to take on certain characteristics associated with that phase of life: to leave paid work, to be less active, more dependent on others, sober in dress and demeanour. Oddly, these notions came to be most widely held in the second half of the twentieth century, which was actually a period in which more people were fit and active to later ages than ever before. Medical opinion by the end of the century held that on average 75-year-olds were as fit as 65-year-olds

50 years before.[12] Curiously, across western Europe the normal age of retirement from work fell throughout the second half of the century, reaching a low point during the economic recession of the 1980s and early 1990s. In the Netherlands, France and Germany, by 1991 fewer than half of all men aged 55 to 64 were employed.[13]

As ever, the actual behaviour of many older people did not conform to the popular stereotype, increasingly so by the end of the century. The growing numbers of active and affluent older people (who co-existed with large numbers of very poor older people) were assisted by burgeoning industries for leisure, cosmetics, cosmetic surgery, drugs (including, for example, Hormone Replacement Therapy, which allegedly rejuvenated post-menopausal women) and travel to destabilize age boundaries and challenge the visible ageing of bodies, age-segregated activities and age-stereotyping. Older people who took advantages of these opportunities were sometimes criticized, by younger and older people, for failing to 'act their age' and 'grow old gracefully', for refusing, in fact, to conform to the stereotype.

Increasingly, however, by the early twenty-first century men and women were being encouraged to work to later ages by governments which had become alarmed by the potential cost of pensions and the shrinking size of the younger workforce as, from the later 1960s, birth rates fell across Europe. This pressure met resistance from many older and younger people, who had become accustomed to the idea of a period of active leisure after an adult lifetime of work. The resistance was more effective in highly trade-unionized France than in Britain, where unions were weaker by this time, or in Sweden, where government and unions were able to negotiate mutually agreeable changes to pensions and retirement ages.

Public conflict between generations

Concern about generations entered the discourse of public politics in Britain most vigorously at times of demographic panic. The first such period came between the 1920s and late 1940s, when most European and other high-income countries experienced the impact of the unprecedented fall in the birth rate of the early decades of the century. In Britain and France this led to especially clearly articulated fears about the economic, social and political effects of the ageing of the population and the intergenerational tensions that might result.[14]

Elsewhere in Europe, especially in the right-wing dictatorships of Germany and Italy, the response to the birth rate decline took the form of seeking to raise the birth rate by discouraging women from paid work and providing incentives to childbearing, such as payments and honours to parents of numerous children, and disincentives, such as higher taxation, to the celibate.[15] France, with its historically low birth rate, had been attempting such incentives since the beginning of the century. Their apparent failure – birth rates per 1000 population fell from 21.3 in 1900 to 14.7 in 1937 – may explain the form that the panic took in France and the lack of faith in the effectiveness of incentives to fecundity such as financial subsidies or childcare.[16]

In Britain in the 1930s the new discipline of demography was developing fast. Demographers demonstrated their newly developed statistical techniques by publishing dramatic projections predicting a continuing long-run decline in the birth rate which, they predicted, would, combined with increasing life expectancy, massively shift the age structure of the population. One projection was that the proportion of over-65s in the population would rise from 7.2 per cent in 1931 to 17.5 per cent in 1976, with a fall in the total population from 45 million to 33 million.[17] In reality the population rose to about 50 million in 1971, following a rise in the birth rate from the 1940s. The leading British demographer, David Glass, studied the effects of the attempts elsewhere in Europe to incentivize fecundity and concluded that they had failed everywhere.[18] There was in Britain in the 1930s little optimism that a new, emancipated, generation of women who had learned how to control births could be persuaded, or bribed by family allowances or tax breaks, to reverse the birth-rate decline.

The outcome was a great deal of gloomy commentary by politicians and some of the most eminent economists and social researchers of the time (such as John Maynard Keynes and William Beveridge) about the likely effects of the birth-rate decline. They mostly assumed major generational differences in behaviour: for example, that investment would decline because old people were spenders rather than savers. But, it was said, even if they consumed more it would not help the economy because they were thought to buy a different and narrower range of goods than younger people. Older workers were said to be less productive and flexible and less capable of learning new skills than the young. It was believed that an older population would be more conservative, politically and culturally, which would discourage innovation. This aroused especial concern in a time of severe economic depression.

These concerns brought to the surface expressions of deeper fears about Britain's weakening international position, sometimes from surprising sources. William Beveridge, a social researcher, academic, at this time Director of the London School of Economics and later an architect of the post-war British welfare state, a Liberal, and already an experienced government adviser, wrote in 1924:[19]

> The questions now facing us are how far the fall will go; whether it will bring about a stationary white population after or long before the white man's world is full ... how far the unequal adoption of birth control in different races will leave one race at the mercy of another's growing numbers or drive it to armaments or permanent aggression in self-defence.[20]

Richard Titmuss, also an academic and after World War II a prominent advocate and analyst of the welfare state, asked in 1938:

> Can we maintain our present attitude to India while we decline in numbers and age ... (and India's population expands)? Can we in these circumstances retain our particular status in the world, our genius for colonization, our love of political freedom and our leadership of the British Commonwealth of Nations ... are we to bring to such a pathetic close, to such a mean inglorious end, a history which with all its faults still shines with the lights of our gifts to mankind and still glows with the quiet patient courage of the common people. If the downward trend in population were to become, as is threatened, a downward plunge, western culture and western ideals would go at the same time.[21]

Societies dominated by older generations were felt to be vulnerable to those in which youth predominated.

At home in Britain, it was feared that intergenerational conflict would emerge, as a shrinking population of younger people was required to pay the costs of supporting a growing older generation, while experiencing frustration as older people held on to power in the economic and political spheres, blocking promotion and stifling innovation.

Some contemporaries, including John Maynard Keynes and David Glass, were more sanguine about the effects of the low birth rate. Keynes argued that it could provide an opportunity for redistribution of wealth and income and for improvement in general living standards since he believed that an excessively large population held standards down. Glass believed that the capacity of older people to contribute to the economy was unknown and probably underestimated and, in any case, that the effects of a low birth rate in Europe could be countered by migration from the poorer countries whose high birth rates so concerned other commentators.

In reality very little was known about the actual social, political and economic effects of an ageing population. A positive effect of the public debate in Britain was that in the later 1940s and 1950s it led to research, especially by industrial anthropologists and psychologists, that was designed to establish whether intergenerational differences in capacities, attitudes and behaviour were really as great as was conventionally asserted. This work established that, on the whole, men (women were rarely studied) could continue to work efficiently at least into their later sixties in a wide variety of occupations, including even heavy manual labour, if they could control the pace of their work. A study of Scottish miners showed that men in their fifties and sixties could cut coal as productively as younger men; what caused them most strain was the walk through the pit to the coalface, when the pace was set by the younger workers.[22] Whatever older workers lost in speed, adaptability and capacity to learn new skills (which was not a lot) was compensated by skill, experience and reliability. Most workers in youth and middle age were understretched and had reserves to call upon as they grew older. Individuals varied as to which of their capacities deteriorated and at what rate, and in part, deterioration was influenced by socially conditioned expectations of capacity at certain ages. Workers in their sixties might, or might not, be less productive than those in their late thirties and forties, but not less so than inexperienced workers in their twenties. Older workers could learn new skills. A long succession of research studies since the 1950s has supported these findings.[23]

The Labour governments of 1945–51 and the Conservative governments of the 1950s tried to persuade employers of the value of older workers, with very little success. Then, as was equally evident in the early twenty-first century, it proved extremely difficult to shift deeply culturally embedded assumptions about the different characteristics of different generations. Workers themselves were equivocal. Male manual workers in particular often welcomed the prospect of retirement at 65 after a hard-working life which might have started at age 12 or earlier, but they were also alarmed at the unaccustomed prospect of unlimited leisure. Even in the 1970s:

> Former Midland car-workers and Jarrow shipbuilders seemed worn out and despairingly lost, cut off from former workmates. They wept on their last day at work. 'I felt terrible'. 'It seemed as though you

were suddenly cut off from life'. They lay in bed in the morning 'puzzled about how to fill the time in'.[24]

Nevertheless, retirement at the state pensionable age spread rapidly through western Europe to become a norm for employed workers by the late 1950s.[25] This owed much to rising living standards and improved state pensions. But those who controlled their own working lives – professionals, senior business people, politicians – were more reluctant to admit their diminishing powers or need for rest as they grew older. Winston Churchill became Prime Minister in 1940 at the state pensionable age of 65. He sustained a punishing workload as an active and effective war leader for five more years. He became Prime Minister again in 1951, aged 77, but his health was failing and he was far from effective. He retired, reluctantly, at the age of 81. In the Soviet Union, Stalin died in office in 1953, aged 74, as did Brezhnev in 1982, aged 76. Charles de Gaulle became President of France in 1958 aged 68 and remained in office for 11 years. Francisco Franco gave up control of Spain unwillingly only when he was close to death at age 83 in 1975. Only recently has the retirement age for British judges been set at 70, ten years later than for other public employees. Politicians still have no retirement age.

By the early 1950s the demographic panic was receding. In most European countries the birth-rate decline was reversed during or shortly after World War II.The rising birth rate was sustained and continued to the late 1960s. In Britain and elsewhere in western Europe, immigration from low-income countries and the entry of increasing numbers of women into the workforce dispelled fears of a shrinking labour pool. The demographic concerns, and the research, of the mid-century were forgotten –until the 1980s, when the effects of a renewed international downturn in the birth rate from the late 1960s began to be noticed. The old fears of the harmful economic, political and cultural effects of an ageing population returned.[26]

One such fear was apprehension – again – of growing intergenerational conflict due to the cost burden on younger workers of supporting growing numbers of older people, all the greater now due to the higher costs of post-war pension and health-care regimes. This was most vividly expressed in a book published in 1991, *Selfish Generations* by the New Zealander David Thomson.[27] The book was based on experience in New Zealand, but claimed wider significance, since the New Zealand case was similar to those of all high-income countries. It argued that modern welfare states had especially benefited those born between

1920 and 1945, who gained from improved provision of cheap pensions and health care, for which younger, later-born generations were paying many of the costs without receiving commensurate benefits. Thomson employed a clear definition of 'generation', arguing:

> Generation here means what the demographers refer to as birth cohort, or all the people born within a specific period. One's generation is as fixed as one's sex, remaining unchanged for life ... social policies have created important breaks in experiences, so that to be born in one year rather than another has been given a special and lasting significance.[28]

He argued that this, fixed, older generation, which had done well out of modern welfare states, would be reluctant to give up their privileges, breeding conflict with younger, less privileged generations. There were similar prophecies of intergenerational conflict in the United States.[29]

Such fears were not wholly lacking in substance, but, in reality, such stark conflict has not emerged, in the United States, New Zealand, Britain or elsewhere, mainly because flows of income and other forms of support between generations are more complex than Thomson suggested. Social policies have not created the major generational breaks that he assumed.[30] The generation which gained from the post-war welfare state has also directly borne many of the costs of its erosion from the 1970s, in particular paying much of the expense of their children's education and housing, which rose sharply from the 1980s. And, certainly in Britain and New Zealand, this same generation experienced in later life cuts in the value of pensions and in the quality of health care and social services due to the same erosion of welfare states. This was less true elsewhere in western Europe, where state welfare experienced fewer cuts at this time. The experience of the former communist countries after 1989 was different again.

Indeed, in the late twentieth and early twenty-first centuries, the evidence of reciprocity between generations was much stronger than that of conflict. In Britain most support (financial above all) flowed downwards from older generations among the better off and upwards (practical and emotional above all) among the less well off,[31] though at all social levels there was strong evidence of substantial intergenerational exchange of both material and emotional support. Despite decades, even centuries, of gloomy commentary on the 'break-up' of the family and the neglect of older by younger generations, social survey evidence persistently shows how stubbornly close intergenerational family relationships remain.[32] The long persistence of the myth that each young generation is more disrespectful of the old – described, and dismissed, by Plato in the opening pages of *The Republic* long ago – itself merits interrogation.[33] This myth is perhaps one of the enduring ways in which Western societies remind themselves of the need to respect and care for older people and indicates enduring awareness of generational difference and intergenerational obligation.

The response of the British government to the renewed panic about the ageing of the population in the 1980s and 1990s was to cut the cost of pensions and other benefits to older people. This was more difficult elsewhere in western Europe where trade unions and other representatives of present and future pensioners had a stake in the administration of pensions and were better able to resist cuts.[34] From the late 1990s the British government in particular sought, again, to encourage businesses to employ older people. Again this foundered on the widespread resistance of employers to clear evidence on the competence of very many older people. The reasons for the strength of this resistance and the preference for stereotyped assumptions about the capacities of older people are unclear. European experience conflicts with that in the United States and Australia, where the abolition of fixed retirement ages and the pattern of working later met fewer obstacles in the later twentieth century. Continuing resistance suggests real, often deeply suppressed, rivalries between generations. The reciprocity between generations in private life does not necessarily carry over into public life, or, at least, into employment relationships. It seems that younger generations resist the notion that older generations may be competent in many spheres of life to late ages until they reach the accepted boundary of old age themselves, when, having internalized conventional stereotypes, they may be surprised by their own sense of continuing competence.

'Private' relations between generations: Families

Relationships between generations became more complex for more people over the course of the twentieth century. Longer life expectancy has meant that it is increasingly common for two – or three, four and even occasionally five – generations to be alive and active together. Older people are more likely to have surviving children, grandchildren and great-grandchildren than in any past time, and to see them and take pleasure in their company. Though the birth rate now is much lower than 100 years ago throughout Europe, a higher proportion of the population are parents, of at least one child, and each child is far more likely than ever before to survive to his or her own old age and to have, and get to know, children and grandchildren.[35] The generations are also highly likely to be in regular touch with each other. They may not live in close proximity, but, in the historically highly mobile societies of Europe, nor was this ever certain. In recent times family members have been able to travel and communicate over vast distances as never before. If a child migrated to Australia, the United States or South America in the nineteenth or early twentieth centuries, as millions of Europeans did, the generations were probably severed forever; now they can be together within 24 hours and in constant touch by phone and email. We still know all too little about the extent and quality of relationships between grandparents and grand- and great-grandchildren, though research is beginning.

It has never been conventional in Britain or in much of north-western Europe for older people to share a home with their adult children or to expect sustained support from younger people until a very late phase of life, when incapacity, normally of short duration, may make dependency unavoidable. Unlike parts of southern Europe, older people have always asserted their residential independence and substantial and growing numbers of them have been able to afford to maintain it. The experience of immigrant groups to Europe is different: especially those originating in Asia often come from cultures in which intergenerational co-residence has been normal. One source of tension between older and younger generation in such communities is the rejection of these traditions by some younger people brought up in Western culture. But they are being rejected by many in contemporary Asia also.

Traditionally in Britain and north-western Europe ageing individuals have valued independence in preference to dependence upon younger people,[36] but this has not meant lack of contact, mutual support or affection between the generations. As we have seen, support, both financial and in kind, has as often travelled downwards as upwards through the generations: older people provide financial help, when they can, and childcare, while younger people give emotional and sometimes physical and financial support. There is no sign that such intergenerational reciprocity has diminished over time, indeed the capacity to reciprocate has increased, with the increased incomes of many older people and the greater fitness to later ages of many more.

Personal experience of becoming the 'older generation'

When interviewed in the later twentieth century, older people expressed surprise that old age was not what they had expected. They had not suddenly crossed a boundary into decrepitude or, conversely, into respectability when they qualified for the pension. They felt no different: 'I don't feel old', they say.[37] They describe, vividly, their experiences in later life and their relationships with younger generations.[38] One woman wrote in the 1990s:

> Now that I am 67 I must consider myself to be 'elderly'. General outlook and attitude must be the deciding factor in placing people in age categories. The old saying 'you're as young as you feel' has some truth in it and we all know people who are old at 40 and some who are much older but have an interest in life and an awareness of all about them, who give an impression of comparative youthfulness in spite of all the lines and wrinkles.

Another 67-year-old woman wrote:

> These days you aren't classed as old until you are 80. I don't feel old, with fashions very flexible you can look fashionable up to any age. My mother is 95 and she wears fashionable clothes.

These statements might be interpreted as just the self-deception of older people, but a woman who was not yet 40 wrote:

> I remember my mother saying 'I may be a wrinkled 57 on the outside, but I'm 17 inside', when I caught her playing hopscotch out on the pavement with my daughter. I'm beginning to understand what she meant ... some people are born 'middle-aged' while some old folk sparkle, are open-minded and have a zest for life ... as a volunteer worker for social services, I have supported women I've regarded as being a generation older than myself and suddenly realized that they are ten years younger than me. They have a poor self-image, are worn down by marital and financial problems, are in poor shape physically ... On the other hand as a member of a keep-fit association, I am often amazed when fellow-members reveal their ages. Women in their 70s with trim, supple bodies glow with vitality and enthusiasm and look twenty years younger.

Even Simone De Beauvoir's generally rather negative account of old age, *La Vieillesse*, (1970, in English *Old Age*, 1972) recounts some quite positive stories. For example, in 1968 a 75-year-old former waitress lived alone in poverty in central Paris, in an attic without gas, electricity or running water, up 'three stories of handsome staircase, then two half floors of steep narrow steps'. 'It is a nightmare for me' she said, but 'she is not bored she says. She walks about a great deal; she reads the headlines at the newspaper stand. When she can she goes to ceremonies in Paris.'[39] De Beauvoir also reported on a survey of French centenarians:

> They were living in the country with their children or grandchildren, or in some cases in institutions or rest-homes ... They had very little money; they were all thin ... They loved their food but ate little. Many of them were strong and well ... there was one who played billiards at over 99 ... They slept well. They passed their time reading, knitting or taking short walks. Their minds were clear and their memories excellent. They were independent, even-tempered and sometimes gay ... They were high-handed towards their 70-year-old children and treated them as young people. Sometimes they complained of the present-day generation, but they were interested in modern times and kept in touch with what was going on ... They did not seem afraid of death.[40]

We can find similar descriptions in many other times and places. The lived reality of generational experience and intergenerational relationships has always conflicted with easy stereotype. Shakespeare illustrated this especially vividly in *As You Like It*. Here Jaques utters one of the best-known stereotypes of old age as he concludes his soliloquy on the seven ages of man with the seventh age:

> Last scene of all
> That ends this strange eventful history,
> Is second childishness and mere oblivion;
> Sans teeth, sans eyes, sans taste, sans everything.[41]

But no sooner is he finished than onstage comes the retainer Adam, who has already described himself, at 'almost fourscore years' i.e. into the 'seventh age' or decade:

> Though I look old, yet I am strong and lusty
> ... my age is as a lusty winter;

Frosty but kindly ...
I'll do the service of a younger man.[42]

The definition and experience of 'generation', as well as the relations between 'generations', are endlessly complex, contentious and shifting, in the twenty-first century as in the sixteenth.

Notes

1. J.M. Winter, *The Great War and the British People* (London, 1985), pp. 65–102.
2. *Security in Retirement: Towards a New Pensions System* (UK government, Department of Work and Pensions, Cm. 6841, May 2006).
3. P. Thane *Old Age in English History: Past Experiences, Present Issues* (Oxford, 2000), pp. 385–406.
4. P. Thane, 'The History of Retirement', in G.L. Clark, A. Munnell and M. Orzag (eds) *Oxford Handbook of Pensions and Retirement Income* (forthcoming, Oxford, 2006).
5. See, for example, T.G. Parkin, *Old Age in the Roman World: A Cultural and Social History* (London and Baltimore, 2003); S. Shahar, *Growing Old in the Middle Ages* (London, 1997).
6. Thane, *Old Age*, pp. 19–28.
7. M. Mitterauer and R. Sieder, *The European Family* (Oxford, 1982), p. 146.
8. D. Troyansky, 'The Eighteenth Century', in P. Thane (ed.) *The Long History of Old Age* (London, 2005) p. 175.
9. L. Botelho and P. Thane (eds), *Women and Ageing in British Society since 1500* (London, 2001); S.R. Ottoway, *The Decline of Life: Old Age in Eighteenth Century England* (Cambridge, 2004), pp. 16–64.
10. Ottoway, pp. 173–221.
11. Thane, *Old Age*, pp. 194–215.
12. T. Kirkwood, *Time of Our Lives: Why Ageing is Neither Inevitable nor Necessary* (London, 1999).
13. M. Kohli, M. Rein, A.-M. Gullemard and H. Van Gunsteren (eds), *Time for Retirement: Comparative Studies in Early Exit from the Labor Force* (Cambridge University Press, 1991), p. 4.
14. P.M. Thane 'The Debate on the Declining Birth-Rate in Europe: The 'Menace' of an Ageing Population, 1920s–1950s', *Continuity and Change*, 5 (1990), 283–305. P. Bourdelais, 'The Ageing of the Population: A Relevant Question or Obsolete Notion?', in P. Johnson and P. Thane (eds), *Old Age from Antiquity to Post-Modernity* (London, 1998), pp. 110–31. A. Sauvy, 'Social and Economic Consequences of Ageing of Western Populations', *Population Studies*, 2 (1948), 115–24.
15. M.S. Quine, *Population Politics in Twentieth Century Europe* (London, 1996).
16. B.R. Mitchell, *European Historical Statistics, 1750–1970* (London, 1978), p. 27.
17. G.D. Leybourne, 'An Estimate of the Future Population of Great Britain', *Sociological Review* 26, (1934). For further discussion of this theme, see Thane 'The Debate on the Declining Birth-Rate in Britain'.

18. D.V .Glass, *The Struggle for Population* (London, 1936).
19. For more on Beveridge, see J. Harris, *William Beveridge. A Biography* (Oxford, 2nd edn, 1997).
20. William Beveridge, 'Population and Unemployment', in R.L. Smyth (ed.), *Essays in the Economics of Socialism and Capitalism* (London, 1964), p. 270.
21. R.M. Titmuss, *Poverty and Population* (London, 1938), p. 53.
22. Thane, *Old Age*, p. 345. R.B. Belbin, 'Difficulties of Older People in Industry', *Occupational Psychology*, 3 (1953), 177–89; 'Older People and Heavy Work', *British Journal of Industrial Medicine*, 12 (London, 1955), 309–19.
23. Including at least 16 publications by the anthropologist F. Le Gros Clark for the Nuffield Foundation in the 1950s, among them *Ageing and Industry* (with Agnes Dunn) (London, 1955). T. Kirkwood, *The End of Age: Why Everything about Ageing is Changing* (London, 2001).
24. Thane, *Old Age*, pp. 403–5, quoting C. Phillipson 'The Experience of Retirement: A Sociological Study' (Ph.D., University of Durham, 1978), pp. 272–3.
25. Kohli et al., *Time for Retirement*, pp. 36–66.
26. World Bank, *Averting the Old Age Crisis: Policies to Protect the Old and Promote Growth* (Oxford, 1994). P. Thane 'Old Age: Burden or Benefit?', in H. Joshi (ed.), *The Changing Population of Britain* (Oxford, 1989), pp. 56–71.
27. D. Thomson, *Selfish Generations* (Wellington, 1991).
28. Ibid., p. 2.
29. Discussed in E.A. Wynne, 'Will the Young Support the Old?', in A. Pifer and L. Bronte (eds), *Our Aging Society: Paradox and Promise* (New York, 1986), pp. 243–62.
30. J. Hills, 'Does Britain Have a "Welfare Generation"? An Empirical Analysis of Intergenerational Equity' (London School of Economics: Suntory Toyota International Centre for Economics and Related Disciplines, 1992), WSP/88.
31. E. Grundy 'Reciprocity in Relationships: Socio-economic and Health Influences on Intergenerational Exchanges between Third Age Parents and Their Adult Children in Great Britain', *British Journal of Sociology*, 52 (2005), 233–55. J. Henretta, E. Grundy and S. Harris, 'Socio-economic and Health Differences in Parents' Provision of Help to Adult Children: A British-USA Comparison', *Ageing and Society*, 22 (2002), 441–58.
32. Thane, *Old Age*, pp. 407–35.
33. Plato, *The Republic*, trans. D. Lee (London, 1987), pp. 61–3.
34. H. Pemberton, P. Thane and N. Whiteside, *Britain's Pensions Crisis: History and Policy* (Oxford, 2006).
35. I.M. Timaeus, 'Family and Households of the Elderly Population: Prospects for Those Approaching Old Age', *Ageing and* Society, 6 (1986), 271–93.
36. Thane, *Old Age*, pp. 168, 302, 477–81.
37. P. Thompson, C. Itzin and M. Abendstern, *I Don't Feel Old: Understanding the Experience of Later Life* (Oxford, 1991).
38. The following quotations are from the Mass Observation Archive, University of Sussex, *Growing Older* files.
39. S. De Beauvoir, *Old Age* (Harmondswoth, 1977), 268–9.
40. Ibid., 605–6.
41. William Shakespeare, *As You Like It*, act 2, scene 7, lines 163–6, Oxford World Classics edition (Oxford, 1998).
42. Ibid., lines 47–55.

11
Soviet Russia's Older Generations

Stephen Lovell

In studies of modern Europe, the history of generations usually means the history of youth. Young people have been the most visible, and vocal, generational actors both at moments of upheaval such as revolution and in periods of state- and nation-building, when socializing institutions such as schools and armies are built and consolidated. All this would seem especially to be the case in Soviet Russia, a polity that was apparently propelled into existence by youthful revolutionary vigour and that paid extremely close attention to its successive junior cohorts as they came on the scene. The Soviet Youth League (Komsomol) ranked as one of the most prominent institutions in Soviet society with more than 40 million members by the mid-1980s.[1]

Yet the Soviet Russia was also conspicuously a revolutionary society that greatly outlived the revolution that brought it into being. It remained in existence for more than 70 years, during which time it experienced events and processes that were bound to redraw the boundaries between the generations and redefine their relative value. In the early 1940s, the Soviet population bore the brunt of a total war that offered a historical point of reference to rival, and even supplant, that of 1917. Soviet society underwent extraordinarily rapid modernization: tens of millions of people moved to the city between the 1920s and the 1950s, and many of them were far better educated than their own parents. Demographic change – the decline in the birth rate – ensured that the USSR after the war became a steadily 'greying' society. As any visitor in the 1970s or 1980s would probably testify, Soviet society was in its late maturity a distinctly conservative place, where babushkas, in the role of sartorial vigilantes, were more likely than youthful enthusiasts to exercise a disciplining influence on their fellow citizens. The correlation between age and authority was no less evident in the upper reaches of the party-state, where Sovietologists had spotted all the signs of 'gerontocracy' by the mid-1970s.[2]

Dozens of articles and several books have been written on Soviet youth, which was undeniably the most salient generational category in Soviet Russia. Old people are much more elusive objects of inquiry: especially in the early Soviet period, they lacked the institutional representation and ideological prominence accorded to their younger comrades. But the relationship between older and younger generations was by no means fixed, not least because the original youthful revolutionary cohort was itself bound to age as the Soviet system advanced to 'mature' socialism. By the end of the Soviet period, the older generation, largely voiceless in the 1920s, was doing much to drown out its juniors in public discourse.

Old age and the emergence of Soviet civilization

In the early Soviet period, old people were few in number – according to the 1926 census, only about one in fifteen Soviet people was 60 or over – and scantily represented in public discourse.[3] If they did figure, then this was primarily as bogeymen (or, more likely, bogeywomen): as symbols of the cultural backwardness that the Bolsheviks were determined to overcome. The only serious attempt in early Soviet Russia to investigate the state of mind of elderly people belonged to the prolific social psychologist Nikolai Rybnikov. Rybnikov's research – which involved circulating a detailed questionnaire to elderly people – was no more than a pilot for a more thorough investigation that never occurred. But his unpublished material gives some idea of the challenge that ageing represented to people in the early Soviet period. Rybnikov favoured the age of 50 as marking the onset of old age, as most people's work capacity declined steeply after that. As he pointed out, the 1920 census had revealed that nearly 20 million people were over the age of 49. Individuals responded to this phase of life in very different ways – some were stoical, others became introverted, and a few defiantly took up gymnastics – but ageing remained a predicament rather than an opportunity in a society where tranquil and well-cushioned retirement was not an option.[4]

There is no reason to doubt that the lot of many old people in early Soviet Russia was a miserable one. This was not a good time to be anything other than physically vigorous. The support networks on which the elderly had previously relied had been badly torn by revolution and civil war. Nor did the situation improve greatly over the next two decades. During the 1920s and 1930s social exclusion was widely practised both as a punitive measure against social 'enemies' and as a way of channelling scarce resources towards the most 'productive' members of society. Less able-bodied Soviet people, above all invalids and the elderly, who did not play a full part in the workforce, were automatically vulnerable. The main historian of Soviet disenfranchisement has found many examples of communities taking away the civil rights of all residents over a certain age (60, 55 or even 50).[5] Nor was the situation promising in the supposedly patriarchal rural family. Intergenerational competition over household resources had been a much-attested feature of peasant life for decades, but in the 1920s the balance seems to have shifted in favour of younger male peasants.[6] By 1927, more than 6000 elderly peasants were said to be housed in special homes, though this provision was acknowledged to be inadequate given the reported reluctance of peasants to take solitary old people into their households.[7]

Even categories of the population that were formally entitled to state support were likely to suffer if they lost their work capacity. The struggle of the Soviet citizen to gain official recognition of his or her pension rights is abundantly evident in the voluminous correspondence between petitioners and state agencies in the 1920s. For example, according to legislation passed in January 1925, teachers in rural areas of the Russian Republic were to receive pension coverage – but only if they could demonstrate at least five years' service in Soviet institutions. This left ample scope for denying pensions to worthy applicants who might have worked in education for 40 years or more, but who fell short of the five-year term of Soviet service by as little as a few months.[8]

From the late 1920s onwards, old-age pensions were introduced for workers in particular industries and professions. But the criteria for entitlement were convoluted and discriminatory, and state pensions were set low. One 70-year-old in Voronezh province, left on his own after his son died in the Civil War, wrote to Soviet head of state Mikhail Kalinin in 1937 asking for confirmation that the loudly trumpeted Stalin Constitution of the previous year included an article on Soviet citizens' right to support in old age. Although he was doubtless reflecting the hopes of many old people at the time, his interpretation of the Constitution was optimistic in the extreme.[9]

Yet, for all that life remained hard, old people were by no means socially insignificant in interwar Russia. Their role as facilitators of Soviet everyday life can hardly be doubted. As the post-Stalin dissident Ludmilla Alexeyeva reflected of her childhood in the 1930s, 'the New Socialist Man – the new kind of man who would be free from vestiges of bourgeois individualism – was being raised by a legion of grand-mothers'. Urban mothers, instead of devoting themselves to childcare, were at this time busy attending meetings and acquiring education that would make their own life chances far preferable to those of their parents. The peasant grandmothers gathered outside the workers' barracks to which they had been summoned from the village were a sight that lodged itself in Alexeyeva's memory of childhood.[10] Elderly women, mostly from the villages, were commonly employed as child-minders by mothers who received two months' maternity leave and never had access to adequate institutional childcare.[11] Elderly *lishentsy* – people who had lost their civil rights in the Soviet period, usually because they had pursued undesirable occupations before the Revolution – had to scrabble to make ends meet. One memoirist (b. 1920) recalled a former senior civil servant being employed as his childminder.[12]

A bigger demographic picture is provided by a pioneering 1930 study of the Ukrainian Republic, which indicated that the labour participation of mothers was made possible by the presence of non-working family members (notably including elderly women, who in the 1926 census outnumbered men in their age group by a ratio of at least seven to five). The author of the study, A.P. Khomenko, noted several negative aspects of this situation: the family was forced to absorb people whose labour was not useful to society, and mothers were forced to go out to work to support elderly relatives, which meant that children were abandoned to the undesirable influence of old women. Yet Khomenko saw little prospect of substantial change until the Soviet state significantly improved its social provisions. And the problem was likely to get worse as Soviet society aged over the coming decades: Khomenko noted that birth control had by 1930 spread to almost all sections of the Ukrainian population.[13]

But old people did not just exist in the interstices of the Soviet state as childminders and home help: they were also, by the 1930s, developing a public profile. The portrayal of old people as undesirable 'remnants of the past', while it periodically recurred in phases of social mobilization such as the Khrushchev era, began to recede as Soviet public discourse began to emphasize the strengthening of the family, to adopt kinship metaphors, to reject 'formalism' in favour of 'tradition', and to look for historical roots as a means of boosting the Great Russian legitimacy of the USSR. In this context, longevity became a matter of state prestige, and older people – in principle at least – became privileged bearers of historical memory.[14]

The post-Stalin era: Developed socialism and the challenge of demography

From the 1950s onwards, old age became a still more explicit preoccupation of Soviet policymakers and public discourse. One important factor in this renewed interest was the demographic circumstance that the number of old people in Soviet society was increasing inexorably. The greying of Soviet society was primarily due not to any great rise in life expectancy but to the falling birth rate. Like other societies subjected to urbanization, industrialization and mass education, the Russians (with exceptions in the 1920s, when the population was recovering from the civil war period, and in the 1930s, in the wake of collectivization and under the pressure of pro-family policies) were having steadily fewer children. The proportion of the population of pensionable age rose from 10.4 per cent in 1950 to 15 per cent in 1970.[15]

Birth rate had never been a major issue in nineteenth- or early twentieth-century Russia. Malthusian fears were not much in evidence, and nor was the opposite concern: that the nation was in danger of dying out. The overriding demographic preoccupation was the shockingly high rate of mortality, especially infant mortality. Everything changed in the mid-1930s, when the Soviet state became overtly pro-natalist. Birth and death figures were taken as the basis for triumphalist comparison with the West.[16] Yet, in their more private moments, the authorities were troubled by signs of demographic slowdown: in 1940, for example, the birth rate was palpably falling, and this was due not only to the arrival of the diminished Civil War cohort at childbearing age but also to a rise in illegal abortions.[17]

Yet, although pro-natalism has been the standard European response to demographic scares, in Soviet Russia it was regularly complemented, and at times even overshadowed, by a concern to reduce mortality. The problem of premature death never ceased to be a preoccupation of Soviet policymakers. Even long after the declared onset of 'developed socialism', many citizens were dying much sooner than they ought to have. Soviet demographers became distinctly coy in the 1970s and 1980s when presenting mortality statistics. In the main demographic journal of the USSR, *Vestnik statistiki*, certain categories of information were silently withdrawn: infant mortality (1976), mortality for other age groups (1978), and causes of death (1985). The figures, had they been published, would have pointed to acute failings in socialist public health. An epidemic of alcoholism and cardiovascular disease was holding male life expectancy down below 65 even before the much-attested mortality crisis of post-Soviet Russia.[18]

It was hardly coincidental that the post-Stalin era saw a marked increase in lifestyle prescriptions for the more mature members of society. The question of how to ensure a long and active life was a regular topic on the pages of *Zdorov'e* (*Health*), a mass magazine established in 1955. Inspiring examples of vigorous longevity both from history and from the Soviet present were combined with practical recommendations on hygiene, diet and exercise. As in the 1930s, energetic older workers and luminaries such as Ivan Pavlov were regularly featured. But *Zdorov'e* differed from the equivalent periodical in the Stalin period both in the sheer volume of material on ageing and in the kind of advice dispensed. Now the old and the ageing were addressed as an audience that required not simple exhortation but reasoned and engaging discussion. The prominent Soviet writer Marietta Shaginian, for example, offered a cautionary tale from her own experience. 'I was wasteful in the use of my natural energy, I overate, I had the stress of my hot temper, and finally I was guilty of that sin so common among us: I completely lacked the correct regime of work and recreation. All this was driving my organism towards catastrophe.' Aged 62, she was laid low for six months by laryngitis. After this, she decided to take drastic measures: she began rubbing herself down with a dry rough towel in the mornings, eventually worked up to cold wet towels, and in this way hardened herself physically. Psychologically, she recommended 'interest in life' as a way of maintaining mental health.[19]

For those less inclined to seek the secrets of longevity so close to home, the long-lived villagers of the Caucasus continued, as in the Stalin era, to exercise great fascination. The 1959 census delivered the strikingly high total of 8890 centenarians (or 45 per 100,000) in the Caucasus and North Caucasus geographical area.[20] A new wave of gerontological fieldwork was not long in coming. In 1960–61 a large sample of Abkhazian octogenarians (1400 people, or approximately 25 per cent of all the people in that demographic group according to the 1959 census) was investigated. And the research carried on into the 1980s, though by then it had taken a more anthropological turn. Researchers were no longer expecting to find a medical recipe for superlongevity, but rather a complex set of genetic, environmental and social factors that enabled Abkhazians to live long and fulfilling lives. These factors included people's geographical immobility (the fact that they rarely strayed far from their native territory), their healthy diet and their constant physical activity, and their wide and supportive network of family and friends. These later studies, conducted under the auspices of the Institute of Ethnography of the Soviet Academy of Sciences, were certainly more intellectually respectable than the fieldwork conducted in the 1930s. But they still appear to have been a little too keen to discover a microcosm of healthy patriarchal existence.[21] As Zhores Medvedev has argued, ethnography is indeed the best route to understanding the Caucasus longevity phenomenon, though not quite in the way chosen by the Academy of Sciences researchers. The Abkhazian communities were characterized by genuine traditions of veneration of old people, and this would have led people to exaggerate their age. There would also have been a strong element of local pride and rivalry with surrounding regions and districts: especially after it became clear that extreme senectitude was a matter of state prestige, each mountain village would have had every incentive to announce as many champions of longevity as possible.[22]

The post-Stalin period also saw an intensification of research in less exotic areas of gerontology. The 1959 census, which showed that the percentage of the population aged 60 and over had risen from 6.8 in 1939 to 9.4, was an important spur.[23] In 1960, the Soviet medical classification of age was changed to take account of the increased life expectancy of Soviet people. Middle age was now extended to 60, those between 60 and 75 were considered 'elderly', old age proper began at 75, while those older than 90 were 'long-livers' (*dolgozhiteli*).[24] Sociologists, too, sensed that traditional divisions between successive stages of the life cycle were not satisfactory. Thirty was no longer bound to be the end of youth and the threshold of middle age, while many people enjoyed an extended period of 'pre-old age' (the 10, 15 or even 20 years after they had raised their children but before they retired).[25]

The proceedings of a conference held under the auspices of the Institute of Gerontology of the Academy of Sciences in 1964 give some idea of the wide range of concerns in Soviet old age policy and research. Here there were close to 100 papers grouped in five sections: social and demographic processes, diet ('questions of nutritional hygiene'), work ('questions of labour hygiene'), recreation (with special reference to physical activity), and medicine.[26] Gerontological topics extended from labour and pension legislation to old people's special requirements in footwear and mattresses.[27] In the first two years of the 1970s alone, around 2500 Soviet articles on geriatrics and gerontology were published.[28]

Given that Soviet gerontology by now eschewed the maximalist assertions of the 1930s – the notion that it would be possible to extend

Soviet life expectancy to well over 100 – practical solutions had to be found to the question of what to do with these increased numbers of elderly and often infirm people. The solution of preference for the Soviet state was, as ever, to integrate them into the workforce. Occupational medicine had since the 1920s been concerned with diagnosing various categories of 'invalidity' and prescribing appropriate forms of work activity for the less than fully able-bodied (above all, victims of industrial accidents and workers with war wounds). By the early 1960s, Soviet diagnosticians were spending much of their time on a category of invalidity that had not received much attention in the 1930s but was now overtaking all others: heart disease. In the early 1960s, a group of researchers at the Leningrad Institute for Assessment of Work Capacity and Organization of Invalid Labour argued that many workers with an identified heart condition could continue to work in heavy industry, but not in the high-temperature workshops. Work capacity commissions were not always making appropriate recommendations for workers with arteriosclerosis: they either reduced the work load to too low a level by taking too 'formalistic' approaches to the categories of invalidity, or they imposed unreasonable burdens such as overtime, work at too high a tempo, and excessive physical strain. Soviet managers were advised to move away from the assumption that a lightening of workers' physical load must inevitably bring with it a shift to less-skilled (and less well-paid) work. Given that the effects of ageing did not set in at equal rates in all workers, a new set of tests were needed in order to assess the work capacity of people over the age of 60. The relationship between age-related infirmity and work capacity required more careful study.[29]

Even if such allowances were made for older workers – which Soviet enterprises, not unlike their capitalist counterparts, were reluctant to do – old people could not in all cases be expected to support themselves. The number of old people living alone had risen steadily: 2.9 million in 1959 (30.9 per cent of the total), 5.0 million in 1970 (35.2 per cent), 6.9 million in 1979 (43.9 per cent). And 90 per cent of the old people living separately from their extended families were women.[30] The enormous differential between the sexes had something to do with women's greater life expectancy, but it was mainly the result of the decimation of the male population in the Great Patriotic War. By the mid-1980s, the situation was becoming worrying for social commentators and policymakers. Home help was supposed to be organized through district departments of social security. A few day care centres were set up. But these measures were not carried out thoroughly, and in any case Soviet citizens were reluctant to deliver themselves into institutional care. There was a slight increase in the number of homes in the post-war years, but the increase in no way matched need, and the condition of the homes, not to mention the quality of their staff, often left much to be desired.[31]

In general, however, Soviet ideology made a virtue out of necessity. The relative weakness of institutional provision might be seen as a strength: as evidence that the Soviet system, unlike the Western, did not push older people into a ghetto. Soviet citizens retained their sacred right to toil even in old people's homes, where they had workshops and allotments at their disposal.[32]

Above all, the evident inadequacy of state support was made good by the family. Although the general trend, from the 1930s onwards, was for households to get smaller – by 1979, the nuclear family accounted for about two-thirds of households – the average size of family, and the proportion of complex multigenerational households, would clearly have fallen even more quickly if the housing situation had been better. At times the process stuttered. Between the 1970 and 1979 censuses, for example, the proportion of extended and multiple-family urban households in the RSFSR actually rose fractionally (from 16.6 to 16.8 percent).[33] The construction drive of the Khrushchev era, while it made available millions of separate family apartments, denied older people agency in obtaining new housing, which in many cases made it impossible for them to live separately from their children.[34] Surveys of the 1960s and 1970s showed that the great majority of urbanites would have preferred to live apart from their parents (if the housing shortage had given them the opportunity to do so), although they still wanted their parents to be close by (in a neighbouring block of flats, or in a flat in the same building).[35]

The tendency to form family clusters in the Soviet city ensured that, while most family units were nuclear on paper, they were multigenerational in their everyday interactions. The irony of this situation is clear enough: a society professing a radical modernizing agenda had turned the 'traditional' structure of the three-generation or extended family into the dominant form of urban living. The old folks took over what was, according to early Soviet policy on the family, to have been the role of the socialist state. Older Soviet people performed much more than their fair share of household tasks. As a survey of the second half of the 1960s demonstrated, older workers in large cities did five or six hours more housework per week than young couples. The weakness of the service sector and the continued underprovision of labour-saving devices ensured that running the household and raising children remained an extraordinarily time-consuming and exhausting business. Yet, with the premium placed on education and technical expertise, young adults were likely to spend more time developing their careers than previously. For this reason, they were calling on their own parents to help more than ever before – even when their parents worked themselves. And the older generation was mostly willing to help, as its own educational opportunities and career prospects were much more limited. Older men, for example, did more housework than they had earlier in their lives.[36]

The exceptionally close everyday relationship between parents and grandparents was reckoned to be a feature that distinguished Soviet society from industrialized societies in western Europe, and this was a source of pride. 'In socialist society, contradictions and differences between the generations are of a non-antagonistic character, so collaboration, contact and mutual support among generations can (and in fact does) attain a scope inconceivable under the rule of private property morality.'[37] Individual material benefit, the development of the personality, and the health of the collective were thus combined in a neat dialectical manoeuvre.

The older generation as an entitlement community

Demography and ideology provide important contexts for understanding the rise to prominence of old age in post-Stalin Russia. But, in order to understand its immediate causes, we need to turn to another domain of Soviet life: welfare.

Accounts of state-society relations in the USSR have tended, for obvious and understandable reasons, to emphasize their confrontational and coercive character. Innumerable commentators have pointed out, following Lenin, that *'Kto kogo?'* ('Who [beats] whom?') was the motto of Soviet politics. Yet a case may also be made for *'Komu chto?'* ('Who gets what?') The USSR was an avowedly modern state that established a monopoly over the distribution of benefits. As many scholars have implied and a few have explicitly argued, the success of the Soviet regime in maintaining itself was due not only to violence but also to the incentive structures it put in place. The Bolshevik dictatorship had a few carrots at its disposal in addition to the powerful sticks that it was always happy to wield.[38]

For the first three decades of its existence, the Soviet benefits system was notable for its lack of transparency and its discriminatory character.

Provisions emerged chaotically, at many different levels of the party-state, thus offering great scope for particularism and special pleading. Large categories of the population were overlooked or specifically excluded. Even in cases where the legislation was unambiguous, its implementation usually was not. The criteria for allocating benefits were often opaque: the 1920s and 1930s were an era when 'proletarians' and 'bourgeois' existed very much in the eyes of the beholder.

In the 1920s, in the near-total absence of pensions legislation to cover old age, the best chance of a decent level of support was a 'personal' pension. In theory, this mark of distinction was reserved for those citizens who had performed 'exceptional services' in the revolutionary cause, but what constituted such services was a moot point. In September 1925, the great-grandchildren of Aleksandr Pushkin applied for an increase in their pension from 70 to 150 rubles. They were turned down on the grounds that they were not especially deserving of state assistance given the number of other needy citizens and the shortage of funds available.[39] In the same year, the RSFSR Ministry of Social Security reported that the definition of 'exceptional services' had been unjustifiably expanded in practice; it had come to mean simply a lengthy work record. By the standards of twentieth-century welfare states, however, the numbers in question were still extremely low. As of 1 October 1924, 2722 citizens in the RSFSR (not including the autonomous republics) were receiving personal pensions, and 1288 of these had their pension removed after a reassessment carried out during that month.[40]

Most effective at lobbying for pensions and other benefits were organizations that represented citizens with a particular standing in the revolutionary state. Notable among these was the Society of Political Prisoners. To receive a personal pension, members of this organization were required to submit themselves to a detailed examination of their revolutionary biographies. As of 1 October 1924 the Society included among its members 158 pensioners who had spent a total of 1884 years in tsarist confinement. By early 1926 the figure had risen to about 200. Anniversaries were an opportunity to expand the number. In 1926, for example, petitions were sent in on behalf of the eight surviving participants in the assassination of Alexander II on 1 March 1881 (the 45th anniversary of this event had just arrived).[41]

In the late 1920s, Soviet society acquired its first specially designated old age pensions (which were reserved for workers in particular occupations). In the 1930s, the categories of beneficiary grew constantly, until the number of pieces of active pension legislation reached three figures.[42]

But pensioners were usually people who had lost the means to sustain themselves for some reason other than old age: war wounds, disease, industrial accident, and loss of breadwinner. In the 1930s Soviet citizens, however old, were meant to work. People who lost their work capacity were likely to find themselves marginalized and poorly supported by the state.

The effect of the war was to make the system of redistribution even more complex and fragmented than it had been in the 1920s and 1930s. During the years of combat, the workforce became noticeably older and more infirm.[43] After the war, tens of millions of people were facing problems such as physical displacement (returnees from evacuation might find their housing either destroyed or occupied), loss of breadwinner, family breakdown, and even starvation. Accordingly, the state was deluged with petitions regarding property, pensions, and so on.[44]

The pensions system was manifestly failing to keep pace with the demands of Soviet society. As well as remaining vastly complicated and unwieldy, it was also failing to provide Soviet people with anything like a decent level of support. Pensions were paid according to norms established in 1928–32: they amounted to 50, 55, or 60 per cent of a salary that was capped at 300 rubles. The minimum pension was 50 rubles in rural areas and 110 in cities; the maximum pensions were respectively 180 and 240. These figures corresponded to the situation in 1932, when the average earnings of workers and employees were 119 rubles; by 1954, average earnings had risen to 699 rubles.[45]

Given that ordinary pensions were financially inadequate for people in most occupations, many of them lobbied for personal pensions. By the end of war the number of personal pensioners in the RSFSR had grown significantly – to 29,146. And the number of people entitled to such pensions was set to rise steeply over the following years. A government decree of May 1944 had greatly increased the number of categories of citizens eligible, and the heroism and human cost of the war were sure to provide many new people to fit the new criteria. In 1945, for example, more than half of the new republican pensions were awarded to citizens who had received decorations. Given these circumstances, voices within the governmental apparatus were starting to argue that an old-age pension was necessary to simplify the outdated legislation on personal pensions.[46]

Another problem was that bureaucratic criteria were much harder to meet in the post-war era: given the widespread loss or destruction of personal documents, many applicants had enormous trouble proving the work record (*stazh*) on which their pension entitlement depended.

By the mid-1950s, local executive committees were constantly asking the RSFSR government to award pensions in 'exceptional' circumstances. The war years, and the post-war upheaval, had left far too many people with work histories that did not fit existing bureaucratic categories. Among the many deserving exceptions was a woman born in 1904, entirely blind in the right eye and with only partial sight in the left eye, who had worked for a total of nearly 12 years. She was denied a pension after the war because more than two years had gone by since she had stopped working. She had failed to make an application within the set term because she had been in hospital between 1942 and 1945.[47]

In 1956, after several years of preparation, a new, 'comprehensive' pensions law was unveiled with much fanfare. It quickly elicited a significant public response. The RSFSR Ministry of Social Security reported receiving from concerned citizens about 800 suggestions for amendments in the month following the publication of the draft law on 9 May.[48] The impact of the law when it took effect was no less impressive. With the passing of the new legislation, hundreds of existing instructions, circulars and decrees became invalid. More importantly, the number of pensioners exploded. By 1 October 1956 they numbered 8,642,931 in the RSFSR; by 1 January the figure had risen further to 9,413,934. The corresponding figures for old-age pensioners were 1,564,260 (in October) and 1,933,359 (in January). The average size of old-age pension increased from 221 to 463 rubles over the first few months of the pension reform.[49]

Despite (or because of) the expansion in the number of recipients, complaints abounded: social security offices were understaffed, staff were undertrained, applicants had been inadequately informed of the paperwork required of them, and mistakes regularly occurred in the computation of pensions.[50] The RSFSR government was receiving up to 20,000 complaints per month in the winter and spring of 1957.[51] In addition, tens of thousands of citizens still eluded all existing pension criteria and fell into the 'miscellaneous' (*prochie*) category.[52]

These practical problems of implementing a complex reform at many levels of a chronically underfunded bureaucracy were only to be expected. What seems more striking in retrospect is the extent to which the issue of pensions entitlement engaged the attention and the energies of so many different sections of Soviet society. Men and women, teachers and metalworkers, Russians and Ukrainians, all had a stake in the pension reform.

The new system drastically changed the generational dynamics in many occupational groups. According to one insider account, university teachers could now afford to retire, as they stood to receive not one-fifth but as much as four-fifths of their former salary. Many older lecturers were glad to relinquish their heavy teaching loads, which made possible a long overdue generational turnover in higher education.[53] Yet the relatively generous pension arrangements available in certain intelligentsia professions seem to have been resented by many workers in more physically demanding occupations. Both before and after the promulgation of the new law, the authorities had to contend with a vast amount of special pleading by people in particular occupational groups, in addition to strong lobbying from trade unions and branches of industry.[54]

Even within particular professions or occupational groups, pensioners did not necessarily speak with one voice. The turmoil of recent European history meant that the new Soviet pensioner had a fractured past. In the months following the pension reform, Moscow was bombarded with requests for clarification from ministries of social security around the Soviet Union. Under what category should invalids of World War I or the Civil War be covered? Should time spent on occupied territory during World War II count towards work record? What about service in the 'bourgeois' Polish army? And in what cases was witness testimony acceptable in order to confirm the length of a person's work record?[55]

One major category of the population, moreover, was entirely ignored by the new pensions law: collective farm workers. In 1956, as earlier in the Soviet period, collective farms were urged to set up mutual aid funds, to pay out welfare benefits their needy members, and to set up homes for invalids and the elderly. But the Soviet state was reticent in pledging practical support, contenting itself with admonitions. As of 1 January 1955, 5,010,700 elderly or infirm workers were to be found on collective farms, of whom almost one-half took no part in agricultural production. These people were rarely looked after properly; in many cases they did not have family to call upon, and 'social aid funds' had been set up in under half of the 50,000 collective farms in the RSFSR. Elderly collective farm parents were legally entitled to support from children who worked in state organizations and enterprises, but in practice this support was often not forthcoming. Many rural people were reported to be disappointed by the new law, as it left them even worse off than before.[56]

Radical disparities within rural society were created in the late 1950s, when many collective farms were converted into state farms. In theory, this made agricultural workers eligible for new state pension rights, but in practice they often found themselves disqualified because their work record was deemed inadequate, or because elderly workers were not accepted into the state farms and so were excluded from social provisions. And in the process they lost what little mutual aid and customary assistance they enjoyed in the collective farm. Their only fallback was the trusty allotment, which they were allowed to retain after transferring from collective to state farm.[57] It is symptomatic of the government's neglect of this issue that the Ministry of Finances seriously underestimated the number of rural claimants when it came to plan for a new law on pensions for collective farmers.[58] The law was finally implemented at the start of 1965, and six months later more than 2.5 million collective farm pensions had been awarded.[59] But these pensions were very low: most of them were set at the minimum rate of 12 rubles.

A further ambiguity of the 1956 legislation was that it did not serve to institute a fixed system of benefits. Rather, it signalled the start of a 25-year period where the regime struggled to devise the pension policy that would best suit its designs. Once the new law had created millions of new Soviet pensioners, the key question was what the Soviet pensioner should be. In particular, should he or she work? In the short term, the new law was a powerful disincentive to work after reaching pensionable age. In Leningrad over the period 1950–56, 70 per cent of pensioners continued working, but after the introduction of the new law, that figure fell to 24 per cent.[60]

Yet to withdraw from the workforce voluntarily before the onset of complete decrepitude was ideologically problematic in a society that continued to exalt labour as the primary source of self-worth for people under socialism. Soviet culture in the 1950s and 1960s betrayed ambivalence on this score. In *The Great Family* (*Bol'shaia sem'ia*), a 1954 screen adaptation of Vsevolod Kochetov's prominent novel *The Zhurbins* (*Zhurbiny*, 1952), the 77-year-old patriarch of a three-generation dynasty of shipyard workers, who has sworn he will never retire, permits himself a sombre monologue after he is transferred from the shop floor to the less onerous job of nightwatchman in the director's office: 'Your working life has come to an end, old man.' His son Il'ia, himself well over 50, rages as his lack of formal training puts him in a weak position relative to his own offspring, who are champions of productivity.[61]

The Khrushchev era, with its emphasis on technological innovation, did indeed make life uncomfortable for workers such as the older Zhurbins. The issues were laid bare in an article in *Izvestiia* written in response to a letter from one woman, a foreman at an electrical factory, that she be allowed to continue work despite reaching the age of retirement. The journalist who replied to her was unsympathetic, 'whether you like it or not, at age fifty-nine a person is already getting over the hill'. The worker in question had been promoted to her present position during the war, but the significant technological changes of the following 20 years had made her training and work habits lag behind the demands of the present. It was time to make way for younger, better-educated colleagues. This individual case prompted the author of the article to more ambitious reflections on the predicament of ageing: 'The old ... does not somehow exist out there on its own, but rather is to be found within us ourselves, in each of us, to a greater or lesser extent. Often ... we are fond of the old ways. They represent our early days, our youth, our former successes. And to remove the old from the path of the new almost always means for us a psychological break that is far from painless.' The only way to avoid the obsolescence attendant upon ageing was to be prepared for it: 'anyone who wants to withstand the ordeal of old age should prepare for it a long time in advance, maybe even from youth'.[62]

Yet the labour legislation that followed in the 1960s and 1970s was more flexible than this brutal assessment would imply. A new law of August 1964 made staying on in work more financially attractive by allowing working pensioners to claim half of their pension as well as their salary (up to a maximum of 200 rubles per month); in some cases (in specific regions and branches of industry) the proportion of the pension paid in such cases reached 75 per cent. In 1970, yet another pension reform made delayed retirement an even more attractive option. Now many working pensioners were entitled to the whole of their pension, and the ceiling for pension and salary combined was raised to 300 rubles per month. The average length of work life after retirement was around five years. Men who took the option of immediate retirement tended to be motivated by the desire to avoid heavy physical work, while women were often motivated by family responsibilities (namely, in most cases, the need to look after grandchildren).[63]

Soviet policy on work frequently resembled an intergenerational juggling act, as the party-state was forced to respond to fluctuating labour flows. In the early Brezhnev era, it had to step in once again to safeguard the interests of youth. Previous legislation on pay and length of working day had made young people straight out of secondary school unattractive to employers. Then, in 1965–6, the problem of finding work for the youth cohort was exacerbated by contingent factors: a baby-boomer demographic bulge, and a reversion from Khrushchev's experiment with vocational training to ten-year secondary education (which doubled the size of the graduating class of June 1966). To meet these problems, the government decided in February 1966 to double the effective youth quota for employment in state organizations and enterprises.[64]

In the longer term, however, the Brezhnev era served to consolidate in Soviet society a sense of entitlement based on age, seniority, and services rendered to the cause of socialist construction. This was very different from the situation in the 1920s, when a few hundred old Bolsheviks were rewarded for their 'services to the Revolution'. The catalyst for the creation of a far broader 'entitlement community' was the reform of the benefits system in 1956, although only the passing of time could turn the old age pensioner into a coherent and established social identity. Crucially, moreover, the identity of 'pensioner' was able to hitch a ride on that of 'veteran'. Between the late forties and the mid-fifties, the war veteran was largely ignored as a category of entitlement by a regime that was keen to keep down the costs of the socialist welfare state and to arrest the development of communities and interest groups independent of the Party. In 1956, however, Soviet society was granted a Committee of War Veterans, which, though designed as an instrument for international propaganda, soon took on many of the characteristics of a lobbying organization. And, from the mid-1960s onwards, as a regime buffeted by de-Stalinization looked to bolster its legitimacy, the Great Patriotic War became the primary historical point of reference for Soviet ideology and a source of unremitting commemoration.[65]

In the last three decades of Soviet history, then, older citizens became the most vocal and united generational actors in Soviet society. As time passed, war service emerged as an empowering identity for Soviet people. Back in 1945, the veterans had been nebulous in generational terms: they constituted an extremely elastic cohort that included everyone from the age of 18 to the age of 55. By the 1970s, as their ranks finally thinned, they appeared much less chronologically diffuse. At the same time, following the remaking of the Soviet redistributional state in the second half of the 1950s, older Soviet people gained an enduring sense that they deserved recognition and reward for their particular contributions to socialist construction, even if these did not come on the killing fields of the western Soviet Union in 1941–5. By the mid-Brezhnev era, the heroes of Stalingrad and Kursk were regularly joined in celebratory public discourse by the 'veterans' of the factory and the collective farm.[66]

Conclusion

The truism that the processes of modernization and urbanization break down families and marginalize the older generation has by now been subjected to much critical scrutiny by historians of old age. The Soviet case suggests that the reverse is closer to the truth: the modern redistributional state makes the older generation socially and politically salient as never before. Perhaps, when we analyse the social ramifications of such states, 'entitlement communities' are more useful analytical categories than 'classes'. Under state socialism, one's relationship to the means of production counted much less than one's access to the means of consumption (that is to say, one's entitlement to a share of collective resources). Old people were never so powerful as a group of social actors as when their existence was recognized by the Soviet pension system. In previous eras of Soviet history, old people, like any other age group, were divided by deep discrepancies in access to benefits. Although the pension reform of 1956 did not eliminate discrimination, it certainly reduced it. And it turned 'pensioner' into an important new social identity. Although the pensioner of 1956 was not primarily an old person, the association between ageing and pensioner status strengthened over the following decades as war invalids themselves aged and died. By the time that the Soviet state embarked on another attempt to reform the social security system in the 1980s, 'pensioner' most definitely connoted 'old person'. And Soviet Russia's older generation was not slow to prove the strength of its sense of entitlement. Between 1989 and 1990, half a million people wrote in to the authorities with comments on the pension law.[67]

The reforms of the social security system were not the only causes of the rising profile of the older generation. The invention and consolidation of the Soviet old-age pensioner proved to be perfectly in synch with that of the veteran. As the Great Patriotic War became established as the defining collective experience of the Soviet 'nation', so the 'war generation', with the passing of time and the diminishing of the cohorts that bore arms, came to coincide with the 'older generation' *tout court*. In other words, if 'veterans' were by no means guaranteed to be old in the early fifties or even the mid-sixties, by the late seventies they certainly were.

The increased prominence of older people in the post-war era was also a solution to the issue of social authority. Here lay an enduring problem for a purportedly socialist regime: how to find an acceptable public justification for hierarchy and authority given that people were supposed to be equal? This question became all the more urgent in the post-war era, when the young were seen to have relinquished their vanguard function (given that they had not played a full part in the Soviet nation's defining collective experience, the defeat of Nazi Germany). By the 1950s, Soviet ideology was routinely trying to square circles. In the field of intergenerational relations, the ambition was to unleash the full energetic potential of youth without in any way destabilizing society or undermining the authority of the older generation. The fundamental incompatibility of these aims gave rise to confusions and contradictions in the Khrushchev era. In the longer run, however, what happened was that Soviet society moved towards the solution proposed by a very early socialist thinker, Robert Owen, who argued that age was the only principle of authority compatible with socialism.[68]

The trajectory of the older generation, then, can be seen as a neat inverse of that of youth. In the early Soviet period, young people were assumed to be a group ready for mobilization and collective action; innumerable conferences, institutions, and publications were organized to speak in their name. Old people, by contrast, had absolutely no coherent social identity. By the post-Stalin era, however, the old-age pensioner came to the fore in social policy, while apathy seemed to have set in among the younger generation. It was symptomatic that, at the thirteenth congress of the Komsomol in April 1958, 52 per cent of delegates were older than 26 (the notional maximum age for membership in this organization).[69] And, when the Soviet system came down, the 40 million Komsomol members dispersed onto as many individual trajectories (from billionaire to drug addict), while Russia's 30 million old-age pensioners became a mainstay of public discussion on the costs and prospects of post-socialism.

Notes

Thanks to Mark Edele, Steven Harris, and Lukas Mücke for commenting on a draft of this chapter.

1. A. Yurchak, *Everything Was Forever, Until It Was No More: The Last Soviet Generation* (Princeton, 2006), p. 81.
2. See, for example, R. Taagepera and R.D. Chapman, 'A Note on the Ageing of the *Politburo*', *Soviet Studies*, 29 (1977), 296–305.
3. Census figure derived from Iu.A. Poliakov and V.B. Zhiromskaia (eds), *Naselenie Rossii v XX veke* (Moscow, 2000), p. 155.
4. Rybnikov outlined his research agenda in 'K voprosu o psikhologii starosti', in *Psikhologiia*, 2 (1929), 16–32. The material he collected on the subject – which includes syntheses of his questionnaire results and translations of

important Western works such as Stanley Hall's *Senescence, the Last Half of Life* (1922) – can be found in the Arkhiv Rossiiskoi Akademii Obrazovaniia, f. 47, op. 1, dd. 38, 39, 40.

5. G. Alexopoulos, *Stalin's Outcasts: Aliens, Citizens, and the Soviet State, 1926–1936* (Ithaca, 2003), pp. 68–9.

6. See, for example, the ethnographic data from Moscow, Smolensk, and Tver' provinces presented in V.A. Murin, *Byt i nravy derevenskoi molodezhi* (Moscow, 1926), Chap. 2.

7. A. Samsonov, *Obespechenie invalidov voiny i krest'ian prestarelogo vozrasta* (Moscow and Leningrad, 1928), pp. 41–2.

8. Gosudarstvennyi Arkhiv Rossiiskoi Federatsii (GARF), f. A-259, op. 9b, d. 688, l. 17; op. 10b, d. 3131, ll. 4–6; op. 10b, d. 3196, ll. 34–5.

9. A.Ia. Livshin, I.B. Orlov and O.V. Khlevniuk (comps), *Pis'ma vo vlast', 1928–1939: Zaiavleniia, zhaloby, donosy, pis'ma v gosudarstvennye struktury i sovetskim vozhdiam* (Moscow, 2002), p. 354.

10. L. Alexeyeva and P. Goldberg, *The Thaw Generation: Coming of Age in the Post-Stalin Era* (Boston, 1990), p. 11.

11. B.A. Engel and A. Posadskaya-Vanderbeck (eds), *A Revolution of Their Own: Voices of Women in Soviet History* (Boulder, 1998), p. 39 (interview with a woman who had her first child in 1939). Descriptions of illiterate and devout nannies are a commonplace in memoirs of pre-war Soviet childhood: see also R.M. Frumkina, *O nas – naiskosok* (Moscow, 1997), pp. 20–1.

12. V.N. Iarkho, *Vnutri i vne Sadovogo kol'tsa* (Moscow, 2003), pp. 13–14.

13. A.P. Khomenko, 'Sem'ia v protsesse perestroiki' (originally published in Ukrainian in 1930), in his *Sem'ia i vosproizvodstvo naseleniia (izbrannye proizvedeniia)* (Moscow, 1980), pp. 67–9.

14. A much fuller treatment of these issues is S. Lovell, 'Soviet Socialism and the Construction of Old Age', *Jahrbücher für Geschichte Osteuropas*, 51 (2003), 564–85.

15. M. Feshbach, 'Between the Lines of the 1979 Soviet Census', *Problems of Communism*, 31 (1982), 34.

16. A. Blum, *Naître, vivre et mourir en URSS 1917–1991* (Paris, 1994), pp. 71–3.

17. A.Ia. Livshin and I.B. Orlov (comps), *Sovetskaia povsednevnost' i massovoe soznanie 1939–1945* (Moscow, 2003), p. 250.

18. Blum, *Naître, vivre et mourir en URSS*, pp. 52, 154.

19. M. Shaginian, 'Sozdai i sokhrani svoe zdorov'e', *Zdorov'e*, 1 (1956), 6–8.

20. As reported in Zh.A. Medvedev, 'Caucasus and Altay Longevity: A Biological or Social Problem?', *The Gerontologist*, 14 (1974), 382.

21. For a sample of the publications, see: V.I. Kozlov (ed.), *Abkhazskoe dolgo-zhitel'stvo* (Moscow, 1987); *Sredi dolgozhitelei Abkhazii* (Tbilisi, 1987); V. Vigvava, *Obraz zhizni abkhazskikh dolgozhitelei* (Tbilisi, 1988).

22. Medvedev, 'Caucasus and Altay Longevity', 386.

23. A. Vostrikova, 'Chislennost' naseleniia SSSR i ego vozrastnaia struktura', *Vestnik statistiki*, 4 (1960), 60.

24. Medvedev, 'Caucasus and Altay Longevity', 383.

25. L. Gordon and E. Klopov, *Man after Work* (Moscow, 1975), pp. 36, 38.

26. *Obraz zhizni i starenie cheloveka: Materialy simpoziuma* (Kiev, 1966).

27. See, for example, *Gerontologiia i geriatriia 1969–1970: Ezhegodnik* (Kiev, 1970).

28. D.F. Chebotarev and Iu.K. Duplenko, 'On the History of the Home Gerontology Development', in D.F. Chebotarev et al. (eds), *Leading Problems of Soviet Gerontology* (Kiev, 1972), p. 35.
29. The relevant reports can be found at Tsentral'nyi gosudarstvennyi arkhiv nauchno-tekhnicheskoi dokumentatsii Sankt-Peterburga, f. 368, op. 2-2, dd. 166, 167, 169, 177.
30. Figures from V.E. Gordin, *Chem starost' obespechim* (Moscow, 1988), pp. 60–1.
31. B.Q. Madison, *Social Welfare in the Soviet Union* (Stanford, 1968), pp. 191–4.
32. N.I. Voitova, 'O perspektivakh razvitiia domov-internatov dlia prestarelykh v Ukrainskoi SSR', in *Obraz zhizni i starenie cheloveka*; Madison, *Social Welfare*, p. 194.
33. V. Tiazhelnikova, 'The Family Household as a Demographic Entity in the 1960s–1980s', in S. Afontsev, G. Kessler, A. Markevich, V. Tyazhel'nikova and T. Valetov, *Urban Households in Russia and the Soviet Union, 1900–2000: Size, Structure and Composition*, IISH Research Paper 44 (Amsterdam, 2005), available at www.iisg.nl/research/ussr.php.
34. S.E. Harris, '"We Too Want to Live in Normal Apartments": Soviet Mass Housing and the Marginalization of the Elderly under Khrushchev and Brezhnev', forthcoming in *Canadian-American Slavic Studies*.
35. See, for example, Z.A. Ian'kova, 'Vzaimootnosheniia nuklearnoi sem'i so starshim pokoleniem i rodstvennikami', in Z.A. Ian'kova and V.D. Shapiro (eds), *Vzaimootnoshenie pokolenii v sem'e* (Moscow, 1977), pp. 97–8.
36. Gordon and Klopov, *Man after Work*, Chap. 3.
37. Gordon and Klopov, *Man after Work*, p. 187.
38. On the roots of the Soviet redistributional state in state–society relations during World War I and the Civil War, see E.E. Pyle, 'Peasant Strategies for Obtaining State Aid: A Study of State Petitions during World War I', *Russian History*, 24 (1997), 41–64, and J.A. Sanborn, *Drafting the Russian Nation: Military Conscription, Total War, and Mass Politics 1905–1925* (DeKalb, 2003). On the rise of entitlement after World War II, see M. Edele, 'A "Generation of Victors?": Soviet Second World War Veterans from Demobilization to Organization, 1941–1956' (Ph.D. dissertation, University of Chicago, 2004). It is to Edele that I owe the phrase 'entitlement community'.
39. GARF, f. A-259, op. 9b, d. 690, l. 3.
40. GARF, f. A-259, op. 9b, d. 698, ll. 16–17, 19, 22.
41. GARF, f. R-533, op. 5, d. 75, ll. 52, 65.
42. 'Za edinyi chetkii pensionnyi zakon', *Sotsial'noe obespechenie*, 6 (1940), 3.
43. Livshin and Orlov, *Sovetskaia povsednevnost' i massovoe soznanie*, pp. 224–6 (a Gosplan memo of 13 December 1944 on the state of the social insurance system during the war).
44. A sample can be found in E.Iu. Zubkova et al. (eds), *Sovetskaia zhizn' 1945–1953* (Moscow, 2003).
45. These points were made in late 1955 or early 1956 in a memo by Kaganovich, head of the State Committee of Labour, to the Central Committee: see GARF, f. 9553, op. 1, d. 93, ll. 250–67.
46. GARF, f. A-259, op. 6, d. 3383, ll. 2–3 (government correspondence on the personal pensions system, January 1946).
47. GARF, f. A-259, op. 7, d. 7426, l. 5.
48. GARF, f. A-259, op. 7, d. 7430, ll. 22–5.

49. GARF, f. A-259, op. 7, d. 7431, ll. 2–4, 11–12.

50. GARF, f. A-259, op. 7, dd. 7431, 7432, 8745.

51. GARF, f. A-259, op. 7, d. 8742, ll. 5–8.

52. GARF, f. A-259, op. 7, d. 8744, ll. 3–5.

53. Iarkho, *Vnutri i vne Sadovogo kol'tsa*, pp. 154–5.

54. Much of this correspondence can be seen in GARF, f. 9553, op. 1, dd. 62, 63, 90, 91.

55. GARF, f. R-9553, op. 1, d. 290.

56. GARF, f. A-259, op. 7, dd. 7433, 8745.

57. GARF, f. A-259, op. 42, d. 1075.

58. GARF, f. A-259, op. 45, d. 2705, ll. 54–5.

59. GARF, f. A-259, op. 45, d. 2706, ll. 40–1.

60. Gordin, *Chem starost' obespechim*, p. 31.

61. Over the course of the film, it almost goes without saying, these intergenerational tensions are resolved and the harmony of the patriarchal family is restored. What is probably most significant about *The Great Family* is not that it shows father–son conflict but that it makes the multigenerational family its absolute focus (with the Party nowhere to be seen). Its early viewers, to judge from one memoir account, valued it precisely for its rehabilitation of the stable domestic world that had been so shaken by the preceding decades of Soviet history: see I. Shilova, ... *I moe kino* (Moscow, 1993), pp. 16–17.

62. N. Sadovnikova, 'Ispytanie starost'iu', *Izvestiia*, 19 December 1962. Thanks to Susan Reid for this reference.

63. A good survey of post-1964 pensions developments is W. Moskoff, *Labour and Leisure in the Soviet Union: The Conflict between Public and Private Decision-Making in a Planned Economy* (London, 1984), pp. 34–44.

64. L.J. Cook, *The Soviet Social Contract and Why It Failed: Welfare Policy and Workers' Politics from Brezhnev to Yeltsin* (Cambridge, MA, 1993), pp. 54–8.

65. See Edele, 'A "Generation of Victors?"'.

66. See, for example, *Veterany kolkhoznogo stroia* (Moscow, 1969), and *Veterany truda rasskazyvaiut* (Tashkent, 1973).

67. A. Chandler, *Shocking Mother Russia: Democratization, Social Rights, and Pension Reform in Russia, 1990–2001* (Toronto, 2004), p. 55.

68. R. Owen, 'Six Lectures Delivered at Manchester' (1839), in idem, *A New View of Society and Other Writings* (London, 1991).

69. A. Kassof, 'Afflictions of the Youth League', *Problems of Communism*, 5 (1958), 18.

Index